T0279183

SECRET
DOLOMITES

*Texts and photographs
by Andrea Rizzato*

JONGLEZ PUBLISHING

Travel guides

With 30 years of experience in the Alpine region, Andrea Rizzato is the author of numerous hiking and ski-mountaineering guides, and also contributes to the main magazines specialising in outdoor activities. Having mostly travelled and photographed the less known and less used routes, he prefers the wilder parts of the mountains that offer a sense of communion with nature. He is also an academic member of GISM, the Italian Association of Mountain Writers.

The author is himself a guide on the routes described in this book and is available for any suggestions or explanations at andrearizzato2018@gmail.com.

*S*ecret Dolomites is a guidebook designed for travellers who wish to avoid those paths that are too busy – even becoming overcrowded in recent years – and set off to discover the countless, almost unknown, but often spectacular sites that the Dolomites have to offer. This guide will be useful for beginners and experts alike, as it reveals places where the mountains still bathe in their original charm along paths immersed in a unique and marvellous nature. These routes pass through ancient villages, cliffs, towers, alpine meadows, and ravines, mostly ignored by books and websites. Often little-known by the locals themselves, these routes contribute to making the Dolomites one of the most beautiful mountains in the world.

The main theme and particularity of these excursion proposals is that, whether they are easy walks on simple paths or hikes on steep terrain along trails, they are all located in areas without tourist infrastructure or ski facilities. These routes show the true nature of the Dolomites, as beautiful as they are fragile, and make us understand that their future preservation depends on us all.

Comments on this guide and its contents are most welcome, as they will help us to update and improve future editions.

Please feel free to write to us at the following address:

Jonglez Publishing, 25, rue du Maréchal Foch
78000 Versailles, France
E-mail: info@jonglezpublishing.com

GENERAL NOTICE

The hikes in this guide range from simple walks suitable for everyone to routes for more experienced hikers, including trails, *via ferratas* and ledges in the heart of a hostile environment, along the tracks of wild animals. None of the routes require knowledge of mountaineering techniques and in principle are not forbidden to beginners, provided hikers are properly informed of the safety precautions to be taken or accompanied by an expert or an alpine guide. Although the routes are not well known and rarely used, especially compared to tourist areas, they all normally have signs, blazes, coloured markers or cairns, useful for orientation in the absence of the classic white and red markers of the CAI (Italian Alpine Club). In such situations, it is essential to be able to move around independently and to only venture out in good weather. Another particularly important point concerns general viability: although the author has recently and personally completed these walks, gathering all the information necessary to produce an up-to-date guide at the time of publication, the routes may change in a matter of hours (due to human intervention or natural events). It is therefore essential to inform yourself before departure and to be prepared for unforeseen circumstances. To undertake these secret hikes, it is very important to have a 1:25,000 topographic map of the area, for a general overview and correct orientation; GPS tracks, when available, are much less effective, especially if they are viewed on a mobile phone screen. Using a traditional topographic map also involves interpreting the terrain correctly and, above all, planning the hike by properly assessing the gradients, slopes, challenges, and the type of environment. Many areas are steep and almost wild, especially in natural parks or nature reserves. It is therefore advised to show caution and respect for the area. We invite you to visit the institutional websites to find out about the specific regulations of the parks concerning their accessibility.

Useful information to plan your hike is provided at the start of every route.

Starting point: useful information to reach the starting point of the hike, in general this is the place to park the car.

GPS: GPS coordinates of the starting point of the hike, usually the place to park the car.

Time: total time of the round trip.

Difficulty: brief assessment of the difficulty of the route according to the usual classification, which is given in a summary table at the end of the guide:

   - **T (Tourist):** generally easy, obvious and well-marked route. The differences in altitude are normally moderate and the paths have no exposed or particularly steep sections.
   - **E (Hiker):** a technically simple, well-marked route, but long and tiring. There may be orientation problems, exposed (but suitably equipped) sections, and sections on unstable and dangerous terrain which must be crossed with care using appropriate mountain equipment, including clothing and footwear.
   - **EEH (Expert Hiker):** a route that has sections on rock or is exposed, with some easy climbing. It requires good general mountain experience, appropriate physical preparation, and is not suitable for people with vertigo. Hikers should prepare their equipment carefully, paying particular attention to clothing and footwear, as well as personal safety. This level of difficulty also includes routes that are complicated due to the lack of signage and difficulty in finding the trails, in areas that are not easily accessible, and where orientation is the biggest challenge: it is essential to know how to read topographic maps.

- **EHE (Expert Hiker with Equipment):** like the EE routes, but with the presence of via ferratas and equipped trails. The scarcity of equipment, the physical effort required, and the considerable exposure of the sections taken involve a level of danger that makes the use of individual safety devices (via ferrata kit and helmet) essential. You may encounter passages that include climbing, but do not necessarily offer fixed equipment. It is necessary to be able to move independently everywhere and to have a good knowledge of the mountain environment.

Note: The above times and levels of difficulty are estimated for a moderately trained hiker and for routes taken in normal weather conditions. It goes without saying that the weather and individual preparation can change the duration and difficulty of each route, sometimes significantly.

Elevation gain: indicates the total ascent; any significant variations are indicated.

Trail markers: an estimate of the quantity and quality of trail markers present on the route.

Cartography: cartography that includes the hiking area. We refer to the 1:25,000 sheets from the Tabacco publishing house. If you use other editions, the place names, as well as the route of some paths, may not be the same as those indicated in this guide. An excellent free map is available on the website of the Kompass publishing house (kompass.de/wanderkarte). Although it does not feature the routes or numbering of the paths and there are no names of accommodations, it is still very useful for studying the routes at home.

STOPPING POINTS

Throughout the Dolomites, even in the lesser known and less frequented areas, there are numerous stopping points, typically alpine refuges (private or part of the CAI), alpine huts, *agriturismi* and bivouacs (prefabricated shelters made of sheet metal or set up in *casere*, typical old, abandoned chalets). The latter are just shelters for spending the night and you need to bring your own sleeping bag and food. For up-to-date information on the various stopping points, it is best to refer to the Internet, as almost all of them have their own website (especially the refuges, *malghe*, *casere* and *agriturismi*) or are described on the CAI website. Another way to spend the night in the mountains is in a tent. This option requires being equipped accordingly but allows greater freedom and autonomy, provided that the rules of conduct are respected. These rules stipulate that you should only settle in a place between sunset and sunrise, without leaving any trace of your passage. It is important to check on the institutional websites as the rules and regulations of nature parks may impose additional restrictions.

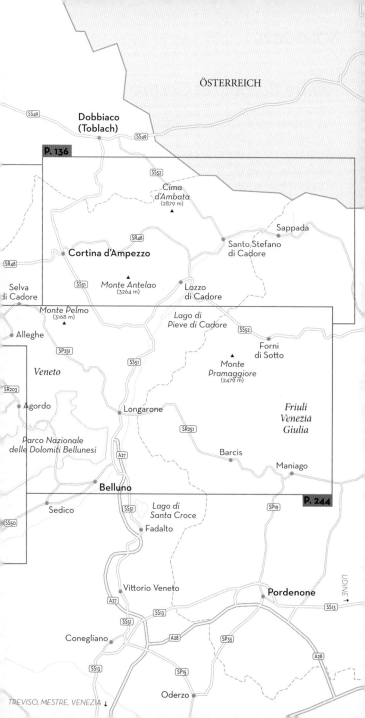

SOMMAIRE

Entre Bolzano et Cortina

Entre Cortina et Sappada

Entre Agordo et Claut

SOMMAIRE

Entre Facade et Feltre

From Bolzano to Cortina

FROM THE BANKS OF THE BLETTERBACH TO THE CORNO BIANCO

The perfect combination of geological discoveries and hiking

Starting point: *Passo di Oclini (1,989 metres)*
GPS: *46.347226 11.451113*
Time: *3 hours*
Difficulty: *Easy, for all hikers*
Elevation gain: *350 metres*
Trail markers: *Excellent*
Cartography: *Tabacco 1:25,000, sheet 029*

Corno Bianco is a popular peak, well known for its beautiful panorama. It is located at the western edge of the Dolomites and rises almost above the town of Bolzano. On summer days, tourists crowd the direct ascent to the Oclini Pass, admire the view from the top and quickly return to the valley, missing the most interesting side of the mountain. The mountain is made up of a light-coloured sedimentary formation which gives it its name, Corno Bianco, meaning 'white horn'. On its north-western slope, erosion has completely exposed an impressive succession of geological stratifications that explain the evolution of the Earth and the formation of the Dolomites.

In its lower part, the Bletterbach Gorge (or Rio delle Foglie) is now a remarkable attraction of dedicated, equipped trails, while towards its summit, the Corno Bianco offers a beautiful panoramic path overlooking the gorge. The pleasant half-day hike combines sites of geological interest and panoramic views.

From the car park at the Oclini Pass, continue along the dirt road west and follow signs to the excellent restaurant Gurndinalm, which you will reach after an enjoyable mountain walk. Immediately before heading down to the alpine pastures are numerous signs leading to the surrounding trails. From there, turn right upwards, and follow the signs to the Corno Bianco. Very soon you will enter the forest and cross the mountain side. The path winds its way through a remarkable landscape towards the western ridge. It leads to the edge of the cliff that overlooks the Bletterbach, which can be admired from above in all its glory. From there, you can already see the large cross on top of the Corno Bianco.

Continue along the edge of the cliff until the marked path that crosses the entire upper part of the ravine. The path winds among sections of mugo pines. At the limestone rocks at the top, follow the direct route to Oclini and climb to the top. It is best to return to the pass via the most direct, clearly marked and popular route.

The Bletterbach Gorge

Located between Aldino and Redagno, not far from the Egna Ora motorway exit, is the Bletterbach Gorge (bletterbach.info). Formed on the slopes of the Corno Bianco about 18,000 years ago, the canyon is almost 8 km long and up to 400 metres deep from the top of the mountain. Over time, it has exposed 250 million years of geological history.

The perfectly preserved rock formations not only tell us what Earth was like at that time but also what mysterious plants and animals once inhabited the Dolomites. There are many trails and guided hiking tours in the Geopark, and most of them are suitable for children.

THE LATEMAR LABYRINTH

A maze of giant rocks at the foot of the most spectacular dolomitic towers

Starting point: *Passo di Costalunga (1,753 metres), between Val di Fassa and Val di Tires*
GPS: *46.404211 11.609167*
Time: *3.5 hours*
Difficulty: *Easy, for all hikers*
Elevation gain: *200 metres*
Trail markers: *Excellent*
Cartography: *Tabacco 1:25.000, sheet 029*

In the Latemar mountain range, Lake Carezza, the area surrounding the Torre di Pisa refuge, and the via ferrata dei Campanili all attract swarms of tourists. But elsewhere, there are still quiet areas where you can wander freely. The Labirinto di Latemar (Latemar labyrinth) is one of those.

This wonder of nature is made up of rocks that fell from the northern walls about 200 years ago. In their fall, the rocks partially destroyed the Latemar Forest and completely sealed off the third Lake of Carezza, or Lake Maggiore, erasing it forever.

This excellent path, which climbs up and through the magical maze, connects the Costalunga pass to the Mitterleger clearing. It is a fun walk among rocks and varied scenery. To the north, among the Dolomites, you can see the splendid and incomparable Torri del Latemar from up close.

From the Costalunga pass, climb slightly north on the ski slopes, then turn right immediately onto the CAI 21 trail toward Mitterleger. Follow the trail along modest slopes until it descends slightly into the forest, and you reach a crossroad. There, turn left onto the CAI 18 trail towards the Forcella Piccola. After a short while you will quickly see a sign to the right, near what is left of the now extinct Lake Maggiore of Carezza, indicating the path to the labyrinth. Follow the CAI 20 trail signs and begin the pleasant climb up this ancient landslide, along a path that will gradually reveal nature and panoramic views. After a while, the route leads west out of the rocks and down to the edge of the woods to the large Mitterleger clearing (1,839 metres). There you will find an old baita (a chalet which was part of the former Lavina Rossa mines, located higher up in the mountain) and a spring. Return to the starting point by following the CAI 21 trail signs that lead along an almost level path.

STALLO DEI CAMOSCI AND THE FORCELLONE

Stray rocks, unstable towers and petrified silences in the heart of the Latemar mountain range

Starting point: *Obereggen, in Val d'Ega (1,530 metres)*
GPS: *46.383996 11.526230*
Time: *5 hours*
Difficulty: *The hike to Forcellone is easy. The descent over scree is perilous and more suitable for trained and safety-conscious hikers. Good visibility is essential. The particularly popular alternative route to the Torre di Pisa refuge is easy, however, even if the terrain is very loose*
Elevation gain: *500 metres, with positive and negative elevation*
Trail markers: *Good throughout most of the hike, but totally absent on the descent of the Forcellone cirque*
Cartography: *Tabacco 1:25.000, sheet 029*

In the western part of the Latemar, the rocky cirques of the Stallo dei Camosci and the Forcellone developed between the Cima di Valsorda, Corno d'Ega and Cima del Forcellone, surrounded by strange rock walls, towers and pinnacles. No one knows how long these limestone formations, that are as thin and brittle as a sandcastle, will withstand time to offer this enchanting landscape and continue to remind us of

the original Latemar, atoll-like platform.

Dark porphyry, on which corals settled over thousands of years, are mixed in the strata and walls, giving them original colours and picturesque shapes. With its horizontal strata alternating between sediments of volcanic origin and scree, under the Corno d'Ega and its crenellated structure, the Stallo dei Camosci is a geological enigma. As for the Vallone del Forcellone, one of the most impressive and colourful depressions of the Dolomites, it is outlined by a thin and fragile rocky hem. Both can be visited by taking an easy loop to the Forcella dei Camosci and the Forcellone, although the latter is recommended for experienced hikers. While it is technically not difficult, hikers need to be particularly wary, as the way down to Obereggen is along loose, rocky debris and there is no path. For an easy loop from start to finish, head to the Forcella dei Camosci and go to the Torre di Pisa refuge (rifugiotorredipisa.it) to see the famous monolith called Torre di Pisa ('Tower of Pisa') and return to Obereggen by following the numerous signs and forest paths.

From the Sporthotel Obereggen, take the chairlift to Oberholz (2,150 metres), a popular access point to the Latemar trails. Ignore the signs for the Passo Pampeago and continue until you reach the tourist facility on the hill and its beautiful view. Take the CAI 18 trail, which travels in long diagonals up the scree slopes of the Corno d'Ega and enters the Stallo dei Camosci. Climb through these magical and captivating landscapes, between scree caves surrounded by unusual rock faces, following an excellent path that leads safely to the base of the Cima di Valsorda. Take a narrow passage with an earthen floor that leads to the Forcella dei Camosci (2,590 metres, 1.5 hours), where the southern slope of the Latemar will appear. Descend towards the huge plateau, where there is a large fork in the road. Ignore going to the right, which leads to the Torre di Pisa refuge, and climb north toward the large depression of the Forcella dei Campanili, clearly visible on the left of the Torri del Latemar. Pass under the eastern wall of the Corno d'Ega and climb to the Forcellone di Latemar (2,582 metres), leaving the main path (be careful, there are no signs). Here begins our little adventure: descend from the northwest on a track through the rocky debris, until the large Erzlahn valley. A depression entirely filled with stones, between walls and strange rock towers, opens up before you. Descend to where the path seems most practicable; the rocks at the bottom make for a sort of rock walkway. Follow the path of your choice to the lowest point of the valley, spotting a few red marks here and there, until you reach the point where the wide CAI 22 trail meets between Oberholz and Obereggen. Turn right into a beautiful forest and follow the paths, signs and other markers to the highest hotels in Obereggen.

The colourful scree of the Forcellone valley which opens up to the top right

CREPE DI LAUSA

An island of tranquillity amid the bustling tourists of the Dolomites

Starting point: *Vigo di Fassa, Ciampedie ski lifts; open every day from 7.15am to 7pm in summer*
GPS: *46.421234 11.671503*
Time: *7.5 hours; 9 hours when returning through the Rifugio Antermoia*
Difficulty: *This is a long hike which includes three moderately difficult sections that require a special via ferrata kit*
Elevation gain: *800 metres return or 1,100 metres if you make a loop via the Passo Antermoia*
Trail markers: *Excellent*
Cartography: *Tabacco 1:25.000, sheet 029*
Accommodation: *Rifugio Antermoia*

As early as 1890, Stefano Dorigoni, a pioneer of mountaineering in the Trentino region, encouraged hikers in his guide to the Catinaccio Group (Rosengarten) to seek out lesser-known areas, like the Torri del Vajolet or del Catinaccio of Antermoia, that were worthy of interest.

Now that mass tourism is overcrowding the refuges and main trails, his words sound almost prophetic and ring truer than ever. In response to his invitation, we head to the peaceful and grandiose sub-group of Larsec (or Lago Secco, 'Dry Lake'), with its jagged cliffs, seasonal lake and stones embedded in the rocky ridges. The climb ends with a panoramic view of the Crepe di Lausa ('Peaks of Lausa'), the long ridge that marks the limit of the Larsec. It is easy to climb to their main summit (2,766 metres) before continuing towards the depression that

is home to the lake and the Rifugio Antermoia, one of the most famous and emblematic places in the Dolomites.

From Vigo di Fassa, climb to Ciampedie (1,997 metres) along the ski lifts. Follow the CAI 540 trail along a gentle incline that crosses the ski slopes and runs for a long distance through the wooded slopes of the Zigolade, until you reach the basin and the Gardeccia refuge (1,950 metres). Follow the signs for the Larsec CAI 583 trail and climb up through the sparse woods on the slopes of the Pale del Mesdì, admiring the impressive Larsec ravines (made up of countless towers and pinnacles). Enter the strikingly steep valley of the Scalette. This is the only access route to the high plateaus of the Larsec. As you wind your way up you will pass two easy trails that overlook a sloping rock face, and a final, steeper section. Just above, you will come to the Passo delle Scalette (2,348 metres) and the banks of the Larsec lake. The lake is seasonal and dries up during the summer, giving the place its name. From the lakeshore, climb the impressive Lausa depression, which extends for a few kilometres at the foot of the Crepe di Lausa, and enjoy the unique scenery of meadows and desolate stretches of rocky debris. At the top of the valley is the Lausa pass (2,700 metres, 3 hours). From there, the view is already spectacular (and includes the Catinaccio d'Antermoia, Sassolungo, Sella, Marmolada), but if you continue on the scree ridge immediately to the right, you can reach the northern summit of the Crepe di Lausa and its uninterrupted views (30 minutes from the pass). If you do not wish to return the way you got up, continue north to the Rifugio Antermoia (2,497 metres) for a well-deserved stop (45 minutes). To return, take the indicated trails, which will take you to the Passo Antermoia and the Rifugio Passo Principe in about 1.5 hours. From there, take the paths to Gardeccia and Ciampedie.

LECH DI DRAGON AND THE MESULES

The rocky glacier, a proglacial lake and a plateau just one metre below the 3,000-metre marker

Starting point: *The Pisciadù car park (1,956 metres), on the road between Corvara and the Gardena pass*
GPS: *46.404211 11.609167*
Time: *8 hours*
Difficulty: *This is a long and strenuous hike with easy sections. Good weather is essential to hike at high altitude*
Elevation gain: *1,000 metres*
Trail markers: *Good*
Cartography: *Tabacco 1:25.000, sheet 006*

T he Lech di Dragon is located on the large scree terrace of the Murfreit, on the slope of the Sella that overlooks the Gardena valley, at an altitude of 2,677 metres. It is a rare site in the Dolomites today, as it forms periodically on the permafrost that covers the terrace.

It is a typical example of a rock glacier between ice and rocky scree.

This small blue spot in the vast expanse of the Dolomites is called a 'proglacial' lake. When the glacier melts, the moraine (an accumulation of debris) acts as a dam which traps the melted water. About 10,000 years ago, at the end of the last ice age, there were many large proglacial lakes. According to old legends, this lake was so large that it was home to a dragon.

Unfortunately, this interesting phenomenon is slowly disappearing due to global warming; the lake has repeatedly failed to form in recent years and, although it recently reappeared, it is much smaller than in the past.

The impressive northern rock faces of the Mesules, which are also the peaks of the plateau of the same name, rise up above the scree terrace, almost uninterrupted until the Sella Pass. You can easily reach the highest peak of this rocky desert, the Sass dai Ciamorces (2,999 metres), by climbing the valley of the same name, just above the Lech di Dragon.

On your return via the Rifugio Pisciadù, take a moment to enjoy a pleasant stop on the banks of the Pisciadù lake, another gem of the splendid Sella Group.

From the car park at the beginning of the Val Setus valley, follow the CAI 666A trail up to the Rifugio Pisciadù. Ignore the signs leading to the Ferrata Tridentina and the Gardena pass and climb between the imposing walls of the Setus valley, which seem to sprout up all around. The path continues along a uniquely beautiful and majestic landscape. After reaching the rocky section that blocks the exit upwards, go beyond it along a simple trail equipped with cables and metal anchors to reach the scree terrace of the Sella, not far from the Rifugio Pisciadù. There is a crossroads with signs. Turn right along the CAI 677 trail towards the Lech di Dragon, where the path blends with the surrounding scree. Follow the trail markers and blazes carefully until you see the lake. The terrain is uneven due to the large rocks that make it hard to identify the path. Depending on the season, the size of the lake can be more or less impressive. Above the lake, the path becomes steeper and climbs between the scree towards the rocks of Sass dai Ciamorces. It winds around the northern slopes to a magnificent scree valley. Go up the long-but-easy track to the Forcella dai Ciamorces (2,923 metres), between the summit of the same name and the Piz Rotic. You will then arrive on the vast Mesules plateau. If the weather is good, the visibility is very high and you can take advantage of this to make the long walk on the summits of the Mesules plateau (from Piz Rotic to Piz Selva) along the Ferrata des Mesules path, at a near-constant altitude of approximately 3,000 metres. The path is not difficult up to Piz Selva but, after, you will have to retrace your steps, as there are no other easy alternatives for the return journey. Once back at the Forcella dai Camosci, continue east along the gravel path, which leads to the Rifugio Pisciadù. After a short walk, you will reach the Sella di Pisciadù, where you can climb the Sass dai Ciamorces. You can reach the summit very easily by climbing any of the numerous peaks that form the vast summit plateau. Back at the Sella di Pisciadù, start the descent toward the Pisciadù lake and refuge, which should already be clearly visible at the bottom of the gigantic scree valley that extends north. Once you have descended the short-but-steep staircase with the help of a fixed rope, follow a pleasant slope over the rocky scree across the grandiose landscape. As you reach the refuge, take the crossroad for the Lech di Dragon and return to the valley along the same route already taken in the Setus valley.

◄ The small Lech di Dragon on the scree of the Mesules seen from the Sass dai Ciamorces. In the background, the meadows of the Gardena pass and the Puez and Odle groups.

BEC DE ROCES

A strange little world in the heart of the Dolomites

Starting point: *Campolongo Pass between Corvara and Arabba*
GPS: *46.519510 11.873769*
Time: *3.5 hours*
Difficulty: *Easy, for all hikers*
Elevation gain: *650 metres*
Trail markers: *Excellent*
Cartography: *Tabacco 1:25.000, sheet 006*

Standing before the Sella Group and its cyclopean walls, the Bec de Roces are strangely shaped limestone pinnacles rising among the mugo pines. In the distance, the sparkling glaciers of the Marmolada and the walls of Pelmo and Civetta are the perfect combination of power and magic. The Bec de Roces are easily accessible in the Campolongo pass and offer pleasant hikes for those who wish to walk around their base freely and discover picturesque silhouettes. The Bec de Roces can also be an intermediary stage as part of a longer hike to the Kostner refuge in the Vallon, and the Boè lake, another important sight in the Sella Group. Although they are quite busy in the summer, there are still quieter spots among these large, sunny expanses to enjoy the exceptional views.

The hike starts at the Albergo Boè (hotel), about 200 metres north of the Campolongo pass (1,875 metres, signs and maps). Follow the CAI 638 trail, which is a shortcut to the longer route on a ski slope, until you reach the Crep de Munt (a cable car from Corvara also takes you there). Climb west, along the same trail. Pass the picturesque Boè lake, a glacial pond in a depression between rocky walls, and continue on the rock slabs of the Plan de Sass near a second chairlift. Once you reach a small plateau, you will see the Rifugio Kostner. Sitting at an altitude of 2,500 metres, the refuge enjoys a beautiful panoramic position between the rocky slabs of the Sella, which can be reached quickly (about an hour from the pass). Leave the paths leading up from the refuge to Piz Boè and follow the signs for the Rifugio Bec de Roces. Go south, and as you descend, take a moment to enjoy the views of the Marmolada, until you reach the Bec de Roces formations. Take your time to discover this magnificent place at your own pace, passing among towers and rocks, like the Sass Quadro boulder. At the base of the boulder, the remains of an Austrian fortification with a wall and stone steps are still visible. Continue along the path until you reach the lawns near the ski slopes where the large refuge is located. To return to Campolongo pass, simply follow the dirt track which, after a sharp left bend, descends between the meadows.

Rocks and trees at the Bec de Roces ▶

Bec de Roces with Pelmo and Civetta in the background

PUEZ MARLS

Discovering the pyramids of the plateau along solitary trails

Starting point: *Colfosco in the val Badia, at the car park of the chairlift to Col Pradat (1,743 metres)*
GPS: *46.557896 11.854609*
Time: *7 hours*
Difficulty: *Simple hike, with a few steep sections near the Forcella del Sassongher*
Elevation gain: *950 metres, with positive and negative elevation*
Trail markers: *Excellent*
Cartography: *Tabacco 1:25.000, sheet 007*

The Col de Puez, Muntejela de Puez, the Col dala Sone, the Col dala Pieres and the Piz Duleda are all remains of very ancient limestone deposits rising atop the Puez plateau. Known as Marne del Puez in Italian, or 'Puez marls', these limestone deposits were formed during the Cretaceous period (around 145 to 100 million years ago) in colourful

strata ranging from red to greenish grey, and often contain ammonite fossils. The combined action of meteorite impacts, and the movement of the Earth's tectonic plates, created these limestone formations. Standing alone on the plateau's pale limestone surface, the volcano-like conoidal depositions, which are less subject to erosion than the surrounding Dolomites, give the landscape an enchanting, almost lunar feel.

Surrounded by spectacular views in all directions of the main mountain groups of the Dolomites, this area is one of the most outstanding features of the Puez Odle Natural Park, created in 1978. Despite the particularly large tourist flow in the middle of summer, which mainly concentrates around the Puez Refuge, it is still possible to walk along deserted paths that are especially interesting from a natural point of view. There are also many easy detours for those who want to wander around the picturesque peaks.

From the chairlift car park, head north on the road up the ski slopes and follow the signs for the Puez Refuge. You will soon come to a crossroad with a main road leading to the Sassongher, an imposing peak that overlooks Corvara and Colfosco at the entrance to the Puez Odle Park. Turn right and take the CAI 7 trail up the scree steps below the jutting rock faces, leading to the Forcella Sassongher (maps and signs) across a few difficult passages. From the mountain pass, the most experienced and trained hikers can climb the beautiful, isolated Sassongher summit. The ascent along a partly exposed and equipped path takes less than an hour. From the fork in the road, head down east into the Juel valley. Turn left at the CAI 5 signs toward the Rifugio Puez and climb up the steep meadows encased between the surrounding rock faces that hide the access to the Puez plateau. As you climb higher you will reach the alpine meadows of the summits and the point beyond which the impressive plateau unveils its beauty. Descend slightly and continue enjoying the incredible environment as you make your way between limestone slabs, meadows and marshes, toward the distant peaks of the Piz de Puez (2,913 metres). On the right you will see the Col dala Sone (2,633 metres) and its original shape: a cone that seems to have been shaped by the hands of an architect. Climb the steep and narrow path to reach the top of it. The hike continues without difficulty to the magnificent depression of the Puez Refuge (2,475 metres). The refuge sits below the Puez pass and its equally original layers of sedimentation (2.5 hours). Once you reach the refuge, it is highly recommended to climb the Piz de Puez. Given that it is the highest of the plateau, this very accessible summit offers the widest panorama of the area. You can reach it by following the marked path that starts at the refuge, continues to the Puez pass, then climbs to the summit over rocky debris (1.5 hours from the refuge). To return to Colfosco, take the CAI 4 trail, which passes by the refuge again and descends to Forcella de Ciampei.

View of the Odle Group from the summit of Piz de Puez

THE SASSONGHER

A deserted alternate path through the Juel valley

Starting point: *Fontanacia (1,490 metres), a small hamlet in La Villa in the Val Badia valley*
GPS: *46.574547 11.889782*
Time: *6 hours*
Difficulty: *This hike is for experts, although it does not present any specific difficulties. A few equipped sections, not very complex, facilitate the most exposed passages in the lower Juel valley and near the summit*
Elevation gain: *1,150 metres*
Trail markers: *Excellent*
Cartography: *Tabacco 1:25.000, sheet 007*

With its obelisk-like size, the Sassongher dominates the villages of Corvara and Colfosco in the upper Val Badia valley. In fact, it is also the valley's symbol. Recognisable even from a distance due to its imposing dimensions that stand out from the foothills of the Puez plateau, it is also a magnetic attraction for tourists who flock to the valley throughout the year, making it one of the most popular and most visited peaks along its main route.

Everyone leaves Colfosco via the Pradat pass and takes advantage of the chairlift, which defaces the slopes on its way to the Sassongher. However, few people venture into the Val de Juel, an enchanting jewel that is still wild, untouched and almost ignored, to enjoy closer contact with nature. In this Dolomite fold that supports the formidable Puez roofs, the climb is captivating, and it is only on reaching the dome that you will probably have to share the rest of the hike to the famous summit with tourists.

From Fontanacia, follow the signs for the Sassongher and take the CAI 7 trail, which zigzags past the first wooded base, some sections of which are equipped with safety cables. Beyond this steep section, you'll be able to enjoy the Juel valley in all its glory: a glacial valley between high rock faces. There the slopes become less steep, and the climb is less tiring. On the left you can see the tapered towers of the Sassongher and on the right the yellow walls of the Para dei Giai, which continue over the scree to the head of the valley where the Sassongher pass opens up (2,435 metres, 2.5 hours). The last section of the summit begins, on a path that is sometimes exposed and partially equipped, but easy despite the loose and crumbly terrain. At the summit (2,665 metres), the panorama is breathtaking, with the streets of Corvara below and the Dolomites unfolding directly opposite (1 hour from the fork).

The Sassongher and its towers, seen from the north

THE LAGHETTO DELLE FONTANE ⑨

The magical water mirror that comes back to life every spring

Starting point: *Vivaio Piccolet (1,257 metres), on the road from Vallada Agordina leading towards Forcella Lagazzon*
GPS: *46.382496 11.918421*
Time: *5.5 hours*
Difficulty: *This hike is accessible to all. It is long and demanding because of the difference in altitude*
Elevation gain: *1,000 metres*
Trail markers: *Good*
Cartography: *Tabacco 1:25.000, sheet 015*

The little Laghetto delle Fontane ('Lake of the Fountains') is nestled on the volcanic ridge between the peaks of Auta and Pezza, in the Marmolada group. If you look for it on a topographic map, you won't find it! This beautiful and calm lake is seasonal. Only the few rare hikers who know when to seize the right moment in the springtime will reach it and fall under its spell.

That's why topographers have never noticed it, given the brief instances it graces the peaks of Mount Pezza, a volcanic rock covered with meadows and stretches of rhododendron. As the snow melts at the end of June and an explosion of blooming flowers in a thousand colours grace this corner of Eden in the Dolomites, the deep-blue lake comes to life. If the mythical King Laurin were to see today how so many alpine areas have been damaged, including several very close by, he would certainly take refuge on the quiet banks of the lake. The hike in search of this lake is rich in panoramas, floral beauties and unique landscapes, and is definitely on the list of what to see in the Dolomites. Make sure to visit the area on a clear, sunny summer's day.

From Vivaio Piccolet, follow the CAI 684 trail that enters the woods to the north (follow the signs for the Baita Pianezza lodge). Climb the slopes of Punta Palazza and cross to the west. At a signposted intersection, turn right on a steep path that climbs steadily through the woods until you reach the wonderful flowery meadow where the Baita Pianezza lodge is located (1,665 metres, 1.5 hours). Here the terrain widens and offers a view of the imposing Pale di San Martino group, which stand out from the landscape. Continue behind the lodge on a narrow path marked in the grass (it is best to follow the signs) which soon widens. After a few bends, you reach the Forcella delle Pianezze. Do not head to the pass: instead, follow the signs and turn right towards the Forcella delle Fontane. Continue east over sloping meadows and pastoral valleys until the majestic and unexpected silvery south face of the Marmolada appears. Continue north, to the right of a stream embedded in the rocky relief at the base of Monte Pezza, to reach the Laghetto delle Fontane and the Forcella of the same name (2,206 metres, 3 hours from the start). For the more experienced hikers, climb over the meadows towards the peaks of Pezza to the east of the lake toward the ridge (there is no identifiable path here) where a panoramic 360-degree view awaits.

◀ The Marmolada and the Laghetto delle Fontane seen from Monte Pezza

The Laghetto delle Fontane near the Cime d'Auta peaks

THE MONOLITHS OF RONCH

Between gigantic dolomitic rocks, on the slopes of an ancient volcano

Starting point: *Ronch di Laste (1,500 metres), a hamlet of Livinallongo accessible from Caprile via a very steep asphalt road*
GPS: *46.447623 11.976609*
Time: *2 hours*
Difficulty: *The loop around the monoliths is easy. The trail to climb the Sass de Rocia is more difficult and requires specific equipment and possibly the presence of a guide or expert*
Elevation gain: *100 metres*
Trail markers: *Good*
Cartography: *Tabacco 1:25.000, sheet 015*

Ronch is a small village clinging to the eastern slopes of Monte Mogon. Just above the few houses that make up the village is a surprising bundle of wonders and a typical example of what the Dolomites have

to offer: gigantic monoliths formed by the limestone of the Marmolada, smooth, compact, vertical and, for the most part, overhanging. A few deep breaks divide them, allowing you to squeeze between the walls along a well-equipped trail that leads to the highest boulder, the Sass de Rocia, which is easily recognisable by its flat top and the Pian delle Stelle shelter. The itinerary along a via ferrata is accessible to most people but is not an ordinary one: there are a few vertical sections to overcome. Those who do not feel up to it can always enjoy a relaxing walk around the boulders, along the clearly marked paths made by the many climbers who climb the walls. In addition to the main point of interest, it is recommended to visit the most distant tower, Sass de la Murada, which offers an amazing view of the Cordevole valley. On its summit, which is inaccessible to hikers, are the remains of a medieval watchtower which in the past communicated with the castles of Andraz and Sommariva d'Alleghe by means of visual signals. It is possible to link this hike with the next one, toward the Malga di Laste, for a pleasant day trip.

From the small car park between the houses of Ronch, follow the signs for the via ferrata and go up through the wood, which soon gives way to the monoliths. The trail, indicated by a sign, begins immediately to the left. Enter the crack between the walls, climb a few steps and a metal ladder to reach a flat spot in the crack, where you will see a small Madonna. Continue the via ferrata using a series of metal supports set into the rock. After climbing to the top of a large tower that stands out from the main mass, cross a metal bridge to reach the flat summit of Sass de Rocia, from where you will soon reach the panoramic terrace of the Bivacco Pian delle Stelle hut. Return to the little Madonna along the via ferrata and, if you wish to continue the man-made route, it is possible to slide down the narrow slit that runs along the bottom. With the help of a cable, descend between the protruding walls to the exit, where the base of the monoliths stands on the slope overlooking Livinallongo. A series of supports leads back to the woods, with a very steep descent that provides a good adrenaline rush (be careful: some of the supports tend to wobble, so check them carefully before. This via ferrata is not as well secured as the previous one). From the base of the rocks, turn right and return to Ronch. If you wish to simply walk around the monoliths, follow the path north from the start of the via ferrata to a signposted intersection. Go down to the right of an isolated tower, at the foot of the rock faces, on a path that leads to the woods below. Once you reach a signpost, you can also climb briefly to the Sass de la Murada to admire the view of the Civetta and the Val Cordevole.

Walking around the Ronch monoliths

Reach the vertical pinnacle by climbing the via ferrata of the Sass de Rocia and crossing the small bridge

MALGA LASTE

The enchanted pasture in the upper Agordino

Starting point: *Ronch di Laste (1,500 metres), a hamlet of Livinallongo
accessible from Caprile via a very steep asphalt road*
GPS: *46.447623 11.976609*
Time: *4 hours*
Difficulty: *Easy, for all hikers*
Elevation gain: *400 metres*
Trail markers: *Good*
Cartography: *Tabacco 1:25.000, sheet 015*

alga Laste (or the alpine pasture of Laste) is on the slopes of the Casiera pass, the long volcanic ridge made up of meadows and rocky parts of Monte Migon, the smallest extension of the Marmolada group. The quiet beauty of the little Livinallongo hamlets, with ancient alpine villages of the high mountains and extensive views of many peaks, including Marmolada, Tofane, Pelmo and Civetta, make this a unique part of the Dolomites. A battery of shells was installed during the First World War to control the Lana pass, which overlooks the whole area and was the scene of bloody battles that changed the landscape. Now the area is peaceful and the alpine pasture, used from June to September with an agritourism service, is part of a scarcely frequented hike suitable for everyone. Starting from Ronch di Laste, this hike can be combined with a visit to the monoliths.

From the small car park between the houses of Ronch, follow the signs for the via ferrata and climb up through the sparse woods. Once you have passed the start of the via ferrata, climb slightly up to the signs at the foot of an isolated, overhanging monolith. Ignore the signposted path to the left and take the clearly visible path that climbs east and quickly enters a larch forest until it crosses the road from Davare. The trail continues slightly uphill to the Rifugio Migon mountain hut, then to the Fernazze meadows. You will then pass by some tabià (typical huts) and climb up a small valley to the foot of the Toront pass, which culminates on a flat area between the Casiera pass and the Mezzodì pass. Before stopping to eat, climb the slopes of the Mezzodì pass, where there is a surprising view of the Marmolada glacier and the barns clustered together down in the Davare valley, another gem of Livinallongo.

RIFUGIO SASSO BIANCO

A high mountain village with a unique view

Starting point: Piaia (1,200 metres), a hamlet of San Tomaso Agordino
GPS: 46.386911 11.983591
Time: 3 hours
Difficulty: Easy, for all hikers
Elevation gain: 650 metres
Trail markers: Good
Cartography: Tabacco 1:25.000, sheet 015

Rifugio Sasso Bianco (the 'Sasso Bianco refuge', or mountain hut, 1,840 metres) stands on a bucolic terrace surrounded by meadows and dotted with barns and ancient huts, known as the Tabià of Ciamp. The hut has an excellent panoramic position over the Pelmo, the Civetta and the Pale di San Martino. The local people of the valley are committed to maintaining and enhancing what was once an alpine village dedicated to grazing and haymaking in summer. Amelia Edwards, an English author and Egyptologist, was struck by the bucolic and evocative beauty of this place, which she came upon in 1872 on her way to the Sasso Bianco. Her book, *Untrodden Peaks and Unfrequented Valleys*, bears witness to her explorations and predicts with brilliant foresight the need we still have today for a change of scenery and to discover new places. There are many hikes that connect this sunny hillside to the other hillsides, scattered on the slopes of the mountain (Giardogn, Malga di Costoia, Tabià Lariz, Casera Bur) and to the summit of the Sasso Bianco (meaning 'white rock face' in Italian), a fantastic, panoramic viewpoint whose name can only be explained when viewed from the north because of its white limestone walls. The mountain

hut is privately owned and offers a simple and authentic welcome that perfectly matches the peace and quiet of the place. We recommend going to the hut from the hamlet of Piaia, which is located on the steep, wooded slopes overlooking the Val Cordevole and facing the Civetta.

From the small car park at the top of Piaia, follow the clearly marked signs and climb between the last houses. The path soon becomes cemented and climbs very steeply, alternating with gentler passages. After passing the few isolated tabià, the forest gives way to a large area from which the refuge cable car leaves. At this point, the path is well-marked and climbs more gently up the slopes. After a picturesque section along a river, you will pass the last ramp and enter the meadows (1 hour and three quarters).

Climbing the Sasso Bianco summit

It is possible to climb from the refuge to the top of the Sasso Bianco (2,407 metres) in about an hour and a half along a highly recommended, easy hike. Follow the signs and head toward the Sasso Nero. Immediately after a short, slightly steep rocky section (which is equipped with a metal cable, for safety in case of rainy weather), you will reach the fantastic, undulating peaks that offer a panoramic view. Continue along the excellent path and make a first detour to the Cima da Pian (sign), a sub-peak that hangs above the villages of the upper Agordino, before descending to a fork that separates it from the main summit. The grassy ridge, dotted with some scree areas, leads to the highest point.

BRAMEZZA

A Turkish influence and the landslide of Monte Piz

Starting point: *Caracoi Agoin (1,250 metres), a hamlet north of Alleghe*
GPS: *46.423022 11.998893*
Time: *2 hours until Bramezza, 4 hours to the landslide of Monte Piz*
Difficulty: *Easy, for all hikers*
Elevation gain: *200 metres to Bramezza, 500 metres to the landslide*
Trail markers: *Good*
Cartography: *Tabacco 1:25.000, sheet 015*

Only a handful of houses remain in Bramezza, an ancient and partially abandoned village located on the slopes of the Sasso Bianco, a little to the west of Lake Alleghe. Compared with the traditional architecture of Agordino, some of the old buildings still standing in Bramezza are clad with Asian and unusual-looking chimneys. It seems that after the Battle of Lepanto in 1571, won by the Venetian Republic against the Ottoman Empire, Turkish prisoners of war worked in the local mines producing coal for the smelting furnaces.

This historical hypothesis is partly confirmed by the local population having slightly darker skin than in the surrounding areas and by the first part of the name of the two settlements below Bramezza (Caracoi Cimai and Caracoi Agoin) being undoubtedly reminiscent of the Turkish words Kara Koy, meaning 'black village'.

Upstream from Bramezza, take a moment to visit the major landslide on Monte Piz. The landslide, which occurred on the night of 11 January

1771, knocked several villages down the slopes of the Sasso Bianco and killed 49 people.

As the rocky debris obstructed the valley and blocked the flow of water from Cordevole, it led to the formation of Lake Alleghe, which is now visited by tourists all year round. Due to the absence of vegetation and obstacles towards the valley, the wide and unobstructed view of the Civetta from the scree is spectacular.

From Caracoi Agoin, follow the signs for the Rifugio Sasso Bianco and continue along a road between the houses that crosses the Ru dei Molini and connects with the dirt road that climbs directly from Saviner di Laste. Follow it for a short while until you reach Bramezza (1,450 metres), where we recommend strolling around the old houses and enjoying the magnificent view of the Civetta, as you look for signs of the village's ancient history and the Turkish chimneys (they offer, in one glance, a view of Lake Alleghe, the Sasso Bianco and the Civetta). From Bramezza, continue toward the Rifugio Sasso Bianco and climb through the woods to the Casera Bur mountain pasture (1,632 metres), which also has a superb view. Continue up the steep eastern side of Monte Piz. After reaching the tables and benches of the stopping point, make your way across the landslide that created the lake (sign). Follow the path that breaks away from the edge and carefully make your way across the collapsed limestone bedrock, now overrun with low vegetation, in an almost unique environment: some cracks, dug out relentlessly by water and frost, are still clearly visible and expose the bedrock. Another area on the edge of the cliff serves as a very pleasant viewpoint.

MALGA BOSC BRUSÀ

An open book on the geology of the Dolomites

Starting point: *Sappade (1,420 metres), a hamlet of Falcade*
GPS: *46.372887 11.874909*
Time: *3 hours if you stop at the alpine pasture, 5 hours if you go to the Sass de la Palazza ridge*
Difficulty: *Easy, for all hikers*
Elevation gain: *450 metres to the alpine pasture, 600 metres to the ridge*
Trail markers: *Good*
Cartography: *Tabacco 1:25.000, sheet 015*

Malga Bosc Brusà (or the Bosc Brusà pasture) is in the heart of a unique geological environment above Falcade, on the mountain ridge between the Passo San Pellegrino, the Valfredda and the Biois valley. This area is particularly interesting for the rock formations on the slopes of the Becher pass, the Pizzo Forca and the Sass de la Palazza. They can be studied like a geology book, opened onto the meadows and overlooking the mountain pasture. The rocks of this ridge form a vast Richthofen conglomerate, with multicoloured, twisted strata upon which the white limestone of the highest peaks of the Marmolada sit. Access to the pasture is easy and pleasant, and there is now a sign for a recently created 'geological path' called Sentiero Geologico di Falcade, or Torrente Gavon, featuring information on the most interesting areas to stop at. The alpine pasture is open during the summer, with an agritourism service. We recommend continuing on the ridge between Pizzo Forca and Sass de la Palazza to admire the geological phenomena and panoramic views.

From Falcade, drive up to the hamlet of Sappade, then to the houses of Meneghina, parking near the Rifugio Barezze. Continue on foot along the road, following the signs of the CAI 631 trail, and cross the bridge over the Barezze waterfall, which gets its source from the Gavon mountain stream that carves its bed for about ten metres in a friable layer of quartz porphyry. We recommend looking at the ravine before you continue along the path that begins to climb the steep slopes of the Bechei pass. As you climb the slopes, you'll notice gaping holes exposing other geological formations on the surrounding steep slopes and towards the Pale di San Martino. After exiting the woods, you will find yourself on the meadows of the Malga Bosc Brusà. Continue your ascent along the same CAI trail for about three quarters of an hour until you reach the grassy area next to the Sass de la Palazza and its superb viewpoint.

FRANZEDAS

The bucolic alpine pasture of the shepherds of Marmolada

Starting point: *Malga Ciapela (1,559 metres), on the road south of Passo Fedaia*
GPS: *46.422180 11.893594*
Time: *3 hours*
Difficulty: *Easy, for all hikers*
Elevation gain: *450 metres*
Trail markers: *Excellent*
Cartography: *Tabacco 1:25.000, sheet 015*

The mountain pasture is in the upper Franzedas valley, in the Marmolada group. It is home to a handful of barns and mountain buildings on the slopes of Mount Fop. The Val de Franzedas, a beautiful glacial cirque, remains a silent sanctuary encased by classic dolomitic towers (even though the Alta Via no. 2 passes through it) and offers remarkable walks with breathtaking views. For a long time the area, which represents the highest alpine pasture in the Malga Ciapela, was home to a high-altitude village that was inhabited every summer. Although the houses are now abandoned, the area is still used for grazing. The best part of the hike to Franzedas is the very end as you reach the Forca Rossa pass, between Monte La Banca and the Becher pass, where the landscape opens onto a spectacular view of the surrounding peaks. During the First World War, the area was an important strategic site, because it dominated the Val Franzedas and the Val di San Pellegrino.

From the Malga Ciapela cable car, follow the paved road that leads to the campsite and the car park for the Rifugio Falier. Continue on foot along the forest road that crosses the Val Franzedas. Do not take the path on the right toward the Val Ombretta and the refuge. Make your way up the numerous twists and turns through the thick forest until you emerge under the walls of the Pale del Fop and reach a crossroads. The signs for the Passo di Forca Rossa continue on the right, while the path on the left will lead you quickly to the Franzedas barns (1,980 metres, 1.5 hours).

La Forca Rossa

From the barns, return to the nearby fork in the road and turn left toward the still-distant valley head. As you walk along the Alta Via path, cross the meadows and sparse woods to your left until you reach the flattened peaks.

After the junction with the Becher pass (which we also recommend discovering), make your way uphill along the bends of a military mule road.

Leave the pass at 2,490 metres and go left on the ridge, ignoring the descent to Passo San Pellegrino, to enjoy the wonderful view (1.5 hours from the mountain pasture).

◄ Monte Agnèr from the Becher pass during the climb from Franzedas to Forca Rossa

The upper Franzedas valley from the Becher pass, with Forca Rossa at the top left

THE EAST OMBRETTA PEAK

The perfect view of the Queen of the Pale Mountains

Starting point: *Malga Ciapela (1,559 metres), on the road south of Passo Fedaia*
GPS: *46.422180 11.893594*
Time: *8 hours*
Difficulty: *A long and strenuous hike. Beyond the Passo Ombretta, there are several steep sections that require good footing and are more suitable for experts. There is a short and easy section above the Dal Bianco bivouac*
Elevation gain: *1,450 metres*
Trail markers: *Good*
Cartography: *Tabacco 1:25.000, sheet 015*
Accommodation: *Dal Bianco bivouac*

Of the three Ombretta peaks, East Ombretta peak is an imposing ridge overlooking the Marmolada. Culminating at 3,343 metres,

the Marmolada has the highest peak and the largest glacier of the Dolomites. With its marvellous silver-coloured wall to the south, its shining limestone and pillars deeply buried in scree that bear witness to key moments in the history of international mountaineering, the Marmolada is the most emblematic mountain of the Dolomites. But the Marmolada is also recognised for its trails, landscapes, extraordinarily beautiful valleys, precious testimonies of the First World War, and its modern contradictions linked to the development of tourism on the glacier side. Trek to the summit of the Ombretta across a precious landscape in the footsteps of the Alpini, the Italian Army's specialist mountain infantry, who crossed it during the First World War. The hike begins at Malga Ciapela, on the Venetian side, but you can also start from Canazei, in Trentino, via the historic Contrin refuge. The time required and difficulty are the same from both ends. If you have two cars, you can make an extraordinary crossing from one side to the other.

From the Malga Ciapela cable car station, continue by car along the paved ro.. that leads to the campsite and the car park where the trails to Rifugio Fal.. (2,080 metres) start. Continue on foot along the forest road and take the pa.. that branches off to the right at 1,638 metres (signs); by taking this direct rou.. you'll avoid making a long detour. The path passes a few waterfalls cascadi.. down from the Pian d'Ombretta just above. In some places there are expose.. overhanging sections that require extra caution. Climb a little further to rea..

Malga Ombretta, at the head of the beautiful valley that bears the same name and stretches out at the foot of the southern walls of the Marmolada. With one final effort, you will reach the refuge that sits atop a hill (1 hour and three quarters). Follow the well-marked path, first through sparse woods and then over the imposing rocky scree sliding down the southern slope of the Marmolada to reach the Passo Ombretta at 2,704 metres. Continue along the ridge line over volcanic rocks toward the Ombretta peaks until you see the Dal Bianco bivouac, a stopping point for climbers on the big wall. Immediately behind the bivouac, cross the sloping rocks along the fixed-rope route until you reach the intersection. This is where you can access a detritus slope that leads to the ridge, near a cave used in wartime. Follow a well-marked path on the side facing the Vernale glacier and continue along a narrow, exposed ledge, carved out by the Alpini where you can still see the iron climbing pitons used to anchor their mountain paths. Leave the track on the right that descends toward the Ombretta Ferrata and make your way across the last rocks to reach the cross on the summit. At 3,011 metres, the summit offers a spectacular view (2.5 hours from the refuge). Carefully descend a few metres from the summit on the Vernale glacier side to see the incredible network of tunnels and caverns the Alpini dug under the summit. Notice the fissures that were consolidated with reinforced concrete and the fixing pins still visible along the bold man-made pathway that went up from the valley.

Arturo Andreoletti and the Rifugio Contrin

On the night of 7 June 1915, the Alpini made a spectacular climb up the Sasso Vernale and chased away the Austrian garrison on the Ombretta pass and peaks. The entire sector was occupied by the Val Cordevole company under the command of Captain Andreoletti, who was behind the construction of a complex network of caves, trenches, barracks and artillery posts to fight the Austrians on Forcella Marmolada and Punta Penia. From that day on, attacks and counterattacks followed one another for two and a half years, until the Italian troops withdrew after their defeat at Caporetto. That same year, Captain Andreoletti organised the destruction of the Rifugio Contrin (which, back then, was the seat of the Austrian command in the upper Val di Fassa) with artillery fire. Shortly after the fighting ended, the ruins of the historic building were donated to the National Alpini Association, presided over by Andreoletti himself, who was in charge of restoring the building in memory of these tragic events. Today, the refuge is one of the most popular places in the Dolomites and welcomes hikers from all over the world (rifugiocontrin.it).

Sasso Vernale from the Cima d'Ombretta

THE VALLACCIA

⑰

The Bivacco Zeni, an eagle's nest hidden between rock walls

Starting point: *The Soldanella restaurant in the San Nicolò valley (1,410 metres), accessible via Pozza di Fassa*
GPS: *46.419888 11.707075*
Time: *4 hours*
Difficulty: *Easy hike with a short and equipped section*
Elevation gain: *700 metres*
Trail markers: *Excellent*
Cartography: *Tabacco 1:25.000, sheet 006*
Accommodation: *Bivacco Zeni*

The Vallaccia is a surprising cirque made of rocky spires and towers, nestled in a peaceful, remote corner of the San Nicolò valley. Uniquely, the view from the bottom of the valley is more splendid than from the peaks! The specific structure of the basin makes it almost invisible from the surrounding valleys and it is only when you reach its centre that you become aware of its special beauty.

Another characteristic is that all the summits are in fact easily accessible via the meadows on the opposite slopes. There are also more intense alpine routes on the calcareous slates of the Vallaccia that are particularly appreciated for their excellent, firm and vertical rock.

On the meadows in the centre of the depression is the Bivacco Zeni, built for those tackling the long climbing routes early in the morning. It is also a beautiful excursion destination for hikers, who can continue along the Sentiero Attrezzato Gadotti ('Gadotti equipped path') toward the Punta della Vallaccia and other minor peaks. The route is recommended for those who would like to extend the climb beyond the bivouac and want to complete a full-day itinerary.

From the Soldanella restaurant or the square a little further up on the left, follow the signs for the Bivacco Zeni. Climb through the lush forest along the CAI 615 trail, which offers impressive glimpses through the fir trees of the Catinaccio, the Torri del Vajolet and on to the nearest Torre della Vallaccia, a projection of the Undici summit. Leave the wooded area and approach the threshold of the Vallaccia, in an increasingly striking environment dominated by rock towers. Once you reach the rocky strip that seems to block access to the upper part of the valley, use the cable and metal supports to reach the flatter terrain of the Bivacco Zeni (2,100 metres, 2 hours).

Reaching Punta della Vallaccia from the Sentiero Gadotti

This trail requires a complete via ferrata kit. It leads over ledges, rocky outcrops and gullies before joining the sloping meadows between the Sasso delle Dodici and the Sass Aut. It passes over the summit of the Sass Aut and descends into an impressive ravine, where a fixed rope will help guide you across this key section, before crossing detritus basins to the Forcella Baranchiè. Once there, climb through the meadows to the extraordinary viewpoint of the Punta della Vallaccia. The long journey down will take you through the meadows to Gardeccia, to the excellent Rifugio Vallaccia and Malga Monzoni. Join the gravel track at the bottom of the valley and follow it to the starting point in the San Nicolò valley. This route requires at least 8 hours of walking, good weather and good hiking experience.

The Bivacco Zeni and the Sassolungo in the background

ALPE DI FOSSES

The definition of perfection in the Dolomites

Starting point: *Sant'Uberto (1,421 metres), on the road between Cortina and Passo Cimabanche (large car park at the entrance of the Natural Park of the Ampezzo Dolomites). Given the considerable elevation gain of this itinerary, it may be convenient to climb to higher altitudes by using the shuttle service to the Malga Ra Stua*
GPS: *46.602410 12.107330*
Time: *6 hours*
Difficulty: *Easy, for all hikers*
Elevation gain: *900 metres*
Trail markers: *Good*
Cartography: *Tabacco 1:25.000, sheet 003*

This is the most beautiful alpine pasture in the Dolomites, a perfect combination of the unique harmony of the landscape and the interaction between humankind and nature. Nestled between the Croda Rossa and the Croda del Becco summits, in the heart of the Natural Park of the Ampezzo Dolomites, this karst plateau offers vertiginous heights, high mountain meadows, peat bogs and ponds. The surface waters are swallowed by a complex hypogeous system that discharges them downstream at the head of the Boite river in Campo Croce, while the ponds spread out on impermeable soils, and represent the most appreciated part of the landscape.

The *Sempervivum Dolomiticum*, a very rare, endemic, fat plant of an intense purplish red colour, blooms in the middle of these stony and sunny mountain pastures. It can take years for the plant to bloom, and after giving the gift of its exceptional flowering (at the start of August), the flower dies.

Rare violets and orchids also bloom along the banks of the ponds, and fossils abound on the rocks, including ancient marine molluscs and ammonites. The hike in Fossa is very easy and allows for detours to discover its vastness.

As you arrive at the Rifugio Ra Stua (1,670 metres, about an hour's walk or quicker by taking the shuttle bus), walk through the meadows lined by forests to Campo Croce. Ignore the path on the left toward Rifugio Fodara Vedla and continue straight ahead until you reach a fork in the road. Turn right toward the Rifugio Biella along the CAI 26 trail. After a steep stretch between mugo pines, you will come out onto the undulating plains below the Piccola Croda Rossa d'Ampezzo and circumvent the Remeda Rossa lake, at the bottom of a bowl-shaped glacier. Continue slightly uphill and descend to the meadows where the tiny Piccolo lake, surrounded by a peat bog, is hidden. You can then reach the magical shores of the Lago Grande di Fosses. Next to it stands the Cason de Fosses (2,149 metres), which serves as a shelter for shepherds and grazing animals. Continue past this shelter over the grassy meadows of the Alpe di Fosses and climb again to the Rifugio Biella (2,327 metres), which enjoys a superb position below the Croda del Becco (3.5 hours from Sant'Uberto). The best view of the Alpe in all its beauty is from the Forcella Cocodain ridge, where you will see the Tofane, the Pelmo and all the peaks of the park. It can be reached in about half an hour by following the Malga Cavallo path. The return journey is easy, along the main access road to the Rifugio Biella, which descends into the valley along the Val Salata and forms a complete loop.

Alpe di Fosses, Col Bechei and the Cunturines of Forcella Cocodain

Lake Piccolo and Lake Grande, along with the Croda del Becco as seen from Lake Remeda Ro

THE CIRQUES
OF COL BECHEI

High-altitude dolomitic sands

Starting point: *Car park of Sant'Uberto, on the road between Cortina and Passo Cimabanche*
GPS: *46.602410 12.107330*
Time: *7 hours*
Difficulty: *The hike is extremely long and demanding because of the difference in altitude. Only a section on the rocky scree before the summit of the Col Bechei can be tricky, as there are often rockslides. It is best to check with the CAI in Cortina before undertaking this hike*
Elevation gain: *1,500 metres*
Trail markers: *Excellent*
Cartography: *Tabacco 1:25.000, sheet 003*

The imposing Bechei pass (2,794 metres) is a singular peak, from a geological point of view. Its walls are made up of crushed and friable yellow and red limestone formations which rest on scree slopes and gorgeous high mountain meadows.

Above all, these summit cirques, suspended between the steep ridgeline and the Fanes valley, are one of the most precious parts of the Regional Natural Park of the Ampezzo Dolomites. A wonderful path, ignored by tourists even in the middle of summer, climbs up the gavel of the Antruiles valley and the glacial valleys of the Taè, crossing the cirques at high altitude. The trail is very well marked and gradually reveals beautiful features that will leave you speechless, leading you in peaceful silence through enchanting landscapes untouched by human intervention.

The only difficulty on this long route, which normally leads to the summit, is a section of large rockslides just before the final slope, which may prove impracticable. Nevertheless, the aim of this splendid hike is not so much the big cross on the Col Bechei as the journey along its fascinating southern flanks.

From Sant'Uberto, follow the signs and the road to Malga Ra Stua as far as the village of Son Pouses. A little further, turn left (following the signs for Antruiles and Lake Limo) to cross the Boite stream. Continue slightly uphill and cross another bridge over the Mezzo valley stream. Climb up to the Casera Antruiles. Follow the signs, go up the Val Antruiles heading toward the extraordinary red wall of the Croda d'Antruiles. At this stage, the path to follow can be hard to identify due to the scree caused by frequent run-off. Higher up, you will reach a bumpy terrain where the track becomes visible again, until you reach the Cadin del Taè mountain. Here the landscape becomes majestic as the slopes of the Bechei di Sotto pass draw nearer. The path winds up the entire meadow that marks the limit of the amphitheatre, creating an easy passage between the rocky bands that seem to block the path. The path opens out onto the high mountain meadows and stretches out at the foot of the coloured rock walls that resemble organ pipes. It climbs onto a flattened meadow near the summit (2,580 metres), where you can enjoy a panoramic view of the Val di Fanes, the peaks of the Vallon Bianco, the Furcia Rossa and the Piz dles Cunturines and Lavarella (3.5 hours from the car park). This spectacular spot, on the wide ridge that connects the Col Bechei to the Taè, can be the finishing point of this hike, unless you want to go further up the steep gravel slopes and the areas of rockfall that you can already see further afield. From the top of the gravel slops, you can see the Col Bechei cross and, after briefly crossing a meadow, walk around a semicircular gravel area. Venture carefully along the CAI trail that struggles to make its way through the fragments of rockfall. After passing another scree slope, the grassy plateau will appear. You'll notice a war shelter and the normal path of the Rifugio Fanes but, to get there, you have to make your way down to another area subject to heavy run-off. Once you have reached the meadows and the easy terrain, join the old military mule track towards Lake Limo and, after a final effort, climb to the summit, where you'll enjoy a unique and unobstructed view.

The colourful rock formations of the Bechei pass

CASTELLO DI BANCDALSE

A fairy-tale castle in the kingdom of Fanes

Starting point: *Sant'Uberto (1,421 metres), on the road between Cortina and Passo Cimabanche (large parking lot). Given the considerable elevation gain of this itinerary, it may be convenient to climb to higher altitudes using the shuttle service to the Malga Ra Stua (information at the visitors' centre of the Regional Natural Park of the Ampezzo Dolomites in Fiames)*
GPS: *46.602410 12.107330*
Time: *8 hours*
Difficulty: *The hike is long and demanding but technically easy. It requires good orientation and competence to advance. It is advised to be accompanied by a guide or an expert*
Elevation gain: *1,200 metres*
Trail markers: *Excellent until Lake Fodara, but absent after. However, the old paths safely lead to the centre of the Vallon Grande. Excellent visibility is required*
Cartography: *Tabacco 1:25.000, sheet 003*

The Castello di Bancdalse (Bancdalse Castle) is a small, rocky plateau between the Val di Rudo and the high plateau of Fodara Vedla in the Fanes-Sennes-Prags Nature Park. It descends for 500 metres toward Pederù, while the eastern slope is bristling with broken towers set on the pebbled streams of the Vallon Grande, at the foot of the Crode Camin.

No one passes through these remote lands, as there are no marked trails. Before the creation of the park, only hunters would go up there to find the chamois. The name 'castle' comes from the salt that was spread on the rocks to attract the goat-antelope.

If you want to enjoy the charm of a discovery hike, which is very rare in the Dolomites these days, you can leave the well-trodden paths near the Rifugio Fodara Vedla and walk along the refreshing springs that flow into Lake Fodara all the way to the sparse pine forests and the enchanted meadows at the foot of the Castello di Bancdalse in the Vallon Grande. More experienced hikers can also reach the Cresta Camin, which marks the southern limit of the amphitheatre, to admire the endless panorama overlooking the entire protected area.

When you arrive at the Malga Ra Stua after about an hour's walk along a marked path (to avoid walking on the road) or by shuttle bus, make your way across the splendid meadows surrounded by age-old forests to Campo Croce, where you will find the springs of the Boite and an important crossroads. Turn left and walk up through the sparse Swiss stone pine forests on the slopes of the Lavinores, enjoying the beautiful views on the Croda Rossa, until you reach the grassy plain of the small Fodara lake (1.5 hours from Ra Stua). Without necessarily reaching the nearby Rifugio Fodara Vedla, walk along the pond on your left and join the track that climbs slightly to the south-west on the slopes of the Lavinores, near the stream that feeds it. Cross the entire northern base of the Lavinores group, passing by waterfalls and springs, between rocks and mugo pines, then continue past the opening over the Piccolo Valley and enter the Vallon Grande. The terrain is initially flat and practicable. To your right, you will see the strange towers of the Castello di Bancdalse. On its northern crest, there is a rocky passage that looks as if it is about to collapse. The faintly visible track that leads to this place disappears in the rocky debris but heads towards the broken Cresta Camin, which closes the passage to the south. If you still have the energy and time, make the effort to climb over the steep scree, preferably on the right, to the notch between the rocks called Forcella del Vallon Grande (2,580 metres, 2.5 hours from Lake Fodara). A little to the east of the pass, it is possible to climb to the wild Cresta Camin, where a branch of larch, the only trace of humanity's passage in this solitary expanse, marks the small summit.

The Sasso delle Nove in the Cunturines from the meadows of Vallon Grande

FORCELLA DEL PIN

On a glacier nestled in red rocks

Starting point: *Passo Cimabanche (1,530 metres), on the road between Cortina and Dobbiaco*
GPS: *46.620356 12.183582*
Time: *7 hours*
Difficulty: *This hike is for experts but is not difficult (crampons are recommended)*
Elevation gain: *1,000 metres*
Trail markers: *Good until the Malga Stolla, few thereafter, but orientation is straightforward if you have good visibility*
Cartography: *Tabacco 1:25.000, sheet 003*

The Forcella del Pin mountain pass is located between Punta del Pin and Croda Rossa d'Ampezzo at the highest point of the spectacular Cadin di Croda Rossa, a wild valley home to one of the last glaciers of the Dolomites.

Its characteristic horseshoe shape, the ochre and deep red colours of the surrounding peaks, with their gigantic, twisted stratifications, and the rock glacier nestled between them, make it a true monument of nature. The entire route to reach it is of incomparable beauty, from the forests at the bottom of the valley to the velvety meadows near the Malga Stolla, through to the moraine valley that leads to the roches moutonnées (rocks created by the passing of a glacier) on which rest rocky debris and firn at the foot of the immense eastern wall of the Croda Rossa. One of the classic routes up this imposing mountain, which is as beautiful as it is crumbly and dangerous, starts at the crossroads. It was mapped out in 1883 by Michael Innerkofler and goes beyond the wall overlooking the Cadin di Croda Rossa, which displays all its power. Although more difficult than the others due to the climbing passages, this route avoids the unreliable sections that make the other slopes almost inaccessible.

As in hike 23 to the Gran Piramide (see p. 98), climb to the plains below Prato Piazza. Turn left on the CAI 18 trail towards the Malga Stolla (1,939 metres, 1.5 hours). Shortly before the clearing where the alpine hut is located, follow the path marked with a few red marks and cairns up the slope between the sparse pine forests and the alpine meadows. You will then approach the Punta del Pin rocks. Turn right toward the visible entrance to the Cadin di Croda Rossa, where you will enter the impressive lock that runs between Punta del Pin on the left and the Campale peaks on the right, leading to the Croda Rossa wall just opposite. The climb depends on the snow conditions, which are normally ideal until mid-June: it is easier to walk on the firn, especially with crampons, than to face the possible invisible cracks in the glare ice at the end of the summer. In any case, when you reach the bottom of the valley, there seems to be no way out: on the right, a sort of slide takes off towards the Forcella Campale, while on the left, the exit to the Forcella del Pin is difficult to find. Head south, on a steep slope normally covered in snow, and you will approach the ridge to the right of the Punta del Pin, at its lowest point. Climbing, you will reach the rocks and finally the famous notch at 2,656 metres, which is easily accessible and allows you to face the other side of the Colfiedo valley (2 hours from Malga Stolla). The Tre Cime, the Cadini di Misurina and the Cristallo all rise up before you impressively. The direct descent to the south, toward Cimabanche, is possible, but is not recommended due to the unstable terrain and the difficulty making progress among the mugo pines.

In the Cadin di Croda Rossa, with the east wall of Croda Rossa in the background

THE COLLAPSE OF THE PICCOLA CRODA ROSSA

The inevitable disappearance of permafrost in the Dolomites

Starting point: *From the Val Pusteria provincial road to the Braies valley following Prato Piazza to the Ponticello Hotel (1,491 metres, parking fee payable)*
GPS: *46.675874 12.148192*
Time: *7 hours*
Difficulty: *Easy, for all hikers*
Elevation gain: *800 metres*
Trail markers: *Excellent*
Cartography: *Tabacco 1:25.000, sheet 003*

In August 2016, a huge landslide broke off from the Piccola Croda Rossa (2,859 metres) and rolled into the meadows near the Malga Cavallo. This impressive collapse opened a breach about 200 metres wide and 30 metres thick, with a total volume of about 700 cubic metres of rock and debris, profoundly altering the morphology of the slope.

The blame was attributed to the disappearance of permafrost, i.e. the ice permanently contained in the mountain's rock, which caused a progressive loosening of the rock. This phenomenon affects all cold areas of the planet and, beyond changing the appearance of these areas, it seems to contribute to global warming by releasing gases into the atmosphere.

To understand what happened to the Croda Rossa, it helps to watch some films shot there when the successive landslides occurred, after a clearly visible crack opened on the summit.

That said, the Croda Rossa massif is known for its extreme brittleness due to the presence of Jurassic limestone and Cretaceous marl, with its characteristic blood-red colour, that generally make up the Dolomites, and make this specific mountain an extraordinary natural monument recognisable from all sides.

The landscapes surrounding the imposing peak are also among the most precious. All of them are unique works of nature, so much so that they are considered the heart of the Regional Natural Park of the Ampezzo Dolomites and the Fanes-Senes-Braies Nature Park. It is now possible to walk along the foot of the landslide, thanks to the recent construction of a path that replaces the one that disappeared under the debris, to admire a new landscape made up of gigantic red and yellow blocks. It is a marvellous alpine setting born of a natural disaster.

From the Ponticello Hotel, follow the CAI 4 sign for the Malga Rossalm, which runs for a long time along the forest road, passing by the Malga de Sotto. The beautiful surroundings, which alternate between forests and clearings, continue up to the Rossalm (2,142 metres) on meadows below the Piccola Croda Rossa (2.5 hours). The malga (alpine hut) offers an excellent welcome, and a possibility to eat, in a charming place. To visit the landslide, which is already visible in the distance, follow the CAI 3 trail to Prato Piazza, which winds up and down in a beautiful natural harmony of meadows, rhododendrons and sparse forests of Swiss stone pines. The round trip from the hut takes about an hour.

What remains of the Piccola Croda Rossa after the landslide

The blood-coloured walls of the Piccola Croda Rossa from the Rossalm

GRAN PIRAMIDE

An exceptional terrace overlooking the Tre Cime, the Cristallo and the Croda Rossa

Starting point: *Passo Cimabanche (1,530 metres), on the road between Cortina and Dobbiaco*
GPS: *46.620356 12.183582*
Time: *8 hours, but can possibly be shortened to 4 hours if you drive up to Prato Piazza from the Val di Braies (convenient, but much less interesting)*
Difficulty: *Easy hike, which requires good training and some concentration for orientation. Good visibility is necessary*
Elevation gain: *1,200 metres*
Trail markers: *Sufficient*
Cartography: *Tabacco 1:25.000, sheet 003*

The Gran Piramide ('Great Pyramid', 2,711 metres) is the little sister of the well-known Vallandro peak, which has become a tourist magnet. With its pyramidal shape, it stands out among the steep ridges of Valchiara, but has managed to preserve its original calm and offers an exceptional panorama, with the chance to climb freely between the rare forests of Swiss stone pines and the meadows separated by remnants of the war. An important Austro-Hungarian garrison was stationed here, with forts and observation posts, one of which is well preserved and can be visited next to the Rifugio Vallandro.

By combining all the connecting paths of the First World War, you can enjoy a quiet tour far from the tourist crowds that unfortunately clog up the Prato Piazza plateau during the summer. This beautiful and pleasant place within the Fanes-Sennes-Prags Nature Park sits at an average altitude of 2,000 metres and has been one of the most important alpine pastures in South Tyrol since time immemorial. There was already mention of it

in documents from the 12th century, describing it as a property of the German bishopric of Freising.

A tarmac road, which today connects it to Braies, has lost some of its original charm. The Gran Piramide, wrongly regarded as a minor peak, is actually synonymous with unexpected discovery and a pleasant return to nature, in its most beautiful aspects.

From the pass, head toward the Croda Rossa, whose incomparable mass overhangs the road, and take the CAI 18 trail towards Prato Piazza (signs). First climb the gravel mound that descends from the heights of Forcella Colfiedo and enter the Canope Valley and the sparse forest, enclosed between the surrounding steep rocks. The path is an easy climb and will lead you to the head of the valley where a beautiful waterfall, fed by the waters of the Prato Piazza plateau, awaits you. The path leads to the left side and passes a scree terrace. After this section, the path quickly leads to the idyllic meadows of Prato Piazza and continues to the right toward the Rifugio Prato Piazza. Without going as far as the refuge, turn right again to the Rifugio Vallandro (2,040 metres, 2 hours). Take the CAI 34 military path to Monte Specie (a beautiful panoramic observatory well worth the detour). Ignore signs to the Vallandro peak and continue along the southern ridge of the Crepe di Valchiara. Follow the markers and large cairns that point upwards on the western side of the ridge as you gain altitude among the alpine meadows. Continue easily up and emerge onto the ridge at around 2,500 metres, where the view is wide open and makes the climb particularly enjoyable. Staying close to the ridge, with detours possible to visit the rocky peaks that make up the ridge (with several war relics), reach the large cross of the Gran Piramide, which is accessible after a final, steeper stretch among the rocks and rocky debris (2 hours from Rifugio Vallandro).

The Croda Rossa as seen from Prato Piazza

PICCOLO SETTSASS

(24)

The unusual mountain that helped uncover the geohistory of the Dolomites

Starting point: *Castello di Andraz (1,726 metres), which can be reached from Cernadoi on the road between Caprile and Passo Falzarego (signs)*
GPS: *46.505068 11.989422*
Time: *5 hours*
Difficulty: *Easy, for all hikers*
Elevation gain: *700 metres*
Trail markers: *Good*
Cartography: *Tabacco 1:25.000, sheet 007*

The Settsass is a wonderful mountain of the Dolomites, especially when viewed from the meadows of the Col di Lana, which slope down to Andraz Castle. The old building is now a real attraction, much appreciated since its recent successful restoration.

Few people know, however, that the Settsass was one of the most studied and visited areas of the Dolomites, especially by scholars from across the Alps who devoted their studies to the local geology and the collection of fossils. The considerable amount of fossilised fauna first attracted Baron Ferdinand von Richthofen and then Edmund von Mojsisovics to the Settsass, who both developed general theories on the formation of the environment of the Dolomites.

Their observations focused mainly on the conformation of a rocky peak detached from the main mountain with an obvious accumulation of corals in brownish marl strata: a relic of an ancient sea floor. The results were published in 1879 by von Mojsisovics, who named the rock Richthofen Riff in honour of his colleague. These rocks again made history when thousands of young soldiers marched over them during the failed battle for the conquest of the Lana pass. An Austrian observatory was set up on the Richthofen Riff and was named Sasso Staccato ('loose rock') or Piccolo Settsass ('small Settsass') by the Italians, a name still used today for the summit.

The ascent to the summit is very easy, and fascinating for its exceptional landscape and wonderful views of all the main peaks of the Dolomites. There are many testimonies of the First World War in the surrounding area.

From the Andraz Castle car park, follow the signs for the Passo Sief and take a forest road that leads slightly uphill to the vast Federe clearings. Dotted with small baite (local cottages) and barns, it is one of the most typical places of the Dolomites. The marvellous jagged walls of the Settsass stand out above, lit up by the morning sun. Climb between the dark walls of the Col de Lana, Mount Sief and the light-coloured rocks of the Settsass and follow the signs to the Passo Sief where the Marmolada, Sella, Odle and the Puez group appear. From the pass, go toward the Settsass, leaving the ridge and the trenches of Monte Sief, to arrive under the Piccolo Settsass. Go around it to the left and up to the saddle that separates it from the main Settsass summit just above. There are many war relics and a trail to the summit with some fun areas through rocky debris (2.5 hours).

Settsass standing tall behind the forests of Federe

On the summit in winter, between war relics and panoramic views

BIVACCO DELLA PACE

One of the most beautiful landscapes in the Dolomites

Starting point: *Capanna Alpina (1,735 metres), accessible from Armentarola in Val Badia, between San Cassiano and the Valparola Pass*
GPS: *46.559717 11.981995*
Time: *8 hours; it is advised to spend the night at the Bivacco della Pace (2,760 metres, sleeps 12)*
Difficulty: *Easy but long. For all hikers*
Elevation gain: *1,100 metres, with positive and negative elevation*
Trail markers: *Excellent*
Cartography: *Tabacco 1:25.000, sheet 003*
Accommodation: *Bivacco della Pace*

The Fanes Grande Alp, in the heart of the Fanes-Senes-Braies Nature Park, is certainly one of the most beautiful landscapes in the Dolomites. Rich in springs, streams, meadows and glacial valleys, it is surrounded by imposing rocky ridges, all of them nearly 3,000 metres in altitude. Isolated and remote from the villages at the bottom of the valley, these peaks were among the last to have been explored by pioneering mountaineers in the late 1800s. Only the First World War and its armed men disturbed its peace. All the ridges were massively fortified and guarded by the Austro-Hungarian army, which faced up to the *Alpini*, the Italian Army's specialist mountain infantry, on the neighbouring Tofane ridges. At 2,800 metres, Monte Castello was a strategic tower between the Fanes peaks, Monte Cavallo and the Furcia Rossa peaks. A post was even built there for a cannon to fight the enemy lines beyond the Travenanzes valley. Now calm has returned, the foot of the walls of Moute Castello is home to the wonderful Bivacco della Pace ('Peace Bivouac'). The old

wooden hut has been renovated and offers all hikers the chance to spend the night in a historic place with an extraordinary view. The terrace where the cannon was located is only a few steps away and, from there, you can see the Tofane and surrounding valleys.

From the car park, go up (no risk of making a mistake) between the branches of the Piz dles Cunturines and the Cima del Lago and climb to the Col Locia (2,069 metres) and the mountain pastures of the Piano Grande and the Passo Tadega. This walk across this exceptional environment is of a rare beauty and represents perfectly how legends describe the paradise that is the Fane kingdom. Beyond the pass, descend to the enchanting mountain pasture of Fanes Grande. There you will find a malga (alpine hut) with the same name, between the meadows and meanders of the fiery streams that converge on the plain (2 hours from the car park). Just before the malga, turn right and walk up the sparse forest of Swiss stone pines that spreads to the grandiose Vallon Bianco, between the Campestrin and Furcia Rossa peaks. Monte Castello is clearly recognisable by its tower-like shape in the centre of the valley. The climb will take you along a moderate slope, on what used to be the path used by the soldiers. Once you pass the large blocks of stone that broke off the Campestrin Nord summit, the path will take you through the rock scree beneath Monte Castello. The Bivacco della Pace is located under these walls (2 hours from the Malga Fanes Grande). From the hut, continue to climb the scree to the right of the walls, then go up a steeper section to reach the fork in the ridge overlooking the Val Travenanzes and the Tofane, where there are still many war remnants. More experienced hikers can push on to Monte Casale (2,894 metres) and Monte Cavallo (2,912 metres) along the old, marked army paths.

Alternative access to the Malga Fanes Grande: the fantastic Fanes Valley, a natural pearl of rare beauty

It is also possible to ascend to the Bivacco della Pace from San Vigilio di Marebbe in the Val Badia by driving up the Val di Rudo to the Rifugio Pederù. From there, continue on foot along the CAI 7 dirt road to Rifugio Fanes (2,060 metres) then to Passo di Limo (2,172 metres). Shortly after the pass, keep to the right and climb to the Malga Fanes Grande (3 hours from Pederù). In summer, there is a paid shuttle bus service from Pederù to Rifugio Fanes. Another possibility is to start from Fiames, north of Cortina: from the visitors' centre of the Regional Natural Park of the Ampezzo Dolomites, follow the CAI 10 trail up the fantastic Val di Fanes, a natural pearl of rare beauty, to Malga Fanes Grande (3 hours).

The Vallon Bianco as seen from the Col Bechei: in the background the Marmolada
and the Piz dles Cunturines
Bottom right, the Malga Fanes Grande

ROS DI TOFANA

The Raibl stratifications and the oldest amber in the world

Starting point: *Rifugio Dibona, accessible by car from the route that branches off the road between Cortina and Passo Falzarego*
GPS: *46.532496 12.070226*
Time: *3 hours*
Difficulty: *This is an easy hike, but it requires good footing and via ferrata equipment. It is best to ask at the Rifugio Dibona about the conditions of the Astaldi trail (an area often subject to landslides)*
Elevation gain: *150 metres*
Trail markers: *Good*

There are many marvellous landscapes and geological treasures to discover at the foot of the imposing walls of Punta Anna, above the Rifugio Dibona. In particular, there is a clearly visible layer of blood-red clay strata, interspersed with rocky stratifications in shades of brown, violet, yellow and green. This is the geological formation of the Raibl. Dating back 220 million years, it is characteristic of the bedrock of the Tofana di Mezzo, with its few solitary and isolated trees on inaccessible escarpments.

This area, called Ros di Tofana due to the predominance of red tones (red is 'rosso' in Italian), is a palaeontological site of considerable importance. It has recently yielded discoveries of exceptional scientific interest, such as Triassic amber, the oldest amber ever found in the world. This material, derived from the exudation of plant resin, has the property of preserving what is trapped inside. In the droplets from the foot of the Tofana, researchers have found multi-cellular organisms exactly as they were 220 million years ago. The discovery led to a new phase of research. The Ros di Tofana can be visited thanks to a pleasant circular route: the Sentiero Astaldi, one of the first equipped routes in Cortina. Although it is not technically difficult, it must be taken seriously and with via ferrata equipment (especially helmets), as it extends over very crumbly terrain.

To extend this short loop, once you have exited the Tofana Valley, you can climb to the Tofana cave, which opens up at the base of the gigantic wall of the Tofana di Rozes. Here too, you have to walk along an equipped path on an exposed but safe and well-maintained ledge. The cave is about 300 metres long and spirals into the bowels of the mountain. Another short, equipped path leads into the cave for a few dozen metres.

From Rifugio Dibona, follow the CAI 421 trail towards Rifugio Pomedes which leads to a spectacular setting at the foot of the rocky bands. You'll see chamois running around as Swiss stone pines, larches and firs defy the forces of nature, clinging to the slopes and rocks. After climbing a hill between the few meadows that do not suffer from the slow erosion typical of the area, you will reach a crossroads. Leave the path leading to the refuge and turn left onto the Sentiero Astaldi. Follow the metal cables that guide you under the walls, with some ascents over rocky debris. The view of the Ampezzo valley and the most important peaks (Sorapiss, Antelao, Pelmo, Croda da Lago, Nuvolau, Marmolada) is spectacular and continues to the end of the equipped path. There, on a grassy hill that also serves as a magnificent viewpoint over the imposing wall of the Tofana di Rozes, you can descend into the Vallon di Tofana and quickly return to the Rifugio Dibona. To get to the cave, follow the track that continues up and joins the road leading to the Rifugio Giussani. Without going up to the refuge, head towards the base of the Tofana di Rozes wall, following the signs for the Rifugio Lagazuoi. You will quickly notice the signs for the cave below the threatening walls. Climb among the scree and up the ledge using a few metal stirrups. Guided by ropes, the path will cross the base of the mountain and, after a final jump on easy stone steps, you can enter the cave.

CADIN DI LAGAZUOI

Away from the crowds at the foot of the Torre Fanis and one of the most spectacular places in the Dolomites

Starting point: *The car park to the ski runs of Col Gallina (2,054 metres), on the road between Cortina and Passo Falzarego*
GPS: *46.520336 12.019183*
Time: *6 hours*
Difficulty: *For experts. This an easy hike, but the terrain is partly comprised of scree and there are some sections without paths*
Elevation gain: *1,100 metres, with numerous counter-slopes*
Trail markers: *Good on the CAI trails, but absent on the section that crosses the Forcella del Mortaio*
Cartography: *Tabacco 1:25.000, sheet 003*

It was the great Austrian pioneers von Glanvell, von Saar and Domenigg who first explored the Fanis group in the upper Travenanzes valley in 1898. The Torre Fanis ('Fanis Tower'), a majestic rocky obelisk, captivated them despite their extensive knowledge of the Dolomites. These three men, who reconnoitred many unexplored places, solved riddles and climbed walls that had never been climbed before, were mountaineering legends.

In von Glanvell's words to describe their first crucial encounter: 'But there, on the right, stands a giant tower, high, very high in the immaculate blue of the evening; a silver ribbon surrounds its tip; below, its walls fall like lead. Yes, it is the mermaid that has drawn us here. We stare silently at this titanic column that, even in the land of the enchanting Dolomites, is incomparable. Without averting our gaze, we walk to meet her.'

This was followed by the discovery of the heights along a route that still commands respect and admiration to this day. After the devastation of the First World War, some parts of the Fanis, such as the Lagazuoi or the Fanis Sud mountain, have become emblematic places for tourists to visit in the Dolomites, while the Torre is still bathed in its original silence. There, in the midst of an imposing natural environment, you can admire its walls up close, as well as those of the Tofane just opposite, that rest on the typical red earth of the upper Travenanzes valley.

Many paths used during the war are abandoned, yet they still lead safely between these monumental mountains along a hike that feels like an exploration.

From the car park, follow a wide path through the vegetation that climbs towards the Lagazuoi and quickly joins the ski slope that descends from

the Rifugio Lagazuoi. Follow the CAI 402 marker on the edge of the track and leave it when the path veers towards the Forcella Travenanzes. From the pass, between the Lagazuoi Grande and the Falzarego peak, there is a superb view of the Travenanzes valley, the Tofane and the Torre Fanis on the left. Take the CAI 20B trail for the Tomaselli via ferrata, which crosses the scree slope to the east of the Lagazuoi Grande and climbs up to the narrow Forcella Gasser Depot, embedded in the ridge of the Lagazuoi di Mezzo. There are still many relics of the First World War on the pass. Descend slightly toward the Cadin di Lagazuoi, one of the most spectacular and grandiose places in the Dolomites, with towers, walls, ravines and the three gigantic Tofane in the background. There, leave the markers, and the crowds of tourists, that all lead to the via ferrata. Find the track that descends into

the Cadin di Lagazuoi, first over the meadows and then toward the base of the Torre Fanis, opposite. Continue toward the gravel that rolls down to the right of the tower from the Forcella del Mortaio (2,446 metres). At the foot of the scree corridor, climb up the laborious yet relatively easy section to reach the notch where, during the war, an artillery piece was installed (3 hours). Go to the opposite side, sliding toward the lower part of the Cadin de Fanis, keeping close to the walls to the right. At 2,200 metres above sea level, join the CAI 17 trail and follow it downhill where it joins the CAI 401 trail, just above the Cason di Travenanzes. From there, continue climbing between the meadows and the typical red geological stratifications on the left flank to reach the mountain pass of the same name. From the pass, return to the car park via the ski slope.

THE ALPINE PASTURES OF POSSOLIVA

The enchanting meadows at the foot of Monte Cernera

Starting point: *The bend at 1,699 metres, in the Zonia valley, on the road that leaves Selva di Cadore and leads to Passo Giau*
GPS: *46.475253 12.039296*
Time: *4 hours*
Difficulty: *This easy hike is accessible for everyone, but requires good visibility to find your way*
Elevation gain: *550 metres*
Trail markers: *Sufficient, though absent on one section, but the path remains easily identifiable*
Cartography: *Tabacco 1:25.000, sheet 003*

Although they are near the busy Passo Giau, the alpine meadows of the Piani di Possoliva and the Val Zonia remain completely shrouded in their original silence, wrapped in the enchanting beauty of an unspoilt and delicate nature. These meadows lie between the imposing Monte Cernera and the volcanic ridge of Zonia, punctuated by erratic rocks and coloured by countless flowers. The view of the shining snows of the Marmolada to the west and the peaks of Nuvolau and Averau to the north make this one of the most typical and peaceful landscapes of the Dolomites. In the Val Zonia there are still a few tabià, the high mountain shelters once used for haymaking and grazing, especially on the working

and hiking trails. In fact, one of these paths is perfect for a delightful walk, with a few short stretches where you can wander freely through the rolling hills of the Zonia valley. Far from the tracks, paths and marked trails, it is a pure joy of a hike.

From the bend in the road, follow the signs for Monte Cernera and Passo Giau and climb through the woods on a forest road to the Val Zonia. Immediately after, ignore the fork in the road to the right for the Andria and continue until you reach the aqueduct artefacts, where the valley begins to appear in all its splendour. At the signposted crossroads, turn right toward Monte Verdal and Monte Cernera. There will be a first stretch across the high grass of the sparse forest (follow the trail markers carefully) which will lead to the lower part of the Possoliva pastures. From there, the most prominent section of the itinerary begins and will require you to abandon the trail markers leading up, instead turning left onto the vast meadows. You can walk around this area, which is free of signs and paths, and climb up the entire impluvium on gentle slopes, after having slipped between two large rocks at the beginning of the route. Once you reach the top of the gentle slope, you can see the head of the Val Zonia, with the peaks over which the Alta Via no. 1 footpath passes. To reach the ridge, cross to the east and follow the classic path to Monte Cernera near the Forcella Col Piombin. You will reach it after a long, flat section and a short climb. Go left on the Alta Via no. 1 footpath to the nearby Forcella Zonia. Just before the pass, take the faintly visible track (signs) that turns left and descends into the wonderful and bucolic Val Zonia toward the Marmolada. Stroll through the flowery meadows to the chalets along the way up to the edge of the forest, from where you can return to the car park

The Marmolada from the meadows of the Zonia valley

ROCCHETTA DI PRENDERA

A not-so-perilous adventure, far from the beaten track

Starting point: *Ponte di Rucurto (1,708 metres), on the road between Cortina and Passo Giau*
GPS: *46.503378 12.076417*
Time: *6.5 hours*
Difficulty: *An easy hike, but with a long elevation. It only requires good visibility and experience walking on rocky debris*
Elevation gain: *800 metres*
Trail markers: *Good until Forcella Ambrizzola. Only cairns beyond this point*
Cartography: *Tabacco 1:25.000, sheet 003*

Prendera is the highest summit of the Rocchette. Together with Ruoibes, Sorarù and Campolongo, it forms a small group of mountains between the Boite valley and the Val Fiorentina. Although these mountains are close to the Becco di Mezzodì and the popular Croda da Lago area, they remain on the fringes of the classic hiking routes.

The Prendera is the only one with a very limited number of visitors, who only come during snowy season as it is a popular destination for ski-mountaineering from Cortina or the Passo Staulanza. The rest of the year, this beautiful and well-preserved area enjoys peace and quiet. The summit owes its name to the Malga Prendera, which stretches out at the foot of the southern walls. These walls reach a height of 300 metres and some of them carry entire towers. The area near the Federa mountain pasture, with its rocky slabs, peat bogs, marshy areas and wonderful forests, is typical of the Federa Lake.

There are two routes to this easily accessible peak, which stands like the prow of a ship facing the nearby Pelmo: the one that starts from the Rifugio Palmieri, ideal for getting away from the summer crowds around the lake, or the one that starts from the Passo Staulanza via the Rifugio Città di Fiume and the Malga Prendera. The view from the summit is exceptional.

From the car park near the Rucurto bridge, follow the signs and climb to the Rifugio Palmieri on the Croda da Lago. We recommend an early start. In summer, the path is very busy, and the real pleasure of the hike is to experience the atmosphere around the wonderful Lake Federa (1 hour and three quarters). From there, the Rocchetta is already visible on the left of the very sharp Becco di Mezzodì. Continue along the small road towards the Forcella Ambrizzola but, before you reach it, turn left and follow the cairns, under the large rocks

The Rocchetta di Prendera and the Becco di Mezzodì as seen from Lake Federa ▶

on the slopes of the Becco. Go around the base of the Forcella Ambrizzola along a path that offers increasingly stunning views at each step, until you reach a knoll beyond which are the Rocchetta slopes, interspersed with meadows and rocks. After easily passing the rocky slabs, climb the scree plateau that separates the Becco from the Rocchetta, from where you will finally see the summit and its cross. Go up the wide ridge, which only narrows at the summit (2,496 metres, 2 hours from the refuge).

Alternative from Passo Staulanza: wonderful meadows

From Passo Staulanza, drive down into Val Fiorentina until you reach a bend on the left, where you can park. Follow the road at the foot of the northern slope of the Pelmo to reach the Rifugio Città di Fiume, which is very popular in the summer. From the refuge, climb the slope above, crossing a long stretch on the western flank of the Col della Puina toward the fork of the same name, along clear and easy slopes. Follow a downhill route through sparse larch forests to Forcella Roan, on the watershed between the Val Fiorentina and the Boite Valley. The Malga Prendera (2,148 metres), already visible near the refuge, can be reached by a moderately steep climb through wonderful meadows (2 hours from the pass). From the alpine pasture, continue toward Forcella Ambrizzola until the first rocks at the foot of the fallen scree of Becco di Mezzodì, the castle with towers on the right at the top of the valley. You will see a large scree slope that starts from the fork between the Becco and the Rocchetta. Go up the slope, following the markers until the small plateau on the ridge, and join the previous access (1 hour from the Malga Prendera).

On the Rocchetta ridge towards the Croda da Lago, the Tofane and the basin of Cortina d'Ampezzo

PENNES DI FORMIN AND THE LAKES OF CIOU DE RA MAZA

Away from the crowds in the region of Cortina

Starting point: *Ponte di Rucurto (1,708 metres), on the road between Cortina and Passo Giau*
GPS: *46.503378 12.076417*
Time: *6 hours*
Difficulty: *This is an easy hike. The climb to the pond is accessible to all, but the climb to Les Pennes is steeper*
Elevation gain: *650 metres*
Trail markers: *No markers beyond the CAI marked trails. Orientation is not a problem if you have good visibility*
Cartography: *Tabacco 1:25.000, sheet 003*

This itinerary allows you to visit two places unknown to many people in the Cortina d'Ampezzo area. The Pennes di Formin are isolated banks of rock on the northern ridge of the Lastoni di Formin, covered by forests. The spectacular larches and Swiss stone pines have been shaped by lightning and are one of the few places where the axe of the woodcutter has never been laid. As a result, some are several hundred years old and are a perfect example of a primitive forest in Italy. The Ciou de Ra Maza pond is a small mirror of water at an altitude of 1,891 metres in the heart of the forest, on the western slopes of the Lastoni di Formin. Although it

is small and cannot be compared with the magnificent Federa lake under the Croda da Lago (which is crowded at every time of year), its charm lies in the contrast it creates with the steep walls of the Formin, which glow red in the morning hours. This body of water is also the scene of ancient legends: it is said the footprints of the Anguanes – female figures with goat feet who come out of their homes to rinse clothes in its cold waters – can be seen on its banks.

The history of the region is also very interesting: it belongs administratively to San Vito di Cadore, which, although geographically distant from this area, has always managed it. To settle old border issues, the wall of Giau was built in 1753 – a straight line of stones on the slopes of the Lastoni di Formin. The few remains of the wall can be visited from the Passo Giau, following the signs and taking the chance to look for the border markers with crosses, the Lion of St Mark (symbolising the Veneto territories) and the Habsburg coat of arms (Cortinese territories). The Ciou of Ra Maza, literally 'the head of the stick', perhaps indicates the section of the border close to the water point.

From the car park near the Rucurto bridge, follow the signs and climb towards the Rifugio Palmieri on the Croda da Lago until you reach the fork in the road near the Cason di Formin (1,885 metres). Then go right into the Formin valley along the CAI 435 trail, gradually climbing from the bottom of the valley, where the mountain stream flows and forms beautiful pools. When the path draws nearer to the rocky bands that support the suspended plateaus of the Pennes on the right, look for a track up a sort of grassy ledge planted with Swiss stone pines. This is the only easy way up. For reference, it is located at 2,040 metres above sea level, as indicated by the black dotted lines on the Tabacco map. Once you have reached the summit plateau at 2,149 metres, you can wander around at your leisure and walk along the ridge to the south toward Mount Formin (1.5 hours). For the lake, 200 metres after the bridge over the Rio Costeana, just after the car park, take the forest road on the right, which will lead you to the southern side of the forest. Once you have passed the remains of the Giau wall, after about 3 km, is a crossroads. Turn left to see the pillars of the Lastoni di Formin, also known as the 'Spurs of Solitude', and you will come across the small pools of the Ciou de Ra Maza (1 hour and 15 minutes from the car park). You can continue along the track towards the plateaus below Forcella Giau and, from there, return to the Passo Giau road, a little downstream from the alpine pasture of the same name (Malga Giau). To return to the car park, follow this same road. You can also make a detour to the Giau wall, which crosses it at an altitude of 1,838 metres (signs).

The Croda da Lago and the Lastoni di Formin; visible on the right is the Passo Pennes
mountain ridge

JOURNEY ACROSS THE MESOLITHIC

A night in a tent

Starting point: *Rifugio Aquileia (1,583 metres), in the upper Val Fiorentina valle*
GPS: *46.436107 12.100675*
Time: *7.5 hours*
Difficulty: *This hike is accessible to everyone, but it requires some practice.*
A tent, mattress and sleeping bag are required
Elevation gain: *1,000 metres, with positive and negative elevation*
Trail markers: *Good*
Cartography: *Tabacco 1:25.000, sheets 003 and 015*

The Journey across the Mesolithic is a long and beautifully scenic route through the millennia to discover the history of mankind in the high mountains. It runs through endless meadows between the Forcella Giau, the Mondeval and the undulating Prendera, at the foot of the Lastoni di Formin, the Becco di Mezzodì, the Rocchette and the Pelmo.

In 1987, near the Malga Mondeval di Sopra, beneath the shelter of a large rock detached from the Lastoni di Formin, is an important burial site dating back about 8,000 years. The site, found in an exceptional state of conservation, is the tomb of an adult man and his many burial artefacts including working and hunting utensils, organic remains, food scraps and resins. These objects have enabled experts, who never before had so many elements to work with, to carry out new studies and make unprecedented discoveries. Today, the 'Mondeval Man' rests in the nearby museum of Selva di Cadore, where a thematic tour has been set up explaining all the aspects of the archaeological site.

Located close to the Alta Via no. 1, the site is quite popular among tourists. To fully appreciate the charm of the area and enjoy the absolute peace of sunset and dawn in the Dolomites, we recommend a two-day excursion with an overnight stay in a tent, which is the best way to live a unique experience under the same starry sky our ancestors admired between two hunts.

From the car park of the Rifugio Aquileia, follow the signs and climb through woods and clearings to the Malga Fiorentina, and further, until you reach the Rifugio Città di Fiume (1 hour). From this busy refuge, continue on the path that climbs toward the slopes of the Col della Puina to reach, after a slight descent, the Forcella Roan. After another moderate climb, you will reach the wonderful plateau of the Malga Prendera (2,148 metres), below the Rocchetta of the same name. From the alpine pasture, climb up its slopes through the meadows dotted with rocks, in a particularly evocative setting. At the edges of the path there are flat areas ideal for tents (a stream nearby will provide a water supply). At the top of the slope is the Forcella Col Duro, with a complete view of the Mondeval mountain pastures, the Croda da Lago and the Lastoni di Formin (1.5 hours from the refuge). From the pass, make a semicircle among the rocks under the Becco di Mezzodì to reach the Forcella Ambrizzola, beyond which the Cortina basin and its mountains are visible. Continue toward Mondeval and descend to the esplanades below the tapering Spiz di Mondeval. There, it is best to head for the Malga Mondeval di Sopra and the rock protecting the Mesolithic burial site. From the alpine pasture, continue along the grassy valleys on a well-maintained path at the foot of Monte Mondeval. Aim for the northern ridge of Monte

Mondeval to quickly reach a terrace that houses the delightful Lago delle Baste (2,281 metres), itself surrounded by a peat bog and pretty streams. This is perfect for a night in the open air, right in front of the Pelmo and the Lastoni di Formin (1.5 hours from Forcella Col Duro). In this case, it is possible to climb easily to Monte Mondeval (2,455 metres), which is a spectacular lookout point. From the lake, continue up toward the already visible Forcella Giau (itself a must, for its beautiful viewpoint), until you reach a crossroad near the large volcanic rocks, rich in fossils. Ignore the Alta Via and turn left onto the CAI 465 trail that descends into the magnificent scenery of the Loschiesuoi valley, as far as the Ponte di Sassi (2,115 metres).

Do not continue down into the valley, instead following signs uphill for about 100 metres to the Sella della Vallazza, between Piz del Corvo and Monte Mondeval, a peaceful and secluded, bucolic place (1.5 hours from the lake). Start the descent toward Malga Mondeval di Sotto, which you will reach after passing the ruins of Casera Vallazza and the meadows of Rio Cordon. Below the mountain pasture is a forest road near a hydroelectric power station. Keep to the left and follow the road through the woods until you reach the Val Fiorentina road, a little below the Baita Flora Alpina. Stay on the dirt roads by the roadside and they will lead you back to the starting point.

From Cortina to Sappada

THE CRESTA BIANCA

Traces of the First World War in an exceptionally beautiful setting in the Cristallo group

Starting point: *The Cimabanche Pass (1,530 metres), on the road between Cortina and Dobbiaco*
GPS: *46.620356 12.183582*
Time: *7 hours*
Difficulty: *This is a long and strenuous hike at high altitude which requires stable weather. At the start of the summer, crampons are recommended, as there may be many exposed sections*
Elevation gain: *1,400 metres*
Trail markers: *Sufficient*
Cartography: *Tabacco 1:25.000, sheet 003*

The Cresta Bianca ('White Ridge') is one of those places in the Cristallo mountain group that is strongly linked to the First World War. In July 1915, Austrian soldiers moved up the northern front and installed a cannon on the highest peaks of Cortina d'Ampezzo, aimed

directly at the Tre Croci Pass. On 2 August, the *Alpini* counter-offensive began. It culminated in the capture of the fortifications and the ridge, which shifted the front line. Entrenched in cruel and static warfare, this new front line remained unchanged until October 1917. The remarkable remnants of war can still be seen today thanks to the well-frequented Sentiero Dibona. The route is very interesting from a historical point of view but is overrun by tourists at the height of summer.

Few people dare to venture to the untouched nature of the Pra del Vecia valley and walk up the Gravon del Forame along the old Austrian military path. There are still many traces of the years of war: barracks, strongholds and paths worth discovering, all set in an exceptionally beautiful landscape at high altitude.

Near the Forcella Grande is a path leading to the small Cresta Bianca glacier, itself protected by the walls of the Cristallino d'Ampezzo and sloping toward the Cresta di Costabella. The war has left its mark: open glacial environments are a rare sight in the Dolomites.

From the pass, follow the signs and walk along the forest roads at the bottom of the valley until you see the sign for the Pra del Vecia valley on the right. Climb up the left side of the valley. This first section, steeped in rocky ledges with little exposure, is home to many streams and pretty areas. Cross the lower threshold in the sparse forest and enter the bottom of a narrow valley with massive rocks under high walls. Exit to the right, where you will find what remains of a path which was created by the soldiers but has since been damaged in parts by snow and rain. It will take you through the mugo pines and over the scree under the Forcella Gialla. Before reaching the Forcella Gialla, cross to the left and, in the middle of wide, hollow sections, enter the Gravon del Forame. Leave the path that climbs toward Forcella Verde to instead join the Sentiero Attrezzato de Pol (equipped path), and climb up the central part of the Gravon del Forame toward the Cristallo peaks, between which the suspension bridge of the Sentiero Dibona is clearly visible. At the bottom of the valley, between rocky debris and snow, keep to the right and climb up to the Forcella Grande (2,874 metres), which is sandwiched between the Cristallino d'Ampezzo on the left and the Cresta Bianca on the right. There you will reach the Sentiero Dibona. The Cresta Bianca (2,932 metres) can quickly be reached by making your way on the rocky debris of the sloping northern wall dotted with war relics (4 hours). We recommend following the via ferrata for a short stretch and visiting the many stations on the southern slope of the Cresta Bianca, overlooking the Cortina basin and its mountains.

THE FONDA VALLEY

An impressive and imposing glacial setting

Starting point: Ponte della Marogna (1,476 metres), on the road between Carbonin and Misurina
GPS: 46.613001 12.226175
Time: 8 hours
Difficulty: It is an easy hike to the base of the channel which leads to the moraine and the glacier. Beyond this point, the hike is very difficult and the help of a guide or expert is needed. In summer, going on the glacier requires a rope, an ice axe and crampons
Elevation gain: 1,350 metres
Trail markers: None. Follow the old soldiers' path
Cartography: Tabacco 1:25.000, sheet 003

V al Fonda is the most colossal of all the gigantic valleys on the northern slopes of the Cristallo mountain group. What makes Val Fonda special is being surrounded by all the main peaks, the highest of which is the Cristallo (3,221 metres).

In its upper part it is home to one of the last glaciers of the Dolomites, now shrunk to nothing but originally very large and criss-crossed by wide crevasses. It was in one of those crevasses that the famous South Tyrolean guide Michael Innerkofler died in 1888, after more than 300 visits. At the time, the classic route to the summit was via the glacier (which gave its name to the entire mountain group). The grandiose environment and the imposing glacial scenery make the valley one of the most important natural monuments of the Dolomites, often photographed from Lago di Landro or the area around Prato Piazza.

In ideal snow conditions, between late winter and mid-spring, the Fonda valley welcomes a multitude of ski tourers who head toward the great depression of the Cristallo Pass (2,808 metres). In the summer, silence reigns in the area as almost no one ventures toward the spectacular meanders of the canyon at the bottom of the valley.

When conditions permit, normally until the first days of June, it is also possible to enter the magical upper amphitheatre after passing a steep channel and continuing to the pass with crampons and an ice axe. When the glacier retreats during the summer and leaves its crevasses uncovered, it is better to give up. However, you can still visit the vast spaces of the moraine.

From the car park near the Ponte della Marogna, go up to the right of the mountain stream that winds through almost flat scree and head toward the walls enclosing the opening of the Val Fonda on to the valley. Enter between the high edges that form the canyon and continue along the side of the stream

as it bends. This first stretch between the rocks is particularly pretty, and quickly leads to a very long, moderately steep slope dotted with rocks that leads to the rocky barrier above which the Cristallo peaks can be seen. As you approach it, the old soldiers' path follows the only passage that allows you to climb up a fissure. You'll notice many remains of the First World War. After a few climbing passages, exit on the lower part of the glacier moraine. Climb again to the left, staying generally on the left side of the glacier, which

can be reached depending on the season and snow conditions. If conditions permit, progress on the névé is normally easy, but if the crevasses are visible, it is essential to be extra careful and take all necessary mountaineering precautions. The climb ends on the Cristallo Pass (many war remnants are still visible), which faces the large southern channel that rises near the Tre Croci Pass. You'll notice the imposing Sorapiss that stands out above the rocks which frame the view of the valley.

GUGLIA DE AMICIS

(3)

The obelisk guarding Misurina that nobody sees

Starting point: *Malga Misurina, easily accessible from Lago di Misurina*
GPS: *46.577996 12.247234*
Time: *4.5 hours*
Difficulty: *This is an easy hike with a steep section when descending the Sella di Popena that requires particular attention*
Elevation gain: *600 metres*
Trail markers: *Good throughout the loop but there are no arrows indicating the detour*
Cartography: *Tabacco 1:25.000, sheet 003*

The Edmondo de Amicis Guglia (*guglia* means 'needle' in Italian) is a 60-metre-high tower on the edge of the Lago di Misurina. Unfortunately, it is impossible to appreciate its elegant profile from there, as it blends in with the other pinnacles at the base of the Pale di Misurina. It is only when you approach its base that this natural wonder fully reveals itself. Tapered like a missile emerging from the rocks and pointing to the sky, there is no doubt it is one of the most extraordinary obelisks of the Dolomites.

A special technique was used for its first alpine ascent in 1906. The guide Tita Piaz, nicknamed 'the devil of the Dolomites' for his perilous undertakings, pulled a rope from the adjacent tower to the top of the spire and reached the summit after a dizzying horizontal crossing in thin air. The legendary mountaineer returned in 1907, accompanied by Ugo de Amicis, who wanted to dedicate it to his father, a writer. It was not until 1913 that the spire was climbed directly, by the talented mountaineer Hans Dülfer, who was one of the first to go beyond grade VI in the Dolomites and who also developed the double-rope descent and crack climbing techniques that now bear his name.

Among the many excursions possible around Misurina, Guglia de Amicis remains unsolicited by many despite being located in an exceptional place facing the lake, the Cadini, the Tre Cime di Lavaredo and the long Sorapiss and Marmarole mountain range.

It is possible to visit the obelisk while undertaking the classic crossing of the Pale di Misurina and the Val Popena, by completing a loop that passes through the Sella di Popena and the ancient refuge of the same name.

From the Malga Misurina, go up to the alpine pasture at the back, following the signs for the Sella di Popena and the former Rifugio Popena. The first crossroads with signs is just above. Turn left to climb the slopes of the Pale di Misurina, following the military path as it bends and twists. At a second crossroads, go right this time, following the CAI 224 trail which will bring you out of the woods but still in the middle of the dense mugo pines. Near a hairpin bend on the left, look for a large stone cairn that points to the right to get to the Guglia de Amicis. The beginning of the path is almost invisible because of the density of the pines, but further on it is easy to spot and stretches toward the Tre Cime, under the Pale di Popena. After a few insignificant mounds, you'll notice a rocky wall and you'll soon see the obelisk. Cross through the gravel to reach the narrow fork that separates it from the other towers. You can even walk around it to enjoy it from all angles (1 hour). Back at the crossroads, we recommend continuing the ascent, which quickly leads to a ridge overlooking the Popena valley, with the Cristallino di Popena and the imposing rock face of Piz Popena, one of the many peaks of the Cristallo that exceed 3,000 metres. From the ridge, the path descends into the Popena valley and then crosses, almost levelling at an altitude, the slopes of the Pale di Misurina, through an area of scree. Reach the grassy plains in the centre of the imposing basin, itself a jewel of the Regional National Park of the Ampezzo Dolomites, and follow the signs that climb a hundred metres up to the spectacular Sella di Popena, where there are the ruins of what was once a refuge. Despite its location and the magnificent landscape it enjoyed, the refuge was never rebuilt. Just in front of the ruins, you'll notice that the descent to Misurina begins. The wooden bridge will help you safely pass by a rockfall, where a steep track allows you to descend carefully on a slippery ground of fine gravel. Soon you will reach the wide and easy path which, if turn left, leads back to the alpine pasture and its beautiful views.

Guglia De Amicis

At the foot of Guglia de Amicis

THE TRENCHES OF THE ALPE MATTINA PASS

The military outpost facing some of the most emblematic scenery of the Dolomites

Starting point: *Rifugio Auronzo, accessible from Misurina on the Tre Cime toll road*
GPS: *46.612262 12.295837*
Time: *5 hours*
Difficulty: *Easy, for all hikers*
Elevation gain: *200 metres*
Trail markers: *Excellent. The trenches can be visited freely*
Cartography: *Tabacco 1:25.000, sheet 010*

I s it still possible to find peaceful havens to admire the many wonders of the most emblematic and frequented place of the Dolomites, facing the gigantic, sail-like mountains of the Tre Cime di Lavaredo? Can we still escape the crowds of tourists that flock to the terrace of the Locatelli refuge and find a quiet corner, respectful of the tragic events that took place up there during the First World War? The answer is undoubtedly yes, because the best viewpoints, slightly off the beaten track, were vital throughout the war, precisely because of their strategic positions at high altitude.

On the slopes just west of the imposing Torre di Toblin there are still paths, trenches and other artefacts that are easily accessible and

shine a light on the tragedy of countrymen killing each other in such a beautiful, harmonious natural setting.

From the car park near the Rifugio Auronzo, follow the road that leads to the Rifugio Lavaredo. At the height of summer, it is best to set off early in the morning as this stretch is overrun by tourists. Walk under the famous walls of the three peaks of the Lavaredo, the Ovest ('west peak'), the Grande ('big peak') and the Piccola ('little peak'), culminating in the Spigolo Giallo, a blade that stretches from the scree of the ground toward the sky. From the Rifugio Lavaredo, which was a key Italian stronghold during the war, climb up to the Forcella Lavaredo, where the three peaks can be seen from their best-known angle. From the pass, continue along the road until you reach the Rifugio Locatelli, whose owner was the guide Sepp Innerkofler before the war. This legendary figure, a connoisseur of the surrounding mountains, joined the Austrian Standschützen (militia) and was killed by an Italian sniper on Mount Paterno, just opposite his refuge. The guns fell silent that day, and operations ceased, as a sign of remembrance, but also to recover the remains and bury them. From the refuge, follow the signs to the Rifugio Tre Scarperi and climb very slightly to go around the Sasso di Sesto to the west, reaching the Alpe Mattina pass in a spectacular setting. From this point, abandon the marked trails and wander freely across the relief of the Val Rinbon below with its many war relics, including a large, well-preserved trench. The last outpost overlooks the Tre Cime, and the view from this privileged vantage point is breathtaking. It was on this ridge, on the morning of 24 May 1915 at 8.45am, that the First World War began.

Dawn over the Cristallo, the Tofane and the Croda Rossa d'Ampezzo, as seen from the Alp Mattina pass

The sun illuminating the walls of the Tre Cime

LASTRON DEI SCARPERI

A flat summit between the peaks of the Sexten Dolomites

Starting point: *The car park at 1,454 metres, at the end of the road that leaves Moso in the Pusteria valley and climbs into the Fiscalina valley. There is a toll to pay*
GPS: *46.666685 12.353908*
Time: *7 hours*
Difficulty: *This hike is for experts, with several steep passages on crumbly ground in the upper part. However, it is accessible to most hikers if they are accompanied by a guide or an expert*
Elevation gain: *1,500 metres*
Trail markers: *Good until Forcella di San Candido, beyond which they are sufficient. The numerous cairns make it possible to identify a safe path, even where there are no markings*
Cartography: *Tabacco 1:25.000, sheet 010*

S tanding tall at an altitude of almost 3,000 metres in the Sexten Dolomites, the Lastron dei Scarperi is a fairly popular mountain. Despite the huge crowds around the huts near the Tre Cime di Lavaredo, the impression of solitude there is breathtaking. Given the exceptional

beauty of the surrounding environment and the views, the feeling is completely legitimate. This is the empyrean of the Dolomites.

This summit is in a place of particular importance, at the barycentre of the giants: the Tre Scarperi, the Popera, the Croda dei Toni and the Tre Cime. To the north lie the Austrian Alps and to the south the Dolomites.

It is precisely for this reason that this summit was of strategic importance to the Austrians during the First World War, and today it is still dotted with vestiges of fortifications and paths laid out by the soldiers. The ascent to the vast summit plateau will take you along one of these military paths created in the early 1900s, which uses the only passable passage through the colossal walls and ravines.

From the car park at the bottom of the Val Fiscalina, follow the signs for the Rifugio Locatelli in the Tre Cime and make your way through the entire Val di Sassovecchio, surrounded by landscapes that are understandably famous for their beauty. The CAI 102 markers will lead you safely to an altitude of 2,314 metres, at the foot of the Crodon di San Candido and just before the Piani lakes, with the breathtaking view of the Tre Cime di Lavaredo in the background. There, leave the main road and the hustle and bustle of tourists and turn right to the nearby Forcella di San Candido (2,381 metres, 2.5 hours). It separates the Torre di Toblin from the Crodon di San Candido and is the finishing point of the climb to the summit. Continue north on an excellent mule track up wonderful sloping meadows, surrounded by imposing rocky peaks on each side. From the mounds near the path you can also enjoy one of the most beautiful views of the Tre Cime. Reaching this view can in itself be the end of the hike if you just want to enjoy absolute peace. At the top of the meadows, you will reach a flat area beyond which the scenery radically changes: you will be surrounded by rocks and notice the Lastron dei Scarperi rising opposite, though its summit will not yet be visible. Descend briefly into the Cadin di San Candido and start to climb again among the rocky debris, passing many war relics. The mule track zigzags then faces a horizontal rocky escarpment where it is important to carefully follow the cairns. When you find the gravel it means you're getting closer to the ridge and the Forcella Sassovecchio, though you won't reach them. Just below, turn left and take a steep, clearly visible corridor, which you should walk along carefully. At the end, near a notch in the ridge, turn left and join a prominent path that quickly leads to the summit plateau. This plateau is characterised by its reddish Raibl deposits and cuts through the sky, leading to the flat summit (2,957 metres) where many large cairns decorate the last rocks (1.5 hours from Forcella di San Candido). With a small difference in altitude, but a significant incline, it is also possible to reach this point from the car park of the Rifugio Auronzo, as in the previous itinerary. To do so, head to the Rifugio Locatelli and descend toward the Piani lakes.

On the red soil of the summit facing the Tre Cime and the Dolomiti del Cadore

MONTE CAMPODURO

From the wild Onge valley to an unknown viewpoint on the Cadore

Starting point: *From Auronzo, go up toward Misurina and, a little beyond the village of Giralba, turn right onto the tarmac road of the Marzon valley as far as the car park near the Cason della Crosera (1,207 metres)*
GPS: *46.592541 12.333665*
Time: *7 hours*
Difficulty: *The hike is easy until the Città di Carpi refuge, then continues along a short, equipped section where a via ferrata kit is recommended*
Elevation gain: *1,050 metres*
Trail markers: *Excellent*
Cartography: *Tabacco 1:25.000, sheet 017*

Monte Campoduro is the main summit of the south-eastern branch of the Cadini di Misurina mountain range. Almost ignored despite its advantageous location above the Rifugio Città di Carpi, which is a popular tourist spot thanks to its easy access from Misurina, Monte Campoduro offers a unique view of the most important peaks and valleys of the Cadore area. The ascent to the refuge through the gentle Onge valley is also completely overlooked. Although it is long, it will reveal to you its charming world of towers and stone walls as you progress. The summit can be reached by an easy and fun, equipped route that requires a little faith in the rock. The final view of the Cadini, the extensive Marmarole range, the Sorapiss and the Croda dei Toni, is surprising and at least comparable to the partial view from the refuge.

From the Cason della Crosera, take the CAI 121 trail which climbs in long diagonals from the Val d'Onge. The modest slopes will allow you to keep your strength until you reach the Tabià Val d'Onge, unless you take some of the shortcuts. There, the scenery becomes even more grandiose, with a view of the towers of the eastern branch of the Cadini di Misurina. Continue further up the meadows in the upper part of the valley until the panorama overlooking the Forcella Maraia (2,101 metres), where the Rifugio Città di Carpi is located (3 hours). From the ridge covered in greenery, follow the CAI 116 trail that heads east toward the rocks opposite Monte Campoduro. After a first steep section on grass, tackle the short, rocky strips and climb with the help of fixed ropes. Once you have climbed out onto the summit ridge, you will find the summit cross (2,244 metres, half an hour from the refuge). To return, you can either turn back to the ascent route or go straight down north into the small valley on a path whose start is hidden among the overgrown mugo pines, and which ends up right next to the Tabià Val d'Onge (if you can't find the small path, it's better to go back via the refuge).

LAGO AIARNOLA

An exceptional wetland biotope in the heart of the Comelico region

Starting point: *Padola di Comelico*
GPS: *46.599795 12.476117*
Time: *3 hours*
Difficulty: *Easy, for all hikers*
Elevation gain: *100 metres*
Trail markers: *Good, clear and unique path*
Cartography: *Tabacco 1:25.000, sheet 010*

The charming Lago Aiarnola (Lake Aiarnola) lies at the bottom of a basin (or 'cadin' as it is called in the local dialect) of glacial origin where surface waters from Monte Aiarnola and the Croda da Campo converge. This lake is the central element of a whole alpine ecosystem densely covered with coniferous forests that are home to ungulates, grouse and birds of prey.

Located at an altitude of 1,573 metres and covering an area of about 3,500 square metres, the lake has an elongated shape and is fed by underground springs, easily identifiable by the water that gurgles to the surface. The surrounding area is a valuable biotope due to several amphibious species such as toads, salamanders and newts. The easy accessibility and the pleasant loop route around it make this lake a highly recommended destination for a half-day walk.

Not far away is the casera (alpine refuge) of the same name, a very old property of the Regole di Calalzo, which is well worth a visit for its beautiful setting and view of the rocky peaks of the Dolomites where it is situated.

From the village of Padola, follow the signs for the Acque Rosse and Casera Aiarnola along the main forest road near the Rio Aiarnola (CAI 152 trail marker). Higher up, the road becomes a path and climbs more steeply through the dense forest. After passing a sort of flat area that overlooks the large basin where the Aiarnola lake and alpine pasture are located, descend slightly to reach the Aiarnola casera (1 hour and 15 minutes). From the casera, follow the forest road toward the Passo Zovo (otherwise known as the Passo di Sant'Antonio), then leave it by turning right at a signposted crossroads. After a few minutes, you'll notice a small path that winds through the forest and leads between massive rocks to the clearings and the lake. A more direct alternative to the lake is possible from the road that connects Padola to Passo Zovo: the itinerary begins a little after the Capitello di Sant'Anna, a few hundred metres before the lake of the same name.

Lago Aiarnola and the Croda da Campo

MONTE CENGIA

One of the most beautiful mountain cirques in the world

Starting point: *A little before Auronzo, head to and drive up the Marzon valley. Park at 1,127 metres, where the path to the Bivacco dei Toni begins*
GPS: *46.589031 12.346074*
Time: *8.5 hours. It is also possible to do the hike over two days, staying at the Bivacco dei Toni*
Difficulty: *A very long and strenuous hike, with an equipped section on steep terrain. Some easy climbing near the summit. For well-trained experts*
Elevation gain: *1,450 metres*
Trail markers: *Excellent, except on the last stretch to the top of Monte Cengia, where there is only an old military track*
Cartography: *Tabacco 1:25.000, sheet 010*

Monte Cengia is an isolated mountain on the ridge between the Croda dei Toni, Monte Paterno and the Tre Cime di Lavaredo. This places Monte Cengia in the centre of one of the most beautiful mountain cirques in the world.

Barely touched by the comings and goings of tourists between the Lavaredo refuge and the Pian di Cengia refuge, Monte Cengia remains an overlooked spot, full of the typical charm of abandoned mountains.

In wartime, it was chosen as the site to welcome an Italian observatory because of its position offering wide, panoramic views and was surrounded by mule tracks and fortifications, which have now almost completely disappeared.

After climbing the monumental Val Marden and crossing the desolate landscape of rocky scree of the Collerana and the bare and magnificently solitary summit plateaus, a long walk along the base of the Croda dei Toni leads to the mountain.

This is one of the most beautiful hikes in the Dolomites, but it is not very popular due to the steep ascent and the many tricky sections equipped with wire ropes.

It is possible to do this hike in two days, sleeping at the De Toni bivouac. The eagle's nest at the foot of the Croda dei Toni will let you enjoy the night landscape of this imposing rock setting.

From the small car park, climb the CAI 106 military mule trail which was used to connect the Marden valley, the logistical headquarters of the Italian army, to the front lines. Now covered in grass, the path rises in regular bends across the forest to a dense and high-altitude wood of mugo pines and then to the flow of scree between the peaks of the Toni and Marden groups, where it continues in a basin bordered by imposing walls on the right side of the valley. At the foot of the Cima d'Auronzo (the eastern branch of the Croda dei Toni), join the CAI 107 trail, a little below the Forcella dell'Agnello. From there you can make a half-hour detour over the pass to see the Bivacco dei Toni (2,578 metres, 3.5 hours). To continue the hike, turn left and enter the stone desert that stretches across the base of the Croda dei Toni, in a solitary, majestic and breathtaking atmosphere. Follow the red markers (essential in case of poor visibility) between the large rocks until you reach a rocky strip. Continue with the help of a daring series of metal cables to reach the sunny terraces near the Forcella dei Toni (2,524 metres). From this crossroads, which allows you to descend to the Val Fiscalina and the Zsigmondy-Comici Rifugio, continue to the Venetian side, taking the CAI 107 trail on the slopes of the Collerena, which is even more spectacular for its views of the Tre Cime di Lavaredo. From there, you'll notice Monte Cengia: the rocky plateau connected to the Collerena, dominating the Salto Valley and the Cengia Valley. Once you have reached the Sella del Collerena (2,491 metres), leave the markers and walk freely toward the summit cross, which is not signposted but can be reached by following what is left of a path, passing over some elevations and depressions. After passing the observation post in the cave, you will reach the main tower of the mountain. A short climbing passage will lead you to the final ridge and the highest point (2,559 metres, 5 hours from the car park). From the summit, although it is possible to descend directly to the Cengia lakes, we recommend retracing your steps to the Sella di Collerena. From there, descend through the beautiful scenery

toward the basin that houses the ponds. That is where you will certainly meet the first groups of tourists. Continue toward the Rifugio Lavaredo. A little further on, leave the main path and turn left onto the CAI 107 trail. At first, it will stretch out between vast meadows before winding its way down from a mule track to a cart track laid out during wartime. After a zigzagging section that feels never-ending, you will reach the Cason di Cengia Bassa, an oasis in the middle of the dense vegetation. Set off again among the trees to reach the paved road of the Val Marzon which will lead you, after about 20 minutes of descent, to the starting point.

THE PIAN DELLO SCOTTER

In the heart of the most spectacular and forgotten valley of the Marmarole

Starting point: *Ponte degli Alberi (1,134 metres), in the heart of the Somadida forest, between Auronzo and Misurina*
GPS: *46.530741 12.282708*
Time: *8 hours*
Difficulty: *This is a long and strenuous, but quite easy hike. Some rocky sections are made easier with the help of fixed ropes*
Elevation gain: *1,200 metres*
Trail markers: *Good until the Bivacco Voltolina, absent after that. As it is necessary to advance by sight, excellent visibility is necessary*
Cartography: *Tabacco 1:25.000, sheet 003*

Between the steep and rugged peaks of the western Marmarole, ignored by modern mountaineers and hikers, barely touched by the Alta Via delle Dolomiti no. 5, the Pian dello Scotter is nestled in an

ncredibly peaceful environment, surrounded by immense rocks, walls
nd stratification. Forgotten by humankind, it is populated only by ibex,
hamois, marmots and eagles. Nature there is still totally untouched and
xpresses itself in all its power, offering a corner of authentic paradise.
Access to the amphitheatre, though unthinkable from the valley, is
ossible via the well-marked path leading to the Voltolina bivouac. It
eads, without any markings or signs, over the meadows in the centre of
he basin. The most adventurous hikers can go as far as Forcella Scotter,
vith its surprising and unprecedented view of the Cadore peaks.

*From the small car park, descend and cross the Ansiei stream on the Ponte
degli Alberi bridge following the CAI 226 forest road into the Somadida
Forest. After passing through the heart of the forest, continue along a very
pleasant, almost flat section that runs between trees until it reaches the Rio di
San Vito. This is where the ascent of the wonderful Val di San Vito, wedged
between the gigantic foothills of the Sorapiss and Marmarole mountains,*

egins. Leave the valley by following the path that climbs steeply to the ight and crosses the Cadin del Doge, dominated by the singular profile of he horn of the same name. At the crossroads with the main path – which oes toward Forcella Grande – turn left at the CAI 278 marker and climb he steep stretch of the Val Grande, where the scenery is both romantic and randiose. Pass an easy rocky section with the help of a fixed rope and reach he gentler slopes of the Val di Mezzo. Ignore the crossroads leading to the Bivacco Musati and the Cengia del Doge and start the last tough climb up he huge rocks of the valley to reach the Bivacco Voltolina, one of the most urprising places in the Dolomites. From the bivouac, the most adventurous art of the hike begins: hikers can proceed as they wish there, as there are ery few tracks and not many visible ones, but there is no risk of getting lost is long as the visibility is good. The hardest and most demanding section is mmediately upstream from the bivouac, where you have to climb up the mpressive expanse of enormous rocks scattered over the glacial threshold of he valley. Exercise patience and attention there and you will arrive at the lat meadows of the Pian dello Scotter. The head of the water-catchment area, which seems to be closed on both sides, is clearly visible. It is possible to reach the depression visible on the right of the long series of peaks that descend from the Cima Scotter (wrongly called the Forcella Scotter, or Scotter pass, because it is in fact not passable). The depression, a cliff over the Boite valley and San Vito di Cadore overlooking the opposite slope, can easily be reached.

The Somadida forest

The hike to Pian dello Scotter begins in the Foresta di Somadida ('Somadida forest'), which extends over 1,700 hectares on the northern slopes of the Marmarole. From the end of the 15th century, the Republic of Venice used this forest and its trees to build masts and ships in preparation for the war against the Turks. During the First World War, it was sacked to build fortifications for the front of the Sexten Dolomites. It became a nature reserve in 1972, with flat trails suitable for everyone, a visitor centre with a small nature museum, and a library where books on natural sciences can be consulted. Some inaccessible areas at high altitudes are still a field of study as they are among the very few places in Italy where humans have never set foot. One of these is the ancient primary forest (in other words, an original and untouched forest) of the Negro pass.

On the Pian dello Scotter with the peak of the same name in the background

THE AIERON RIDGE

Like an eagle soaring above the villages at the heart of the Cadore region

Starting point: *The La Pineta bar in the Val d'Oten (1,044 metres), which is accessible from Calalzo di Cadore by the main road. From there you can also continue along the dirt road to the car park before the Rio Diassa (1,133 metres).*
GPS: *46.477604 12.333102*
Time: *6 hours*
Difficulty: *This is an easy hike until the Chiggiato refuge and the Forcella Sacù. Beyond that, the hike is for experienced hikers only*
Elevation gain: *1,200 metres*
Trail markers: *Excellent until Forcella Sacù, irregular after that*
Cartography: *Tabacco 1:25.000, sheet 016*

The Cresta d'Aieron (or 'Aieron Ridge') is the first rocky ridge above the Chiggiato hut in the heart of the Marmarole. Although less impressive than the surrounding ridges, its location gives it a strategic vantage point to enjoy surprisingly wide views of the rocky landscape.

All the peaks of the Marmarole and the Antelao pyramid are visible to the north, while the Cimon del Froppa, the Croda Bianca, Monte Chiastelin and the esplanades of the Pian dei Buoi rise to the east. Beyond the Piave valley, the ridge formed by the Cridola, the Monfalconi, the Spalti di Toro, the Preti and Duranno peaks (the Oltrepiave Dolomites) can all be fully appreciated.

The Cresta d'Aieron is also the only summit that can be reached quickly and without any difficulty from the Chiggiato hut, along an itinerary surrounded by still wild, untouched nature, offering otherworldly emotions. This hike is a perfect opportunity for those who have energy and are looking for an easy adventure off the CAI marked paths, among edelweiss and nigritella flowers.

From the car park, follow the CAI 260 trail toward the Rifugio Chiggiato. The trail steadily climbs up a slope in long diagonals on the western side of the Negro pass. After a less steep section with beautiful views of the Antelao and the grandiose Oten valley below, follow the steep climb up a slope through a dense forest until you reach the splendid panoramic meadow and its characteristic refuge (1,911 metres, 1.5 hours). If you arrive early in the morning, you should make a quick detour into the surrounding area to enjoy the magnificent views of the nearby mountains and valleys. From the refuge, follow the signs for the Rifugio Baion and the Bivacco Tiziano up a gentle climb to the north where you will quickly reach the grassy expanse of the Forcella Sacù (1,914 metres), where you will find numerous signs. Pay no

attention to the signs for the Rifugio Baion (right) and the Bivacco Tiziano (left) and look out for a red marker on a cut log in the meadow opposite. You will notice the Cresta d'Aieron rising immediately above. Take an excellent track through the mugo pines, which zigzags up, watching for the rather irregular red markings to guide you. Although the path is strenuous, it is easy to follow until you reach the first rocks. Then the path will veer off to the right and start to climb again in a wide, steep but easy grassy corridor ending with a spectacular, grassy flat section. The gigantic walls of the Cimon de Froppa will appear before you, along with those of the Cresta degli Invalidi

and the Croda Bianca, dominating the imposing Froppa valley that rises in the centre. The difficult part of the itinerary begins there: first, carefully cross a very steep meadow, then advance on a scree ledge, slightly exposed above rocky mounds and leading east, behind the summit. Follow the marks and cairns and climb between meadows and some rocks to reach the fantastic final ridge and the summit (2,306 metres, 1.5 hours from the refuge). The view over the refuge and the lake of the centre of Cadore in the Piave valley is breathtaking. Look out for the metal box containing the guest book hidden under the stones.

MONTE CHIASTELIN

A pioneer ascent of the Cresta del Drago

Starting point: *Rifugio Baion (1,828 metres), accessible by car from Lozzo di Cadore on the steep road to Pian dei Buoi (tarred only up to Pian dei Buoi). In the middle of summer, it is only possible to ascend in the morning and return in the afternoon*
GPS: *46.498800 12.384929*
Time: *5 hours*
Difficulty: *This is a very nice hike, but it is difficult, not because of the few passages on the rock, but because of the delicate terrain and the narrow track between the walls. It is recommended to take a helmet and be accompanied by a guide or expert*
Elevation gain: *750 metres*
Trail markers: *Good until the actual start of the hike, absent after that point*
Cartography: *Tabacco 1:25.000, sheet 016*

This is the highest point of the three mountains that dominate the background of the Baion refuge. Flanked by Torre Chiastelin, Pupo di Lozzo and Monte Ciarido, it forms the jagged profile of the eastern Marmarole which, from the valley, resembles a dragon resting on the Pian dei Buoi.

The classic path to the summit from the rather steep southern slope is a marvellous, craggy route not yet distorted by signposts and metal cables. The surprising access to the final peak is via a narrow, exposed ledge, allowing you to pass certain otherwise inaccessible walls. It is impossible not to admire the work of the pioneers who found this providential passage, which can only be seen once you get to it. The climb is one of the most recommended hikes in the Dolomites. It will require you to learn how to read the terrain and offers the rare pleasure of discovery without having to rely on signs or markers.

Although the itinerary is relatively short and presents a limited difference in altitude, it is complicated due to several (easy) climbing passages on rocks that are not always stable. The itinerary also requires excellent visibility and a good sense of direction as there is a real risk of losing your way in the upper half.

From the refuge, follow the Rifugio Ciareido path until it comes out of the woods and reaches the crossroads marked for the Sentiero del Pastore. As you leave the refuge path, turn left and climb over beautiful meadows toward the cliffs that dominate the area, following the red markings and cairns. The path crosses rocky strips that cut the slopes and then goes east, under the rocks. At this stage, before embarking on a crossing, it is important to find the exact spot where you should stop following the red markings and begin to climb toward the summit. This place is approximately below the

vertical of the summit (the third on the right of the Chiastelin peaks).

To guide yourself, look for a huge concave rock wedged between the walls and head toward it. As you climb the slopes, follow the few cairns and head to the scree terrain by approaching the rocky band under the stuck rock. An old, useless nylon rope will indicate the easy passage to climb and the passages to follow, to the right, over a difficult terrain along a discreet path just below the vertical of the summit. Once you reach the spectacular terrace, from which you will see the majestic Torre Chiastelin, the path seems to stop among precipices. However, you will notice a cairn on the rocks, above and to the left, which you can reach after a short grade I climb. From there, it is easy to spot a smooth but exposed narrow ledge running north. It grows narrower at the end (but you can hold on to it with your hands) and includes a passage out in the open. At the foot of a grade I+ chimney, climb it to reach the eastern back of the summit, mainly scree, where a track leads to the summit (2,570 metres, 2.5 hours from the refuge).

PUPO DI LOZZO

A stone doll in the Cadore skyline

Starting point: *Pian dei Buoi, which is accessible by car from Lozzo di Cadore along a steep road. In the middle of summer, it is only possible to ascend in the morning and return in the afternoon*
GPS: *46.512407 12.404803*
Time: *4 hours*
Difficulty: *Easy, for all hikers*
Elevation gain: *200 metres*
Trail markers: *Good*
Cartography: *Tabacco 1:25.000, sheet 016*

Pupo di Lozzo is a tower that stands out, isolated in the rocky ridge of the eastern Marmarole. It resembles a gigantic stone doll. Observe it from the path between the Ciareido and Baion mountain huts, and it appears to have an enigmatic profile with a barely sketched out smile. This singular monolith has become the symbol of this area of Cadore and is a popular destination for climbers thanks to its beautiful rock and its intact environment. An excellent way to admire it, and a great place for a snack, is to make the short and easy journey between the Ciareido refuge and the Baion refuge. Panoramic views, archaeology and local flavours come together on this interesting hike accessible to everyone.

Although it is not very well known, the Baion is a highlight among the huts in the Dolomites and is renowned for the specialties that its historical manager prepares with passion. The surrounding area is a real paradise of meadows and forests. This is where, by a nearby marsh, various flint artefacts dating back to the Mesolithic period (some nine thousand years ago) were found in the year 2000.

Prehistoric hunters used to settle in this strategic area, where they could observe and surprise the herds of ungulates grazing on the slopes of the Marmarole. The Ciareido refuge, built by a military garrison in the characteristic manner of the late 19th century, is also worth a visit. Located on a secluded and panoramic hill, it is a true gem of the Pian dei Buoi plateau. For several years now, it has even been open in winter when it snows and is safely accessible from Auronzo along small dirt roads.

From the car park at Pian dei Buoi (1,825 metres), follow the signs and climb up a small road on the slopes of Monte Ciareido. After several chalets and a few huge rocks, you will soon reach the Rifugio Ciareido (1,969 metres). At the crossroads, slightly below the hill where the refuge is located, follow the wide CAI 272 trail of the Alta Via no. 5, which crosses the high meadows and goes around the slopes of Monte Ciareido. That is where you'll be able to see the Pupo, rising into the sky between Ciareido and Torre Chiastelin. The path descends toward meadows and arrives at a new crossroads with the Sentiero del Pastore. Turn left and descend through the woods to the Rifugio Baion. To return to the Pian dei Buoi, follow the access road to the dirt hut, which is lower down in the woods than the path on the way up.

Pupo di Lozzo

The Ciareido refuge, near the Comelico peaks

THE UPPER GLACIER OF ANTELAO

The last frozen jewel atop the King of the Dolomites

Starting point: *The La Pineta bar, in the village of Praciadelan in the Oten valley (1,044 metres). Accessible from Calalzo di Cadore via the tarmac road*
GPS: *46.472168 12.338501*
Time: *8 hours*
Difficulty: *This is a long and challenging hike for experts. The only difficulty lies in overcoming the rocky climb to the glacier, where there is a short vertical via ferrata*
Elevation gain: *1,550 metres*
Trail markers: *Good*
Cartography: *Tabacco 1:25.000, sheet 016*

The first studies of the Antelao glaciers were carried out by the geographer Marinelli in 1897, a few decades after the end of a cold phase that lasted from 1500 to 1850 which caused the glacier to expand considerably. Marinelli carried out topographical surveys, established the temporary limit of eternal snow and set the first markers to measure frontal variations on the two main glaciers, which are still monitored today by researchers at the University of Padua. In 1850, the snout of the upper glacier was estimated to start at a height of 2,100 metres above sea level. Today, it begins at 2,580 metres above sea level, which

shows a drastic reduction in its volume.

These data provide us with objective measures of the relentless global warming and, in the case of the Dolomites, of the disappearance of deposits even at high altitude. Its neighbour, the lower glacier, facing the Oten valley, has now almost disappeared, and is covered with rocky debris. If conditions do not change, the upper glacier and other glaciers in the region will have all disappeared by the end of the century. This is why it is urgent to schedule a visit to the last remaining frozen jewel on the Antelao (3,264 metres). The King of the Dolomites is second in altitude only to the Queen Marmolada. Nowadays, its spectacular blue crevasses have nearly disappeared. In their place, equally charming blue basins have been formed, where the impetuous meltwaters are collected and then engulfed in the valley. Above, the last frozen cap appears to be resisting, in the shadow of the northern walls, and continues to offer a grandiose landscape.

From Praciadelan, follow the signs for Pian Antelao and Rifugio Antelao and, after crossing the Val d'Oten mountain stream, climb into the wooded Antelao valley on the CAI 258 trail. The track winds its way, wide and regular, but quite steep, to the gates of Antelao, a prelude to one of the most secret wonders of Cadore: the romantic and secluded Pian Antelao. Descend a little on the vast and long green plateau between the Crode Mandrin and the Ciaudierona mountain. Enjoy a bucolic stroll across the plateau to the small Cason Antelao, where cows and donkeys graze in the summer. Keep to the right and enter the sparse forest. Start climbing again at a good pace, heading toward the slopes that descend from the moraines of the upper glacier which, at this stage, is not yet visible. On the alpine meadows, the woods will start thinning out. Leave the path leading to the Rifugio Antelao and take an excellent track, gradually gaining altitude, in an increasingly open and panoramic environment. Once you have passed the upper limit of the vegetation, approach the polished rocks of the ancient glacier and the rocky debris leading to the only difficult section: a vertical climb of about 20 metres, well secured by supports and metal cables. After this passage, the snout of the glacier, the small fusion lakes and the summit of the Antelao await. Continue up to the Forcella del Ghiacciaio, from where you can also see the Tofane, the Sorapiss and the Marmarole. For the more experienced, it is possible to descend carefully to the opposite slope where another via ferrata dips over smooth, rocky slabs, skims the lower glacier and ends at the Rifugio Galassi. From there, the return journey to the starting point takes a long time across the entire Oten valley.

The lake at the foot of the glacier, with the Antelao in the background

CRODA MANDRIN

Exploring the Dolomites off the beaten track

Starting point: *From Pieve di Cadore, drive up to the little village of Pozzale and follow the signs for the Rifugio Prapiccolo (1,366 metres). Continue along the dirt road and park a little before the now closed little shelter in the woods*
GPS: *46.456008 12.346824*
Time: *6 hours*
Difficulty: *A demanding hike for experts (uncharted terrain and steep sections)*
Elevation gain: *900 metres*
Trail markers: *Good until the Antelao refuge, completely absent after*
Cartography: *Tabacco 1:25.000, sheet 016*

Croda Mandrin is a steep mountain, crushed on all sides, sitting atop the gently undulating terrain that is home to the Antelao refuge. From the summit, the view of the gigantic Antelao pyramid is unique and spectacular, as is the complete panorama of the Marmarole group, the Oltrepiave and Comelico Dolomites, the Civetta and Bosconero.

Wilderness still reigns, protected by the absence of information indicating the ways to the summit. There are no paths or markers; only the tracks left by the chamois will guide the worthiest hikers to this exclusive spot. Despite its modest altitude, the Croda Mandrin is one of those destinations that will fully satisfy hikers who still believe in adventure hiking and the unique character such hikes offer.

The itinerary is a short loop from the Antelao hut along two grassy corridors leading to the final ridge. Both are steep and challenging, but there are no exposed or climbing passages. We recommend that you only venture out there if you are experienced or accompanied and have good visibility.

From the small car park located below the abandoned Prapiccolo hut, follow the road and the CAI 250 markers for the Rifugio Antelao. Taking the shortcuts through the forest, exit onto the charming meadow near the Forcella Antracisa, then turn right onto the road that climbs from Pozzale. After a short time, you will reach the refuge (1,796 metres, 1 hour and 15 minutes). Immediately after the refuge, continue toward Forcella Piria, going up the meadows and steep woods of Croda Mandrin. When you reach a sort of grassy, flat terrain, leave the main path that would lead you to the area around Pian dei Cavai and take the track that breaks off to the right to cross a forest of mugo pines horizontally at the base of the mountain (you are now on the slope overlooking the refuge). Once you have passed a sort of notch in the rocks, you can clearly see a meadow corridor which, from the mugo pines, leads directly to the ridge (it is from the refuge that you can best observe this corridor). Leave the path at a loop and tackle the corridor directly on its steepest slope. There are no signs, but the path is clearly visible due to the passage of animals, so continue by sight until the ridge. At that point, turn left onto a grassy ledge from where you will see Monte Antelao. Go around a low wall on crumbly ground leading to a large scree shoulder on the north side of the mountain, following the little marked tracks that lead to the ridge and, by extension, the summit (2,273 metres, about

Below the summit, toward Monte Antelao

2 hours from the refuge). For the return journey, we recommend returning to the shoulder and descending south-west down the steeply sloping meadow to grassy, flat terrain at the top of a boulder-cluttered bowl surrounded by rocks. Go around a few peaks below the ridge (Antelao side) to climb back up a few dozen metres, where you will find an opening. From there, it is possible to pass to the opposite side (Piave valley) through a characteristic hole created by the rocks themselves. Passing there will confirm you are on the

right path. You'll find yourself at the top of a small corridor of greenery and rocky scree that points south toward a plateau overgrown with mugo pine and erratic rocks. Descend easily, despite there not being any landmarks, until you come across a faint track that cuts into the vegetation. Turn right and you will quickly reach the Pian dei Cavai and Forcella San Pietro. Follow the marked path that leads back to the path between the Rifugio Antelao and the Forcella Piria (1.5 hours from the summit).

THE CHAPEL OF SAN DIONISIO ⑮

An easy hike with an exceptional view

Starting point: *From Valle di Cadore (857 metres), follow the signs and the partially asphalted road that climbs in bends through a forest on a steep slope until Rifugio Costapiana (1,610 metres). It is also possible to use the paid shuttle service*
GPS: *46.404211 11.609167*
Time: *4 hours*
Difficulty: *Easy, for all hikers*
Elevation gain: *450 metres, with positive and negative elevation*
Trail markers: *Excellent*
Cartography: *Tabacco 1:25.000, sheet 016*
Accommodation: *Rifugio Costapiana (1,610 metres, renowned restaurant) and Rifugio Antelao (1,796 metres)*

The picturesque little chapel dedicated to San Dionisio, martyr and patron saint of Cadore, stands on the hill of the same name on the slopes of Monte Antelao. Built in 1508 and renovated in 1910, it has been the destination of pilgrimages by the valley's inhabitants for centuries. Its grandiose panorama has also been admired by important personalities, namely Queen Margaret of Savoy in 1882, and King Albert of Belgium, an avid mountaineer, in 1914. In 1916, General Cadorna chose this hill to establish a defence plan for the Cadore front. This plan foresaw the use of the many fortresses on the surrounding hills but remained unfinished due to the withdrawal at the battle of Caporetto.

There are many legends about how and why this chapel was built in such a secluded place. The most likely one is that Dionisio chose this

hill to isolate himself and meditate, and that the first chapel was built in gratitude after the battle of Cadore. In this battle, which took place near Pieve di Cadore in 1508, the Venetian armies commanded by Bartolomeo d'Alviano faced the German armies of Maximilian I, who wanted to reach Rome by annexing the territories of La Serenissima in order to declare himself emperor. The German invasion was prevented and gave Venice the impetus for further expansion. The hill and the church have now become symbols of peace and offer an easy walk, accessible to all, with an incomparable view. The proximity of the Antelao refuge, a historical accommodation in this bucolic corner of Cadore, completes the excursion with a gastronomic stop.

Behind the Rifugio Costapiana, take the wide mule track CAI 251, which climbs toward the Colle di San Dionisio. At the crossroads with a sign for

the Forcella Antracisa and the Rifugio Antelao, turn left and climb a slightly steeper slope through woodland that becomes progressively more sparse, until you reach the final ridge and the summit meadow where the chapel stands (1,946 metres). After a pause to admire the view and ring the bell, continue toward the Rifugio Antelao that sits at the top of the meadow, toward the Col della Croce (1,967 metres), recognisable by the cross on the summit. Take the narrow, marked path that descends, with a few steeper sections, toward the Sella di Pradonego, through a sparse north-facing forest. Descend quickly and exit onto the meadows where the refuge is located. To return to Costapiana by making a pleasant loop, it is advisable to descend a little along the CAI 250 road toward Pozzale until you reach the area around Forcella Antracisa. Once there, take a path to the right (signs) which, after a modest climb, lead back to the crossroads under the Colle di San Dionisio. Return to the starting point by following the path you have already taken.

THE GEOLOGICAL PATH
OF THE QUATERNÀ PASS

The remains of an old volcano

Starting point: *Rifugio Casera Coltrondo, accessible by car from the tarmac road that branches off the road between Padola and the Monte Croce di Comelico pass*
GPS: *46.663153 12.450007*
Time: *4.5 hours*
Difficulty: *Easy, for all hikers*
Elevation gain: *650 metres*
Trail markers: *Good*
Cartography: *Tabacco 1:25.000, sheet 010*

The Quaternà pass is the remains of an ancient volcano. It has survived because it is made up of solidified lava more resistant than the type that surrounded it, which has disintegrated over time.

Climbing to the top of the hill means reaching the old central chimney, walking on the metamorphic rocks formed by the very high pressures and temperatures to which the minerals were subjected some 300 million years ago. The dark phyllades can also be seen on the slopes of the mountain. Veined with white flint and with typical thick folds, these are the oldest rocks of the Comelico, dating back more than 500 million years. They can be seen on a long stretch of the route around the hill which, in addition to its geological interest, offers a unique historical setting and a panoramic one. The elements that embellish these slopes are of rare beauty, in particular the rhododendrons in July, the mysterious fort on the border with South Tyrol, the trenches near the summit and the superb views of the Sexten and Comelico Dolomites. Pope John Paul II climbed to the summit on 13 July 1987 during one of his visits to Cadore.

From the car park of the Rifugio Casera Coltrondo, follow the dirt road which will rapidly take you up to the Casera Rinfreddo. From there, continue on the slopes of the Quaternà pass, leaving the woods. At a fork in the road, turn left onto a military mule track (signs). Gradually climb toward the volcanic cone, with the large cross at its summit. As you follow the regular hairpin bends you will gain altitude in a clear panoramic setting, overlooking the Cima Bagni and Popera mountain ranges, until you reach the Costa della Spina ridge at the Sella del Quaternà (2,379 metres). The view stretches to the Digon valley below, to the Cresta Carnica and the cliffs of Longerin, Palombino and Peralba. From there, near the remains of the Italian trenches, there is a short, steep path on the left that leads to the summit cross (2,503 metres) through old passages used by soldiers and overlooking the rock formations of the volcano chimney (2 hours from the start). Once you have descended from the summit, pass over meadows and scree to reach the Silvella pass (2,329 metres), between Comelico and Val Pusteria, and begin the descent into the Vallorera toward Malga Nemes. Follow the road for about 500 metres before leaving it when a small path marked CAI 159 goes to the left (signs). After an initial gentle descent, this beautiful track will cross the slopes of the Quaternà pass at an altitude in a magnificent setting, between rhododendrons, alders and larches, leading to some ruined military fortifications on the ridge. From there, with a panoramic view of the Malga Nemes below and the Sexten Dolomites, continue the pleasant descent along a path that leads back to the Casera Coltrondo.

VAL VISSADA

An authentic jewel of the Comelico

Starting point: From Presenaio di Cadore, follow the signs and climb to val Visdende until Pramarino. After the agritourism centre of the same name, continue on the dirt road until Forcella Zovo (1,606 metres), where there is a private refuge and parking
GPS: 46.602639 12.591691
Time: 3 hours
Difficulty: Easy, for all hikers
Elevation gain: 450 metres
Trail markers: Good
Cartography: Tabacco 1:25.000, sheet 001

Val Vissada is an authentic jewel of the Comelico that brings together all the characteristics of the Dolomites in one place: vast, high mountain meadows, limestone spires and towers, and endless panoramas that reach as far as the Carnic and Julian Alps.

The valley is surrounded by the picturesque Crode dei Longerin, a disintegrating coral atoll which resembles a less grandiose version of Latemar. A curious coincidence has placed them at the extremities of the Dolomites, stretching over volcanic terrain and covered with forests. In the heart of the Crode dei Longerin stretch the idyllic Piani di Vissada ('Plains of Vissada'), which are home to cattle pastures in summer and where huge, erratic rocks form an enchanting and primitive setting.

In the lower part of the alpine basin, away from the path, is the ancient Cason di Vissada, a small lookout point facing the looming peaks. There are numerous hiking opportunities from there.

From Forcella Zovo, follow the CAI 169 path that crosses the forests of Monte San Daniele at high altitude, skirting the slopes of the Vissada valley. Once you reach the Rio Vissada, where a beautiful waterfall cascades over the flat terrain below, enter the upper Vissada valley, which is more accessible and bucolic. Go up the vast, grassy impluvium until you reach the undulating terrain of Forcella Longerin (2,044 metres, 1.5 hours). There you can enjoy a superb view of the Visdende valley opposite and the Torri dei Longerin, whose gothic forms overlook the meadows and scree. There are signs and CAI 195 markers at the fork for the Cima Sud dei Longerin ('Southern summit of the Longerin', 2,523 metres), which can also be reached via the scree and meadows. The hike along paths and tracks (1.5 hours from the fork) is not difficult and is recommended.

Monte Schiaron: an extraordinary viewpoint

According to a local legend, Monte Schiaron (2,246 metres) owes its name to the large iron rings (*sciara* means 'ring' in the dialect of the province of Belluno) set into the rock to moor boats in the days when the Visdende valley was just a huge lake. Its dominant position on the Austrian border and the surrounding peaks made it a guarded outpost during the First World War. The remnants of the war are still clearly visible today near the summit, which is an extraordinary lookout point despite its rounded shape and densely wooded slopes.

The Schiaron closes the Vissada basin to the east and is worth a visit once you reach the Forcella Longerin. From there, follow the marked path that runs along the ridge, then pass the rocky cap by a few steps on a steeper slope (about 1 hour from the Forcella).

Strangely shaped towers on the Longerin

The Longerin and the Plains of Vissada

The Longerin peaks in winter

MALGA DIGNAS

Old alpine traditions in the charming Visdende valley

Starting point: *From Presenaio di Cadore, follow the signs and climb Val Visdende until Pramarino. There are free parking spots in the village of La Fitta (signs)*
GPS: *46.624040 12.626549*
Time: *3 hours. This is a short hike but we recommend spending the night at the hut to enjoy the warm and friendly welcome of the Casanova family, who will also be able to guide you to the most beautiful areas in the surrounding environment*
Difficulty: *Easy, for all hikers*
Elevation gain: *350 metres*
Trail markers: *Good*
Cartography: *Tabacco 1:25.000, sheet 001*
Accommodation: *Upon reservation. Excellent agritourism*

The Malga Dignas (the alpine pasture of Dignas) stands at the eastern end of the Cresta del Palombino, in the Visdende valley. These thousand-year-old pastures, which are still used today along with the hut, belong to the Regola di Casada. The strategic position of the Malga Dignas makes it an almost obligatory stop for hiking and mountain biking or, in winter, for snowshoeing and ski-mountaineering. It is a wonderful crossing point on the famous Strada delle Malghe ('road to the mountain pastures') through the entire valley. The farmhouse is also excellent for its agritourism. You can enjoy local dishes prepared by the Casanova family, who also offer, upon reservation, some beds for the night. If you ask the owners, you can visit the stables and see the

animals for a full immersion into the typical activities of the mountain pasture. This is not just a tourist refuge but a real working place, where people still carry out the ancient tasks so typical of the high mountain economy. Above the alpine pasture, the ridges of the Austrian border stretch out and offer many detours. The quickest and most advisable route is via the Forcella Dignas, a pass with a carriageway leading down to the Gail valley.

From Pramarino (1,300 metres), continue north on the road that enters the beautiful forest of the Val di Londo. At the Ciadon crossroads, turn right and walk along the Costa Spina into the Val Dignas. At the edge of the wood, after a few twists and turns on the meadow, you will reach the mountain pasture (1,686 metres, 1.5 hours).

Forcella Dignas: an incredible view over the Visdende valley

From the mountain pasture, continue along the Strada delle Malghe as it twists its way up the upper Dignas valley. At the crossroads, continue to the left and climb toward the head of the valley on the well-preserved military road, which offers wonderful views over the Visdende valley, as far as the Forcella (2,094 metres). Many war stations and small barracks are visible in the area which, until just a few decades ago, was controlled by the Guardia di Finanza, the Italian border and customs police. Slightly below the fork, on the Austrian side, is the cosy Austrian refuge Neue Porze Hütte. We recommend walking along the panoramic ridge to the west, where you can see far into the distance (1.5 hours from the alpine pasture).

PASSO DEL MULO

War memorials between the beautiful Olbe lakes and the Visdende valley

Starting point: *From Cima Sappada, drive up the carriageway toward Sorgenti del Piave until you reach Baita Rododendro (1,450 metres), where you can park*
GPS: *46.594271 12.720716*
Time: *6 hours*
Difficulty: *Easy, for all hikers*
Elevation gain: *900 metres*
Trail markers: *Good*
Cartography: *Tabacco 1:25.000, sheet 001*

Passo del Mulo (the 'Mule Pass') is a notch between the Ferro ridge and Monte Lastroni, between Sappada and the Val Visdende valley. The wonderful Olbe lakes are reflected on the southern slope, while the green Carnica ridge and the pale limestone of Peralba and Monte

Avanza stretch out to the north. The pass owes its name to an episode of the war: thanks to a thick fog, four Austrian soldiers managed to break into Italian territory and capture an *Alpini* soldier and his mule ('mulo' in Italian). They passed through the rocky fork in the road that became known as the Passo del Mulo. The animal continued to serve, but in the Austrian ranks, on Monte Peralba.

The Olbe lakes, on the way up to the Sappada pass, are three mirrors of water set in grassy plains under the ridges of the Ferro crest. They are one of the most popular destinations in the area.

It is thought the Italians dumped two cannons and war material into the larger lake, which is more than 20 metres deep and has a funnel-shaped profile, after they had to withdraw following the Caporetto breakthrough.

Due to the weeds and the very dark depths that make it difficult to explore, underwater research has never confirmed the rumour spread by the villagers, feeding the story surrounding those tragic days.

From the Baita Rododendro guesthouse, follow the CAI 138 mule track which crosses the Piave over a small bridge and climbs for a long time on the left side of the wild Vallone del Rio della Miniera. Higher up are the first meadows, where the small road that climbs up from Sappada begins (we do not recommend taking this road, as it runs alongside the ski slopes). Instead, turn right to enjoy the fantastic views of the Carnic and Julian Alps to the east. You will then quickly reach the Casera d'Olbe. It stands at the foot of Monte Lastroni, in the middle of picturesque meadows, and has characteristically original architecture, with its stables on the side of the main building. After the casera, you will cross more meadows and, after a

final stretch, reach the chapel on the edge of the largest lake (2 hours).
We recommend taking a short detour to visit the second lake, which is smaller but surrounded by a superb carpet of greenery and peat bogs, and the third, which is very small but close to the towers of the Ferro crest. From the chapel, walk around the right side of the lake until you reach a marked crossroads. Leave the path for Monte Lastroni and turn left following the CAI 135 signs. The path climbs steadily up over meadows, while the landscape widens toward Monte Siera, the Clap and the Terze, until it reaches the watershed. There, you can visit the fortifications and other military ruins before crossing a scree slope to reach the Passo del Mulo (2,356 metres, 1 hour from the lake).

SAPPADA VECCHIA

A long loop through villages, traditions, alpine architecture, culture and nature

Starting point: *Sappada Borgata Granvilla, on the parking of the parish church*
GPS: *46.564986 12.678458*
Time: *5 hours*
Difficulty: *Easy, for all hikers*
Elevation gain: *450 metres, with positive and negative elevation*
Trail markers: *Good*
Cartography: *Tabacco 1:25.000, sheet 001*

Sappada (Plodn in the local dialect) is a famous tourist resort and the highest municipality in Friuli, on the border between Cadore and Carnia. Since 2017 it has been included in the list of 'Borghi più belli d'Italia', the most beautiful villages in Italy.

It extends over meadows along the upper Piave valley, surrounded by impressive limestone rocks, and includes no less than 15 typical villages that make it one of the most interesting municipalities in the Dolomites.

Few other areas can claim to have such lively and well-preserved alpine architecture, traditions and culture, and sun-kissed houses waiting to be discovered and enjoyed all year round.

The origins of Sappada date back to the 11th century, when a few families from the neighbouring Tyrol settled in the valley, creating a German-speaking linguistic bubble in the heart of the Venetian mountains (at that time, the territory belonged to the Republic of Venice). The first inhabitants of the valley arrived in small numbers and later formed villages connected to each other. The German dialect is still widely spoken today, and is even taught in elementary schools so that it can be passed on from generation to generation.

The typical architecture of Sappada is characterised by wooden houses, built using the old Blockbau technique (stacked logs), with facades adorned with traditional fieldwork, wood panelling and spectacular flower arrangements on balconies and terraces. Simply strolling through the streets and small squares, where even the fountains and the many small chapels are impeccably decorated, it is easy to see how Sappada enjoys creating a welcoming atmosphere for guests.

To fully enjoy the valley and the villages, you need to hike around the area. It takes a good day to get to all the points of interest, including the climb to a spectacular viewpoint. The first part of the excursion runs through the typical streets and meadows, while the second passes through the majestic forests that tend to follow the Piave River. There are many opportunities to eat in bars or restaurants.

Monte Siera from the viewpoint at Capanna Bellavista

From the parish church, follow the main road toward Cima until you reach the first small square surrounded by shops. Go up to the left of the newsagent shop in Borgata Pill and stay on the highest alleyway which borders the Cappella di Sant'Antonio in the village of Bach. Built in 1726, it is the oldest church in Sappada, miraculously escaping the 1908 fire that destroyed many of the surrounding houses. On the square a little further on are some beautiful houses decorated with flowers and local handicrafts. With the Hotel Bladen to your right, continue down to the wooden bridge over the Rio Mühlbach, where the Sentiero delle Cascatelle ('path of the waterfalls', see following itinerary) begins. Stay on the road and climb into Borgata Cotterne, with its beautiful and refreshing fountain. This is where Sappada Vecchia ('Old Sappada') begins. It consists of the oldest and most picturesque villages in the area. Follow the road through Hoffe, Fontana, Kratten and Ecche before reaching Puiche with its wonderful little church overlooking the whole valley. Continue through the meadows along a dirt road that crosses the Rio Fauner and leads down the provincial road to Borgata Cretta, at the bottom of the valley. For a section of the route, walk on the pavement along the provincial road and cross over the Piave. Immediately after the bridge, turn left along the river to reach one of the most important places: the perfectly restored large mill on the Piave. Follow the asphalt road that passes by the mill uphill to reach the carriageway from Cima that leads to the Sorgenti del Piave (or 'Piave springs'). From there, return to the valley along a wonderful walk through the meadows, with a view of the imposing peaks of the Siera, the Clap and the Terze. Shortly before Cima is a sign on the left indicating the Capanna Bellavista. Follow this sign and, after a long climb through the woods, you will come to a viewpoint above a cliff overlooking the valley, protected by fences. For the return to Cima, we recommend a path (signposted) that leads directly down through the woods to the houses. After visiting the historic houses of what is probably the most characteristic village of them all, pass the provincial road near the church and continue along the flat meadows dotted with barns, until you reach the ski lifts of Monte Siera. You will soon spot the signs for the CAI 318 trail, which you should follow for a while through the enchanting woods of Monte Siera until you come across a forest road. Follow the road to the right and descend on a steep slope to the Piave, near the Baita Mondschein. Pass through the meadows, along the golf course and reach a dirt road. It will lead up to Borgata Palù then to Granvilla, completing this long loop.

A typical house in Sappada Vecchia

THE PATH OF THE WATERFALLS IN SAPPADA

A surprise path along the Rio Mühlbach canyon

Starting point: *Sappada Borgata Bach*
GPS: *46.567212 12.687668*
Time: *1.5 hours*
Difficulty: *Easy and equipped hike that includes a section on a steep slope in the woods and a vertical ladder*
Elevation gain: *100 metres*
Trailer markers: *Good, with a unique, clear route*
Cartography: *Tabacco 1:25.000, sheet 001*

The short, easy Sentiero delle Cascatelle ('Path of the Waterfalls') is spectacular and leads to enchanting corners of nature, ideal for those seeking a few hours out of the hot summer sun. It is one of the most recommended activities in the Sappada valley, along with a visit to its typical villages and meadows along the Piave River. The path takes you through the last stretch of ravine that the Rio Mühlbach (or Rio del Mulino, 'River of the Mill') carved out of the greenish marl limestone of the Buchenstein formation, exposing very colourful stratifications. At the very top is a high and powerful waterfall, the largest of all the waterfalls that follow each other down the valley until the Piave. The loop ends with the Via Crucis, which offers clear views of the entire valley and its mountains.

In the village of Bach, cross the Rio Mühlbach on a characteristic wooden bridge with flowers and turn left. This is where the Via Crucis begins and the Ethnographic Museum is located. There the trail starts with wooden bridges hanging over the meandering river canyon (the source of which lies a little below the Olbe lakes, another place to discover in the area). Continue along the river, which in some places can be very close, admiring its water features until you reach a rock with wooden steps and ramps. This leads to the upper waterfall, about 20 metres high, which sprays droplets of water on those who try to bathe in the emerald-coloured pool at its base. The trail now becomes narrower and steeper, zigzagging up the wooded slopes immediately to the right of the waterfall, beneath the layered canyon rocks. After one final little effort, climbing a short metal ladder to the meadows where a small church and three crucifixes stand, you'll finally come out into the sunlight. This well-maintained place of faith is the point of arrival of the Via Crucis, a cherished spot for locals (the centuries-old pilgrimage to Santa Maria di Luggau in Austria starts there every year). Descend this path, enjoying the different stages along the way, until you reach the wooden bridge over the Rio Mühlbach.

The Acquatona chasm

A little downstream from Sappada, toward the Comelico, near a bridge and a well-marked car park, you can admire and visit the impressive chasm dug by the Piave River on the slopes of the Terza Piccola, another popular spot near the village, which is also appreciated in winter for its frozen waterfalls. After crossing the chasm on the wooden bridge, it is possible to descend to the bottom thanks to a path equipped with ladders and railings. Although it is intended for tourists, this route requires safe footing and the ground must be dry, as it is particularly slippery after a rainfall.

Sappada seen from the Via Crucis, at the end of the Path of the Waterfalls

PASSO DELL'ARCO

A hidden portal between the Cadini del Clap

Starting point: *From the church of Sappada, descend to the bottom of the valley and pass the Baita Pista Nera lodge and its ski lifts. A little further on is a sign to a small car park near the Piave (1,200 metres)*
GPS: *46.561527 12.687963*
Time: *5 hours*
Difficulty: *This is an easy hike with several exposed horizontal sections, secured by wire ropes. The descent is on a steep slope*
Elevation gain: *700 metres*
Trail markers: *Excellent*
Cartography: *Tabacco 1:25.000, sheet 001*

The Passo dell'Arco is a striking, rocky window that opens onto the ridge between the Creton dell'Arco and the Col dei Mughi in the Clap group. It is a beautiful destination for a pleasant hike, in a setting typical of the Dolomites.

The hike offers beautiful views of the Sappada valley, the Carnic Alps, the Dolomites and the neighbouring peaks of the Clap. Along this hike, it is also possible to enjoy the views of unusual natural landscapes, like the ravines and waterfalls of the Rio, the enchanting forests of the Casera Siera area and the more distant Cadin delle Vette Nere. It is possible to return to Sappada along an interesting loop via the Cadin di Fuori and Lake Zieghel.

After crossing the Piave, follow the CAI 316 forest road which climbs steeply through the forest toward the walls of Monte Siera. Ignore the possible detours and continue to the end of the road. Continue along a path with several easy equipped sections above the Rio Siera ravine that offer a view of the beautiful peaks that border the Cadin delle Vette Nere. After a few crossings and steeper sections, the slope of the path becomes gentler. Take the detour to the right, directly toward the Passo dell'Arco. You can also take the longer and more interesting route by first walking to the picturesque meadows dotted with larches, on top of which stands the Casera Siera (1,633 metres). On the meadow below the casera, there are more signs for the Passo dell'Arco, leading to the path you previously left behind but at a higher altitude. On the CAI 137 mule track, follow the regular twists and turns in a fascinating environment with alternating forests and views of the splendid walls of the Creton dell'Arco, the Robianco peak and the Vette Nere, until you reach the Passo dell'Arco (1,907 metres, 2 hours). From this rocky gateway, we recommend following the track that stretches toward the summit of the Col dei Mughi, a magnificent balcony overlooking the Sappada basin. From the pass, descend along the opposite side of the Cadin di Fuori. As you go down, be careful of the first steep section, even if it is well secured by a wire rope, until you reach a crossroads. Do not take the path that climbs to the left toward the Bivacco Damiana. Instead, continue to descend on narrow paths winding through woods and bushes until you reach the sport fishing pond and the Ziegelhütte (1,186 metres), where the road leads to the sawmill and the tarmac road to the campers' parking area. From there, you'll find the starting point on the right.

On the Arco

THE VIA FERRATA SIMONE AND THE VIA FERRATA DEI 50

Climbing among the towers of the Clap Group

Starting point: *From the church of Sappada, descend to the bottom of the valley and pass the Baita Pista Nera lodge and its ski lifts. A little further is a sign to a small car park near the Piave (1,200 metres)*
GPS: *46.561527 12.687963*
Time: *8 hours*
Difficulty: *This hike includes difficult via ferratas, in particular an exposed vertical section on the Ferrata dei 50. Some places on the way down from the Creton di Culzei are not equipped and are grade II. The hike is for trained and experienced hikers or hikers accompanied by a guide*
Elevation gain: *1,400 metres*
Trail markers: *Good*
Cartography: *Tabacco 1:25.000, sheet 001*

If you are looking for a moderately difficult via ferrata in a grandiose setting that is not particularly busy even in summer, you should discover the new via ferrata Simone at Creton dell'Arco and the Ferrata dei 50 at Creton di Culzei, in the Clap group.

The route, which includes the two equipped paths, starts at the Passo dell'Arco (detailed in the previous itinerary) and straddles a magnificent ridge as far as the large summit plateau of the Creton di Culzei. This memorable experience amid the rocks of a wild and imposing landscape

enables you to discover the valley along its partially equipped classic route, the northern corridor of the Forca dell'Alpino and the Bivacco Damiana, far from the crowds who, in other parts of the Dolomites, would take this type of hike by storm.

As for the previous itinerary, go directly up to the Passo dell'Arco (1.5 hours) without passing through Casera Siera. From the signs pointing to the Creton dell'Arco, climb up steep, loose meadows until you reach the walls on which the first equipment is installed. Climb a rocky outcrop and make your way along a corridor and a steeper section on a wall to the right. When reaching the Creton dell'Arco ridge, continue along the wide ridge to the summit (2,357 metres), where a breathtaking view of Monte Siera, the Julian Alps on the horizon and the Sappada mountains (1.5 hours from Passo dell'Arco) await. To reach the Ferrata dei 50 in its intermediate section (it actually begins on the southern slope, near the Rifugio dei Gasperi), descend on the south-western side of the summit as far as the fork below and climb toward the ridge toward the Cima di Robianco, following the cairns and red markers. Once you reach the Ferrata dei 50, you will have to overcome a particularly difficult section: a vertical chimney which you can climb up with the help of supports and by holding on to the exposed wall on the left. After this key passage, you will reach the summit plateaus. Continue to climb until you reach the last gap which will let you access the summit of the Creton di Culzei (2,460 metres, 1 hour from the Creton dell'Arco). For the descent, follow the classic route: descend directly to the north and you will soon find fixed ropes installed to facilitate access to a downwards corridor. Descend the entire length of the corridor with the help of the equipment and, after a short ascent in a small corridor blocked by a rock, you will arrive above the Forca dell'Alpino. In a final descent section, you will need to tackle the wall facing the pass which, toward the end, requires some grade II climbing without equipment (a few metres). From the col, descend on the gravel facing north, following the track between the scree-covered slopes marked by the CAI. Pass the boulder embedded along the way with the help of four metal handles and continue along the wide corridor flanked by impressive walls, which eventually lead to the Cadin di Dentro. There you will find the Bivacco Damiana. Before reaching it, follow a track that stays high on the meadows to go around the right side of the valley and catch up with the bivouac path at the Forcella della Chiesa. After a final climb with the help of a few fixed ropes, reach the pass, again enjoying the views of Sappada it offers. Descend into the Cadin di Fuori to the crossroads near the Passo dell'Arco. This is the highest side of the rocky portal. For a quicker return to the valley, it is best to climb up briefly to the pass, then descend to Sappada, taking the route back in the opposite direction.

On the Arco ridge toward Monte Siera, the Creta Forata, the Julian Alps, and the Pesarina valley below

The Sappada valley and its mountains from the Creton dell'Arco

FORCELLA DELLA TERZA PICCOLA

The great beauty of a small mountain

Starting point: *From the church of Sappada in Borgata Granvilla, go down to the sawmill and park near the Rio Storto*
GPS: *46.560700 12.675322*
Time: *4 hours*
Difficulty: *Easy but strenuous hike*
Elevation gain: *1,000 metres*
Trail markers: *Good*
Cartography: *Tabacco 1:25.000, sheet 001*

La Piccola is the smallest of the three peaks that make up the Terze group – rugged but grandiose limestone mountains between Carnia, Comelico and Cadore. Unlike its sisters, it has the characteristic towers and battlements so typical of mountains in the Dolomites. It is also widely known among local enthusiasts that the most beautiful view of Sappada and the surrounding valleys can be enjoyed from this peak, due to its ideal position on the Piave. The great beauty of this small mountain is revealed above all in the northern valley, nestled between the towers and culminating above the Forcella della Terza Piccola, the peak of Terza Piccola. There are also pleasant detours to be made around the pass to discover unusual scenery: strange, twisted spires and oddly shaped rocks complement the views of the surrounding peaks. Experienced hikers can also attempt the ascent to the summit, but on a normal route with grade I+ climbing passages on friable and partly exposed terrain.

From the car park, continue on the road that crosses the bridge over the Rio Storto. Follow the signs and take the path for the Passo della Digola, which climbs steeply up a first section through the woods. Further up, take the forest road toward the pass and follow it until you see a sign on the right. Leave the main road and follow the CAI 311 signpost to the Eichenkofel valley. It will soon lead to another forest road that stretches through the woods, narrowing to a path as you go. Continue on opening terrain, then cut the eastern flank of the bastions that border the Vallone della Terza Piccola and enjoy the spectacular view of the entire Sappada valley. Beyond this point, the path becomes a clearly visible military mule track and, after a section that has been cut into the rock, you will reach a crossroads with signs. Leave the mule track and turn left to climb a very steep slope surrounded by the beautiful peaks that border the Cadin della Terza Piccola. In a marvellous and wild setting, make your way across the meadows to the Forcella della Terza Piccola (2,165 metres, 2 hours from the car park).

The strange, teeth-like silhouette of the Forcella della Terza Piccola

View from the Vallone della Terza Piccola toward the wild group of Rinaldo and Monte F

MONTE BRENTONI

A dome in the heart of the wilderness of the Dolomite

Starting point: *From Laggio di Cadore, drive up to the Valico di Cima Ciampigotto and park in the small car park on the Rementera pass, before the Rifugio Tenente Fabbro (signs)*
GPS: *46.488113 12.578450*
Time: *5 hours*
Difficulty: *This hike is for experts, and includes an equipped vertical rocky section for which a via ferrata kit is recommended*
Elevation gain: *800 metres*
Trail markers: *Good*
Cartography: *Tabacco 1:25.000, sheet 001*

Monte Brentoni is the main summit of the group of mountains of the same name. It is an imposing, rocky mass between Cadore, Comelico and Carnia which, despite being directly above a very popular area, still boasts almost complete wilderness. It has two completely different faces: to the south it is a conical dome typical of the Dolomites, while to the north it resembles a great white pyramid with smooth, stratified walls.

These gigantic, painting-like rocks look like washboards – old planks of wood cut with an axe and used in the old days to wash laundry at a fountain. The classic route to the summit is tiresome but well worthwhile as it offers an enchanting, wild backdrop, a final section of climbing on a characteristic dihedral with a wire rope, and an extraordinary panorama.

Few peaks in the Dolomites can boast such a central position in the eastern Alps. With a single glance, you'll be able to see the Dolomites, the Carnic and Julian Alps, the Venetian and Friulian Prealps and even a glimmer of the Adriatic Sea.

From the car park, follow the forest road that descends gently toward Forcella Losco, where there is a fountain. Go straight on through the meadows following the CAI 332 signs to get around Monte Losco and climb to the Forcella Camporosso pass, where there is an important crossroads. Ignore the path that goes to the right toward Forcella Valgrande and take the CAI 328 path on the left, which leads out of the forest and winds through the marvellous, flowery meadows under the dome of Monte Brentoni. From this sunny hill it is possible to admire a unique view of several mountain groups (such as the Cridola and the Monfalconi) and the Carnic Alps (the Bivera and the Tiarfin). When you reach the plains at the base of the great southern ridge of Monte Brentoni and some of its towers, there is a crossroads indicating the classic route. Leave the path leading to the Bivacco Spagnolli and go to the right, following an excellent track that first climbs over meadows, before quickly approaching the rocks and advancing to the left of the mountain walls. The path points to the rocky ridge to the right of the towers and you will even have to make your way up rocky steps with the help of short, fixed ropes. Just below the ridge, go right to a fork between the summit of Monte Brentoni on one side and the Valgrande on the other. That is where the climbing section begins. With the help of fixed ropes stretching over the rocky dihedral above, and the via ferrata kit, climb the vertical part, which is about 30 metres long, then take an easy clearing corridor. As you exit this corridor, you will reach the summit (2,547 metres, 2.5 hours).

Arriving at the summit, toward the Civetta, the Antelao, the Marmarole and the Sorapiss

At the summit, with the Comelico mountains and the Austrian Alps in the background

Monte Brentoni from the meadows of Forcella Camporosso

FORCELLA VALGRANDE

Solitary mountains between the Dolomites and the Carnic Alps

Starting point: *From Laggio di Cadore, drive up to Valico di Cima Ciampigotto and park at the small car park at Col Rementera (1,776 metres), before the Rifugio Tenente Fabbro (signs)*
GPS: *46.488113 12.578450*
Time: *5 hours*
Difficulty: *This is an easy hike in a remote area with very few tourists*
Elevation gain: *400 metres*
Trail markers: *Excellent*
Cartography: *Tabacco 1:25.000, sheet 001*

Forcella Valgrande is a pass of the Brentoni group and takes its name from the grandiose valley deeply embedded between Monte Cornon and Monte Brentoni to the edge of Santo Stefano di Cadore.

Despite its remarkable scenery, it will never be a classic destination for hikers because this rough and rugged area lacks refuges and convenient access. However, it brings together the characteristics of both the Dolomites and their rough rocks, and the soft and verdant rocks of the Carnic Alps.

Although it is located in the busy Cadore region, with the Tre Cime di Lavaredo in the distance, the mountain remains unspoiled and wild.

and is perhaps one of the last refuges for solitary dreamers and nature lovers.

From the car park, follow the forest road that gently descends toward Forcella Losco, where there is a fountain. Go straight through the meadows following the CAI 332 signs to get around Monte Losco and climb to the Forcella Camporosso pass (1,913 metres), where there is an important crossroads. Ignore the path that goes left toward Bivacco Spagnolli and turn right to follow the Sarende pass on the beautiful CAI 332 track between the steep walls. Reach the slopes of Monte Brentoni and advance almost to the top under the singular towers of the Val d'Inferno, then carefully pass some rockfalls while remaining on the path. With a spectacular view of the Terze group to the east and the Bivera group to the south, you can reach the mugo pines below Forcella Valgrande (2,044 metres) after a final climb (2.5 hours). If you have two cars, it is also possible to make the crossing to Santo Stefano. In this case, make your way across the wild and enchanting meadows under Monte Cornon toward the centre of the impluvium. Cross the sparse forests until the simple Casera Drota delle Père that sits below the pale, sloping rocks of Monte Brentoni. Immediately below the guesthouse, take the military mule track that descends for a long time through the harsh and fascinating Valgrande to the Capitello di Sant'Antonio (899 metres), at the edge of Santo Stefano (2.5 hours from the fork).

SAN GIACOMO

The typical beauty of the Carnic Alps

Starting point: *Casera Razzo, on the road between Laggio di Cadore and Sauris*
GPS: *46.478271 12.608119*
Time: *3.5 hours*
Difficulty: *Easy, for all hikers*
Elevation gain: *300 metres*
Trail markers: *Good*
Cartography: *Tabacco 1:25.000, sheet 002*

Adorned with meadows, the hill was dedicated to San Giacomo by the inhabitants of the Tagliamento valley and stands in a peaceful, bucolic area on the slopes of Monte Tiarfin in the Bivera group. These mountains belong to the Carnic Alps and perfectly represent their typical beauty. They even have the advantage of being opposite the Dolomites. Looming over the Tagliamento valley with a harmonious and distinctive presence, the jagged ridges of the Cridola, Monfalconi,

Spalti di Toro and Pramaggiore, commonly known as the Oltrepiave Dolomites, are clearly visible from the grassy and flowery hilltop dotted with larches. Even the walk to the top, at the edge of the woods and in the middle of the high mountain meadows, is a relaxing stroll.

From the Casera Razzo car park (1,739 metres), follow a pastoral path toward Casera Chiansavei, which winds up the slopes of Monte Tiarfin, offering an unobstructed view of the Brentoni, the Terze and, rising just opposite, Monte Bivera. Ignore the fork in the road and the path to the left toward Casera Mediana and cross a ridge with a sign for Forcella and Casera Tragonia. Leave the road and turn right to climb the CAI 209 path over meadows below the clearly visible pass. Make your way across meadows and sparse larch trees. Once you reach the Forcella Tragonia, leave the signposted path down to the lodge and go left, on the grassy ridge of the Colle di San Giacomo, whose gentle profile is already visible. A beautiful, airy and panoramic walk will quickly take you to the velvety meadows of the summit (2,058 metres) and its small cross (about 2 hours).

At the top of the Colle di San Giacomo toward the Dolomites of Oltrepiave

CASERA DOANA

Alpine pastures and panoramas for every season

Starting point: *From Laggio di Cadore, follow the road to the Piova valley toward the Casera Razzo until the small car park in the Piova valley (1,559 metres)*
GPS: *46.488001 12.566879*
Time: *3 hours*
Difficulty: *Easy, for all hikers*
Elevation gain: *250 metres*
Trail markers: *Excellent*
Cartography: *Tabacco 1:25.000, sheet 002*

The Casera Doana (alpine hut) stands on a raised hill between Monte Verna, Colrosolo and Cima Camporosso – modest elevations at the edge of the Bivera group. The hill offers wide, sunny spaces with a clear view of the Cadore mountains and the Oltrepiave Dolomites.

The easy access from the road that connects Laggio di Cadore to the Sella di Campigotto, and the fact it is possible to easily reach panoramic viewpoints at high altitude close by, make it a pleasant and rewarding destination for those looking for easy hikes outside the classic tourist routes. In fact, most of these hikes are practicable all year round.

Not far away is the Casera delle Pecore (1,865 metres) and the lookout point on the nearby summit of the Cima Camporosso, which is popular for its views and flowers. In summer, the Casera Doana offers an agritourism service.

From the car park, descend gently to cross the Val Larga river on a small bridge. Follow the forest road through a wooded valley to a saddle at 1,840 metres. After this point, cross the almost flat meadows to the alpine pasture and the farmhouse (1,911 metres, 1 hour and 15 minutes). From there, continue to the already visible Casera delle Pecore.

Colrosolo: another popular viewpoint

Colrosolo (2,139 metres) is another panoramic viewpoint in the area which is appreciated for its unusual views of the Tiarfin peaks to the east and of the entire Dolomites.

From the lodge, head east toward the flat meadows between Colrosolo and Monte Verna that can be rapidly reached along the small, unmarked track. Without passing it, stay on the Val Larga and continue to the right on a path that runs along the eastern slope of the summit and climbs to the ridge. Follow a track along the ridge that ends at the remote summit. It can also be reached by following a small path directly along the ridge that rises steeply next to the Casera Doana.

The Cadore Dolomites and the Casera delle Pecore

From Agordo to Claut

COL NEGRO DI COLDAI

A beautiful and romantic spot near Parete delle Pareti

Starting point: *Palafavera in the Valzoldana, a little above Pecol*
GPS: *46.400535 12.101373*
Time: *5 hours*
Difficulty: *This is an easy hike, which only requires a little attention when leaving the Alta Via no. 1 to find the way to the summit. Good visibility is necessary*
Elevation gain: *600 metres, with a few counter-slopes*
Trail markers: *Good until Forcella del Col Negro, absent after, but the path to follow is obvious*
Cartography: *Tabacco 1:25.000, sheet 015*

This pass is a little-known summit of the Val Civetta, between the Coldai and Tissi mountain huts. It is set in a delightfully romantic environment away from the crowds, which tend to flock to the iconic Coldai lake. From the meadows on the summit, between edelweiss and solitary larches, you can enjoy the best view of the mighty north-western wall of the Civetta. The biggest wall in the Dolomites is a genuine natural monument and an internationally recognised icon of extreme mountaineering. It is one of the few places in the mountain range where, even in the middle of summer, there is not a soul to be found. No one can imagine how spectacular the panoramic view is from its summit, which hovers between Lake Alleghe and the Civetta. Its location near the two mountain huts gives it a perfect vantage point from which to admire the sunset, when the alpenglow colours the immense rocky organ pipes in red and yellow.

From the car park just below the Palafavera ski lifts, follow the signs for Rifugio Coldai and climb the forest road to the Malga Pioda mountain pasture. Continue on a wide, winding mule track under Monte Coldai and tackle a final, steeper section that overlooks the Ziolere valley. The path will lead to the meadows near the refuge, facing the mountains of Val Zoldana and Cadore (1.5 hours from the car park). From the refuge, go up the Forcella Coldai and make your way around the lake on the right, following the clearly visible Alta Via trail. When you are at the top of the moraine, with the lake nestled to the south, descend a few dozen metres on the opposite side, toward the basin that opens up on the right. Leave the Alta Via and descend toward the small, grassy valley enclosed by the clearly visible Negro pass to the west. After crossing the meadows dotted with rocks, walk freely to the base of the sloping meadow wedged between the Col Negro and a rocky outcrop on the left, which separates it from the Forcella del Col Negro. Climb this steep slope to reach a flat area that will let you access the summit meadows. You can climb freely along a delightful and intuitive path to the main summit (2,248 metres), which seems to be suspended above the Lake Alleghe. Col Rean and the Rifugio Tissi are visible to the west (1 hour and 15 minutes from the Coldai refuge).

CANTONI DI PELSA

The unique charm of the Dolomites

Starting point: *Capanna Trieste in the Val Corpassa (1,135 metres), accessible by car along the asphalt road from Listolade, a little north of Agordo*
GPS: *46.343803 12.031520*
Time: *8 hours*
Difficulty: *This hike is for experts. The terrain is steep but there are no climbing obstacles. You need to be sure-footed, and good weather is essential*
Elevation gain: *1,200 metres*
Trail markers: *Excellent until Rifugio Vazzoler, but only markers and cairns after*
Cartography: *Tabacco 1:25.000, sheet 015*

haracterised mainly by huge, rocky masses and uniform, compact walls, the Cantoni di Pelsa are part of the Civetta group. In contrast, the structure of the Cantoni (meaning 'sharp angles' in the local dialect) is complex, expressive and jagged. They are a real patchwork of towers, bell towers, spires, ridges, forks and corridors which, altogether, form one of the most striking parts of the Dolomites.

Their geological origin comes from the sediments of the land below, which caused fractures in the banks of dolomite rock. These banks were then later shaped by glaciers and climatic changes. You'll find an elephant with a trunk, eyes and ears, a perfectly shaped arch displaying the rock stratifications, human-like shapes resembling hunchbacks and hooded monks, and needles of all shapes and sizes. The culmination of all these

structures is Torre Venezia: a dolomite missile that seems to stand out from the rest of the mountain and has resisted the landslides around it for decades. A track descends between these nooks and crannies, revealing wonders all the way up to the ridge near the Torre Venezia, where the Arco di Pelsa stands tall.

This beautiful climb is unknown to many people and is undoubtedly one of the most unusual and secret hikes in this guidebook. It is a must for experienced hikers and guides.

From the car park, it is possible to reach the Rifugio Vazzoler (1,714 metres), a historic stopping point for hikes in the area, by following the dirt road that continues beyond Capanna Trieste. From Rifugio Vazzoler, go toward Rifugio Tissi along a short stretch of road but, as soon as you spot an open gate on the right next to a private house, leave the dirt road and go right. This is where the adventure begins. Follow the unmarked but well-trodden path that leads to the foot of Torre Venezia. Climb up a ridge covered with mugo pines and meadows, in a setting that becomes increasingly spectacular as you make your way toward the iconic tower, on a small path of scree, which becomes steeper but never difficult. When you arrive below the east wall, an essential cairn indicates where to leave the well-marked track from the classic route to the tower and continue straight on. The tracks are now less visible and more uncertain, but the direction to take to reach the Forcella delle Mede (2,326 metres) is obvious. You will then have to climb a very challenging scree slope between vertical rock faces. Be careful to choose the most solid sections. When the slope starts to narrow, it is better to go on the right side, near the walls. Climb the whole scree slope until you reach the fork. At that stage, there is no risk of making a mistake. Immediately below the pass, go to the left, advancing on a steep slope at the base of the Dente della Henrietta. After the only slightly exposed but short passage, exit onto the extraordinary ridge, with a view of the Croda di Pelsa and countless other peaks. With their shapes that seem to defy the laws of gravity, you'll notice the Aghi rising up from the Pelsa plains. You can end the climb at the large cairn, close to the Croda di Pelsa. The panorama is breathtaking (4.5 hours from Capanna Trieste). To reach the Arco di Pelsa, on the other hand, you must continue toward Torre Venezia, descend slightly to the right and cross the ridge until you reach a small arm. You'll see the portal in all its scenic splendour framing the Torre Trieste in the background. The landscape is particularly striking. To get in front of the portal from this incredible balcony you just have to continue carefully, making your way on the stratified and sloped terraces (about half an hour).

The Arco with Torre Trieste in the background

MONTE ALTO DI PELSA

An exclusive terrace on the great Civetta

Starting point: *Capanna Trieste in the Val Corpassa (1,135 metres), accessible by car along the asphalt road from Listolade, a little north of Agordo*
GPS: *46.343803 12.031520*
Time: *7.5 hours*
Difficulty: *This easy hike is long and strenuous. Good visibility is required to not lose track of the path near the summit and in the first part of the descent*
Elevation gain: *1,400 metres*
Trail markers: *Good until Forcella dei Sech, sparse thereafter*
Cartography: *Tabacco 1:25.000, sheet 015*

Monte Alto di Pelsa is an imposing, isolated bastion on the south-western slope of the Civetta group. It stands opposite a series of towers and peaks between the main summit of the Civetta, the Ghiacciaio del Giazzer, the Cima della Busazza, the Cantoni di Pelsa and the Moiazza. Hikers can walk along the ridge between flowery terraces and open views in the peace and quiet of a site that remains uncrowded, even in the middle of summer, just a few hundred metres from the crowded Alta Via 1, between the Vazzoler and Tissi mountain huts. Though it is tiring, the hike is easy for those who wish to climb to one of the most beautiful, spectacular and admirable places in the Dolomites. Monte Alto di Pelsa offers the most beautiful views of the breathtaking Torre Venezia and the fanciful spires of the Cantoni di Pelsa. The steep slope facing Val Cordevole still bears many traces of the hard work of generations of woodcutters, shepherds, charcoal burners and hunters, while the Casera di Pelsa and the Pian della Lora conceal historical evidence dating back to the Mesolithic period: flint flakes and other objects have been found on the meadows. Just like the more famous historical traces from Mondeval, these items were brought by prehistoric hunters to their high-altitude dwellings, which they built near what used to be a small lake.

As with the previous itinerary, climb to the Rifugio Vazzoler. Continue along the dirt road to the Rifugio Tissi, passing under Torre Venezia to reach the crossroads that indicate the direction to the Casera di Pelsa. Leave the Alta Via no. 1 and turn left onto a pastoral path leading to the alpine hut. Before reaching it, you will notice signs for Cencenighe and the Ferrata della Palazza Alta near a large meadow. Enter the vast forest of mugo pines on the slopes of Monte Alto di Pelsa and walk through it almost in a straight line toward the south-west, with the landscape becoming increasingly clear over the Civetta and the Cantoni di Pelsa. You'll notice Torre Venezia towering above. When you reach a flat area where the signs split in two, continue to the right, ignoring the route to the via ferrata, and head toward the ridge, always following the signs and the wide path across the mugo pines. Once on the ridge, leave the path that continues toward the Sech ravine and descends to Cencenighe and instead continue on the thin track toward the summit, which is now clearly visible and free of vegetation. Climb without difficulty the steep meadows punctuated by rocks until the wide, bare summit (2,417 metres, 4.5 hours). By following the many cairns and washed-out red signs, you can descend via another route, which is very interesting because it starts on the large summit slopes. After a long downhill crossing heading north, you will reach the first mugo pines and the track, which is quite steep, that leads to the Forzele esplanades, just below Torre Venezia. Once you are back on the Alta Via of the Dolomites, easily return to the Rifugio Vazzoler.

Civetta as seen while climbing Monte Alto

THE LABYRINTH OF MOIAZZA

Follow the golden thread between the rocks of Moiazza

Starting point: *From Forno di Zoldo, drive up to Passo Duran. Once you reach the little village of Le Vare, after Chiesa di Goima, follow the signs on a forest road toward the Malga Grava. Just before reaching it, near the CAI signs, park at 1,520 metres (small clearing on the right)*
GPS: *46.357083 12.090956*
Time: *5 hours*
Difficulty: *For experts, despite being short and not very challenging*
Elevation gain: *600 metres*
Trail markers: *Good until the ruins of Casera Moiazza, but minimal after*
Cartography: *Tabacco 1:25.000, sheet 015*

Thanks to the little-known Moiazza labyrinth, it is possible to climb to the Grisetti bivouac on Van della Moiazza by an alternative route to the CAI paths. It is an original route that stretches in a complicated round trip within a rocky bastion at the foot of the Crepe della Moiazzetta. This bastion has cracks all along its length, and even some unsuspected canyons created by the effects of atmospheric factors, which the locals aptly call a labyrinth. Although this hike is easy on the whole, it has very few markers and some short, more athletic sections of climbing. The key passage also involves squeezing through a very narrow crack just 40 cm wide, and larger people may find it difficult to get out of the heart of the mountain.

This trail is a wonderful experience for those used to discovering inaccessible areas, following a delicate and precious golden thread between wild vegetation and rocky crevices.

From the small car park on the carriageway, follow the CAI 578 trail marker, which descends and crosses the Ru della Grava, before climbing up the steep side of Van della Moiazza, with a beautiful view of the gushing Moiazza waterfall in the distance. After a narrow corridor of scree surrounded by rocks, climb to the ruins of the Casera Moiazza (1,754 metres, 1 hour). A sign indicates the direction to the Bivacco Grisetti, about ten minutes away. As soon as you reach a clearing between the mugo pines and the sparse forest, leave the CAI path at a stone cairn. Go right. At first the track will appear faint, but it will soon turn into a clearly visible path between the mugo pines and larches. Head for the rocky bastion opposite. Once you are below the bastion, do not enter the corridor that goes up, but follow a section of successive ascents and descents to the north, then go around the stone ramparts and find a crack where the labyrinth begins. Make your way between the high walls where the floor is cluttered with large, embedded stones, and cross a few jumps until you reach the key passage: a narrow fissure which you have to cross at an angle. Continue for a short distance until the canyon starts to dissipate, slowly replaced by the mugo pines of the Van della Moiazza. After a final, slightly exposed passage, you will reach the Sentiero Angelini which, if taken to the left, will bring you to the Bivacco Grisetti (2,060 metres, 1.5 hours from the ruins) in 15 minutes. From the bivouac, return to the ruins of Casera Moiazza, following the signpost CAI 559.

On the path to the labyrinth

SPIZ DE ZUEL

Great views at a modest altitude

Starting point: *From Forno di Zoldo, drive up to Passo Duran. Once you reach the little village of Le Vare, after Chiesa di Goima, follow the signs on a forest road to the Malga Grava car park (1,627 metres)*
GPS: *46.363006 12.090519*
Time: *3.5 hours*
Difficulty: *Easy, for all hikers*
Elevation gain: *400 metres*
Trail markers: *Excellent*
Cartography: *Tabacco 1:25.000, sheet 025*

The Spiz de Zuel, or Agnelessa, is a forest-covered dome on the eastern slopes of the Civetta. Isolated from the great walls of the Civetta and other surrounding peaks, it offers an excellent viewpoint, easily accessible on forest roads.

It is one of those mountains that can be climbed in all seasons and offers many hikes for climbers of all levels to discover the beauty of high

altitudes without fear. The presence of the Malga Grava alpine hut at the start of the itinerary also offers the possibility of enjoying a meal after this pleasant hike. For now, these places are still unaffected by mass tourism and deserve to be visited with respect so as not to spoil their simple, original beauty.

From the car park, follow the signs heading north along the clearly visible forest road toward the Spiz de Zuel, whose summit is not yet visible above the dense forest. Follow the road closely as it winds its way on modest slopes through the woods. With a few twists and turns, the path leads to the Forcella della Val del Top, which can be visited for its panoramic view of the Pelmo, a few minutes' walk away, and continue gradually uphill to reach the double summit of the Spiz de Zuel (2,033 metres). On the open alpine meadows, head toward the small depression between the two peaks. You will have to choose which one to climb to complete the ascent: the one on the left is home to radio transmission facilities, while the one on the right has a table and benches, perfect for enjoying a wide view.

THE LACH DI PELMO ⑥

Pastoral landscapes and cyclopean walls

Starting point: *Coi di Zoldo (1,500 metres), park at the car park near the church*
GPS: *46.383114 12.132693*
Time: *3.5 hours*
Difficulty: *Easy, for all hikers*
Elevation gain: *550 metres*
Trail markers: *Excellent*
Cartography: *Tabacco 1:25.000, sheet 025*

The Lach, or lakes, are the characteristic marshy depressions on the slopes of the Spalla Sud del Pelmo. They offer a magnificent lookout point among alpine meadows and connect the Mandre plateau under the majestic, stratified walls of the Pelmo and Pelmetto, which are separated by the imposing gravel-covered gash of the Fessura. The highest mountains of the Dolomites are visible all around: the Civetta, the Marmolada, the Sella, the Sorapiss and the Antelao form a harmonious ensemble. The singular rocky tower of the Dambra can be admired from the prominent two-part 'canopy' summit, under the Spalla Sud del Pelmo. Its shape is reminiscent of old wooden bedframes, known locally as dambra. It is possible to visit these places from the village of Coi di Zoldo by making a short loop past the village's typical wooden chalets. Even in the middle of summer, this side of the Pelmo is not overrun by tourists, most of whom pass through the Staulanza pass

and the Venezia Refuge.

From Coi di Zoldo, go up to the highest houses, where you can see the typical wooden tabià ('chalets') and the signs for the Rifugio Venezia. Take the forest road CAI 473, which follows a grassy hill overlooking the Civetta and, near a hut at the edge of the wood, turn right toward the refuge. Immediately after, at another fork in the road, turn right again at the CAI 473A signpost to the Lach. The path across the meadows will continue through a splendid forest of larch trees and lead to the Sass de Formedal. Once you have reached an extraordinary clearing dominated by the Pelmo and Pelmetto monoliths, cross the entire meadow and enter the sparse larch wood, which soon gives way to high mountain meadows and the Lach esplanades, which are often swampy in early summer. Before joining the nearby path that leads to the refuge from the Staulanza pass, climb to the meadow-covered summit at 2,020 metres. It can be considered the final destination and offers spectacular views of the Cadore mountains (1.5 hours). Returning to the well-trodden path, you will soon come across the CAI 472 marker. Ignore the sign indicating the direction of the Rifugio Venezia and go left toward the Passo Staulanza, plunging into the vast Mandre mugo pine forest, until you come to a crossroads with a sign at 1,908 metres. Turn left toward the valley and descend quietly through clearings and sparse woods, first following the Ru de la Fessura (which finds its source in the corridor between the Pelmo and Pelmetto). Pass a beautiful traditional hut and the rock called Sass del Drago, where what appear to be dinosaur footprints have been found. Return to the forest road and then to Coi.

Antelao, the second highest peak in the Dolomites, as seen from the Lach

THE VILLAGES OF ZOLDO ALTO

Discovering the ancient villages of the upper Val di Zoldo

Starting point: *Coi di Zoldo (1,500 metres)*
GPS: *46.383114 12.132693*
Time: *About half a day*
Difficulty: *This easy hike between houses and meadows is accessible to everyone*
Elevation gain: *About 100 metres*
Trail markers: *Excellent*

The history of Val di Zoldo – largely linked to the Serenissima Republic of Venice – goes back a thousand years through generations of lumberjacks, miners, blacksmiths and carpenters. It is only recently, after decades of emigration, that its economy has shifted toward tourism, skiing and precision eyewear craftsmanship (Longarone and Agordo, two nearby towns, are renowned internationally for their eyewear expertise).

The typical high mountain villages are the witnesses to this manufacturing and craft tradition. Most of them are well preserved and worth a visit, especially on sunny days, when you can appreciate the colours of the flowers on the facades of the houses, and the woods and clear views of the surrounding peaks. Visits to these villages alternate between easy, relaxing walks and short car trips.

It is possible to start the visit at Coi di Zoldo, which can be reached by car from Mareson, a hamlet above the Forno di Zoldo on the way to the Passo Staulanza. Coi is above all remarkable for its rustic wooden tabià ('chalets'), decorated with rich friezes on their front façades, and the direct view they offer of the monolithic walls of the Pelmo and Pelmetto, amid a uniquely beautiful environment. Turn right onto the path that leads to the Rifugio Venezia, after visiting the small church and the mills on the Mareson road, which were in operation until the 1970s. It is better to continue along the same road, which leads to other beautiful chalets, this time with the Civetta in the background. From Coi, go to Brusadaz, with its ancient Costa mill, active since 1693, and the mines of San Pellegrino and Da Doff, whose entrance is still visible. Back in Costa, park before the main village and continue on foot along the small road that passes the houses and enters the woods. Continue until you reach the Mas di Sabe massif, the oldest in the Val di Zoldo, which dates back to the 16th century and is still in good condition. From Costa, drive down a winding road passing through Fornesighe, which is also worth seeing for its wooden architecture, until it joins the provincial road of the Val di Zoldo. Go to Forno di Zoldo and follow the signs for Zoppè di Cadore (even though it is on the Zoldano slope), which can be reached after a long, winding climb. Zoppè, intimately linked to Mount Pelmo and its forests, has preserved all the distinctive features of high mountain villages. The beautiful church of Sant'Anna, built in 1530, houses a painting attributed to Tiziano Vecellio and is a prelude to the walks, all of which are signposted, to the historic Rifugio Venezia on the southern slopes of Pelmo.

The Spiz di Mezzodì from the meadows above Coi

SASSOLUNGO DI CIBIANA

Easy climbing in the footsteps of pioneers and hunters

Starting point: *Passo Cibiana (1,530 metres), pass road between Forno di Zoldo and Valle di Cadore. Parking near the Baita Deona*
GPS: *46.404211 11.609167*
Time: *6 hours*
Difficulty: *This hike is for experts, with some easy climbing passages (grades I and II, not exposed) and various sections on steep, loose terrain. A climbing and mountaineering helmet is recommended*
Elevation gain: *1,000 metres, with positive and negative elevation*
Trail markers: *Good*
Cartography: *Tabacco 1:25.000, sheet 025*

The Sassolungo di Cibiana is a beautiful summit of the eastern branch of the Bosconero. It is quite popular among local hikers but is not yet part of the classic Dolomite circuits, despite its two access paths and the incredible panoramic view its summit offers.

Hikers with a minimum of experience on rock and scree terrain should not miss this original and exciting destination, especially since the entire route is well signposted, with the possibility of making a pleasant loop around the summit. The route involves overcoming the rocks on the west wall, including some passages with wall climbing, then descends along the normal path on the south ridge, which has long been popular with hunters. The route is not exposed, and the surrounding environment is varied and pleasant. Good, stable weather is essential, as the hike passes through some areas that can be very dangerous in heavy rain or storms.

From the car park, follow the CAI 483 dirt road to the Rifugio Bosconero, which passes by some characteristic tabià ('chalets') then enters the forest. After an uphill stretch, you will reach a crossroads. Turn right onto a path that leads past the Casera Copada Alta to the crossroads on the Pian d'Angias (1,873 metres). Turn left for the Casera Campestrin and cross the large scree that rolls down from the Sfornioi. This path goes first to the Forcella Bella Impradida and then to the Forcella Bella Alta (2,112 metres). Descend to the south. The path will zigzag down for about a hundred metres, until you come across a clearly visible crossroads, indicated by a cairn (but without a sign). Leave the CAI path for the Casera Campestrin and go to the left, climbing up under the rising rocks and heading toward the Sassolungo wall. In a splendid and wild setting, you will brush past some of the ridge's incisions

until you reach the deep *Forcella Ovest*, at the foot of the Sassolungo. A red arrow on the rock indicates the path diverges, and it will take you to the vertical rocks, on which you will find good holds to climb a first boulder. Cross north on a ledge that leads directly to the wall. Follow the red mark and cairns, alternating between easy climbing passages and sections on rocky debris. The key passage of the climb is on a small rock face. To pass this obstacle, you will need to go through a hole. Beyond, you will encounter mostly rocky debris until you reach the summit dome that is characteristic of this summit. Follow the ridge to reach the big cross (2,413 metres) and its magnificent panorama (3 hours from Passo Cibiana). For the descent, it is advisable to follow the southern ridge closely, carefully following the cairns and red marks, on easy ground. When the ridge becomes impassable, descend to the left, first on rocky debris and then on some rocky jumps, until you return to the side facing the Bivacco Campestrin. From there, the descent is more difficult and the terrain steeper, but the path is clearly visible and will guide you to the best passages until the key section: a short drop and then a small, exposed crossing on a ledge. It is protected by a nylon rope. Descend into a crumbly corridor full of rocky debris and return to the meadows near the Forcella Ovest of Sassolungo. From there, you can easily return to the starting point.

Cibiana and its murals

Cibiana is a small village in the Alto Cadore, a little to the east of the pass of the same name.

With its 60 or so murals that adorn the facades of old houses, it became a real open-air museum in 1980, thanks to the original initiative of Osvaldo Da Col and Vico Calabrò, a painter from the Agordo area.

The aim was to breathe new life into the village and preserve the memory of old traditions, even if some of the frescoes were painted by foreign artists from all over the world.

Each work of art tells the story of the house in which it is located as a sort of collective painting to keep traditions, trades, stories and legends alive in the minds of those who see them.

SFORNIOI DEL BOSCONERO

A perfect lookout point to admire the alpenglow

Starting point: *Passo Cibiana (1,530 metres), pass road between Forno di Zoldo and Valle di Cadore. Parking near the Baita Deona*
GPS: *46.404211 11.609167*
Time: *5 hours*
Difficulty: *This hike is for experts up to the Sfornioi Nord, with some grade I+ climbing on steep, loose terrain. The climb to the summit and its cross above the Forcella delle Ciavazole is easy*
Elevation gain: *900 metres, with positive and negative elevation*
Trail markers: *Sufficient*
Cartography: *Tabacco 1:25.000, sheet 025*

The Sfornioi mountains form the northern ridge of the Bosconero group. Largely bordered by long ledges and broken walls, they culminate with three distinct summit towers: North, Middle and South. The North Tower (2,410 metres) is the only one with a normal path accessible to experienced hikers and offers a most satisfying climb, rich in beautiful scenery. At the end of the afternoon, the glow of the sun as it sets on the mountains transforms them into glowing blades in an astonishing setting. The triad formed by the Sasso di Bosconero, the Sasso di Toanella and the Rocchetta Alta is especially breathtaking. Those who do not wish to go all the way to the top can retreat to the terrace called Forcella dei Gendarmi or dei Pupe, where some small spires (the Pupe) seem to defy the laws of gravity.

An alternative, which is just as satisfying and easy, is to stop at the clearly visible cross on the way up. From there it is also possible to enjoy the alpenglow at sunset and return without difficulty through the woods at the bottom of the valley.

At the Passo Cibiana, park at the Baita Deona (sign) and follow a small road through flat meadows in view of the Sassolungo di Cibiana and the Torri di Campestrin. A little further on is a sign indicating the way to the Rifugio Bosconero. Go up through the woods to a crossroads with a sign, where you should leave the road (which leads to the Casera Copada Alta at 1,692 metres) and take the path to the right. Further up, reach a crossroads on the Pian d'Angias (1,873 metres) and follow the CAI 485 signpost which, after a short, steep stretch, reaches the Forcella delle Ciavazole (1,994 metres) in a magnificent setting (1.5 hours). On this level, the Alta Via no. 3 passes by and descends to the Rifugio Bosconero, where it follows a signposted path to the south-east that runs through the mugo pines and climbs safely to a sub-peak with a large cross. Those who are not experts in rocky and exposed terrain can stop there. Or, from the cross, continue on a track just below the ridge line, on crumbly gravel, paying attention to the exposure below. Once you arrive at a wall at the foot of the highest rock of the North Sfornioi, climb it carefully on a faint trail (exposed grade I section), following the few red marks. On the ridge, continue on a convenient ledge that runs along the entire summit until you reach another ridge. Go to the right, on the normal path to the summit (don't miss the cairn at the entrance of a chimney). This is where the most difficult part of the climb begins, with corridors and rock jumps leading to the summit (a good hour from the cross, with grade I+ climbing passages). Back at the base of the summit, follow the path leading to the ridge which, after a quick turn, will reach the lofty Forcella dei Gendarmi, guarded by two singular spires suspended in the void and facing the Bosconero valley.

The peaks of Bosconero, as seen from Sfornioi Nord

THE SASSO DI BOSCONERO

On the roof of the Zoldo trinity

Starting point: *Pontesei car park (825 metres) in the Zoldana valley, a little downstream from Forno di Zoldo*
GPS: *46.339586 12.223741*
Time: *7.5 hours. It is recommended to do the hike over two days, sleeping at the Bosconero refuge, an old casera that blends in wonderfully with the surrounding wilderness*
Difficulty: *A long climb for experts, and very demanding after the Bosconero refuge. Good footing is necessary in some places*
Elevation gain: *1,650 metres*
Trail markers: *Good until Forcella Toanella, absent after, but the path to the summit is clearly visible*
Cartography: *Tabacco 1:25.000, sheet 025*

The Sasso (2,468 metres) is the highest peak of the Bosconero group and one of the most isolated viewpoints in the Dolomites. From its summit you can see all the mountains of the eastern Alpine arc. The landscapes from these shattered blocks of rock are fantastic and, despite the modest altitude, are as good as those of its giant neighbours, such as Pelmo and Civetta. Together with the Sasso di Toanella and the Rocchetta Alta, it forms a triad of imposing vertical rocky sails, very similar in some respects to the Tre Cime di Lavaredo and which blush just as fiercely at sunset.

The path to the top passes right at the foot of these walls, in the heart of a wild and steep landscape. It winds through steep and gravelly terrain, but does not pose any particular problem and is perfect for trained and experienced hikers.

From the car park, follow the signs and the path to the Rifugio Bosconero, which climbs steeply through the woods on the right side of the Bosconero valley. Once you reach the Pian del Mugon, where you can see the casera of the same name, continue up to cross the stream at the bottom of the valley. Shortly after a last gap, cross to the left and reach the clearing of the Rifugio Bosconero (1,457 metres, 1.5 hours). Take the path just behind it, which enters the increasingly sparse forest, toward the grandiose north face of the Rocchetta Alta. Higher up, climb the gravel that rolls down from the Forcella Toanella, which will eventually appear before you, embedded between the mighty walls of the Sasso di Bosconero and the Sasso di Toanella. Ignore the less obvious track near the Lares del Belo, which continues toward the Forcella del Matt, and climb the difficult dark gravel corridor, on an inconspicuous track, all the way to the fork (2,150 metres). Leave the Alta Via no. 3, which continues toward the Rocchette della Serra on the Viaz de le Ponte, and immediately turn left. Climb the grassy, rocky slope that runs from the fork toward the Sasso di Bosconero, on the left of the impressive scree that falls from the vicinity of the summit (do not venture onto the clearly visible track that cuts right over the scree, directly toward the Viaz del Orso). Continue along the slope where the ground is more solid, and a small path makes it easier to advance to the top of the slope. Follow the cairns and continue along the broken rocks. Below the summit, follow a clearly visible path that crosses the Bosconero valley on a slightly uphill ledge. Be careful with some exposed spots and crumbly terrain. Pass the last rocks (al

curiously crushed and cracked) without any particular difficulty until you reach the summit (2.5 hours from the refuge).

Lares del Belo, the thousand-year-old larch

The Lares del Belo is an imposing larch. It is probably the oldest tree in the province of Belluno, with an estimated age of about 1,000 years. It is named after a hunter from the Zoldo area who was stationed nearby at the beginning of the 19th century, waiting for the chamois to pass.

The larch is not exceptionally large, which makes it all the more resistant and adaptable as it stands in a setting of rocky scree and mountain walls that only let the sun's rays in during the summer. Perhaps it is precisely these mountains, which rise over 600 metres, that have protected it from lightning and violent winds over many seasons. Lay your hands on the reassuring folds of its old bark as a way of greeting this grandfather of the Dolomites, which has seen many generations of hunters and mountaineers go by and still offers its fresh green hues in spring and hints of red as it prepares for winter.

It can be reached quickly via a short detour before tackling the gravel corridor that descends from the Forcella Toanella

The original stone cairns on the summit

VAL TOVANELLA

A little-known forest listed as a nature reserve on the slopes of the Bosconero

Starting point: *Termine di Cadore (471 metres)*
GPS: *46.302219 12.319434*
Time: *6 hours*
Difficulty: *Easy but tiring hike*
Elevation gain: *1,150 metres*
Trail markers: *Sufficient*
Cartography: *Tabacco 1:25.000, sheet 025*

Val Tovanella is a state reserve created in 1971 in the southern sector of the Bosconero, a little upstream from Longarone. It spans an area of more than 1,000 hectares, mainly covered by coniferous forests. In the past, this was a wood reserve for the fleet of the Republic of Venice. Val Tovanella is a perfect environment for large ungulates, especially deer and roe deer, and for their natural predators, eagles, martens and lynx. Bears were seen there for the first time in the Eastern Dolomites in 1995 and seem to roam freely, given the total absence of human activity.

In the past, the valley was criss-crossed by many paths used by hunters, coal merchants, woodcutters and shepherds, who even set up summer pastures for their animals. Because it is very steep and difficult to access, the area is almost completely abandoned now, despite the few paths that are still visible, marked and well maintained by the Corpo Forestale dello Stato, thanks to a recent effort to improve access in the area. It has made access to the forest and all the way to the old casere possible as part of an original hike that feels like old times.

Near the church of Termine, take a path that climbs between the old houses (next to a fountain is a sign with directions). Go up between the ruins, past the railway, then turn left. Beyond the Piave, you can admire the Pissa, an impressive stream of water that gushes out of the slopes of Monte Borgà. Weave your way up the wooded hillside along an old mule track flanked by moss-covered dry stone walls, until you reach a casera on the Tosute pass and a small road that climbs from the cemetery. Follow it all the way, skirting the Varda pass and crossing some streams until you reach the Pescol clearing, where there are two casere: one closed and reserved for the Corpo Forestale, the other open, and serving as a good refuge for hikers with its two beds. Above the meadow, spot the southern towers and the summit of Sasso di Bosconero (3 hours). If you continue the hike, you can either go to Casera Fason (1,318 metres), which is also well situated in the Bosconero mountains, or to Casera Busnich. In both cases, follow the signs and climb through the forest at the back. At the first crossroads on the left, you can reach Casera Fason in half an hour, while if you continue straight, you will reach Casera Busnich. Carefully follow the red and white markings on the trees (on this stretch the path is almost absent, but the signs are clear) until you cross the mule track that climbs from Castellavazzo and Olantreghe. Take this path on a steeper climb out of the woods to find the Casera Busnich (1,563 metres), on a hill at the top of the old mountain pasture (1 hour and 15 minutes from Pescol).

RIFUGIO ANGELINI

An alpine refuge from another time nestled between the pinnacles of the Spiz di Mezzodì

Starting point: *From the small church of Sant'Antonio near Forno di Zoldo, follow the road of the Val Pramper (which is almost completely paved) to the car park at Pian de la Fopa (1,210 metres)*
GPS: *46.321997 12.167226*
Time: *3.5 hours*
Difficulty: *This is an easy hike, with a short section on rocks secured by metal cables. Another solution is to climb to the refuge from Forno di Zoldo by the mule track (see box)*
Elevation gain: *400 metres*
Trail markers: *Good*
Cartography: *Tabacco 1:25.000, sheet 025*

The Rifugio Angelini sits on the western edge of a small clearing under the vertical walls of the Spiz di Mezzodì, where the ancient Casel Sora 'l Sass was located. The Casel Sora 'l Sass was the name of a casera (alpine hut) on a raised rocky outcrop in the Pramper valley where milk was processed. The Casel was already mentioned in a topographical survey

of 1888 and, like almost all the casere in the Dolomites, it was abandoned after the Second World War. It was only a renewed interest in mountain hiking that allowed it to be preserved, first with a restoration in 1971 by the CAI Valzoldana section, then with its conversion into an alpine refuge. Small and welcoming, even if it offers only the essentials, the refuge is perfectly integrated into the landscape and accessible only by footpaths. It is now regarded as one of the few authentic refuges in the Dolomites and was named after Giovanni Angelini, an illustrious admirer and connoisseur of these mountains. His research and documentation work was recorded in the precious *Guida ai Monti d'Italia, Pelmo e Dolomiti di Zoldo* (Guide to the Italian Mountains, Pelmo and the Zoldo Dolomites) of the Italian tourism organisation Touring Club Italiano, a monumental work in which all the hikes, climbing routes and difficult chamois paths are described in surprising detail. As you leaf through the guide, you'll be impressed by the countless hiking possibilities offered by the refuge and the Spiz di Mezzodì, despite the fact it is a small and modest group of mountains.

From Pian de la Fopa, follow the road at the bottom of the valley until you reach a small bridge on the left. Nearby is a CAI 534 sign for the Rifugio

Angelini. Take a path over the rocks of the Giaron della Pala dei Lares, which rises from the imposing and magnificent towers of the Spiz, until you reach a crossroads for the Bivacco Carnielli. Ignore the path to the bivouac and turn left, along the bottom of a corridor surmounted by imposing, protruding walls. Cross the corridor and tackle a rocky ramp equipped with a steel cable to climb up the base of the Spiz, above which are forests and where the walls close in. A path winds its way up this gallery for a long time, with splendid views of the Valzoldana mountains, to the clearing and the refuge (1,588 metres, 1.5 hours). From there, we recommend taking a small detour to the Piccolo Belvedere ('little lookout point') to enjoy the exceptional panorama, which is otherwise obstructed by bushes and other vegetation around the refuge. Follow the sign next to the winter shelter and head gently down the hill until you reach the surprising terrace made of rocks and meadows suspended above Val Pramper (10 minutes). We recommend returning downstream on an alternative route, which is a little longer but easy. Take the CAI 534 path that descends to the Casera di Mezzodì along a steep slope in a valley amid forests. Leave the meadow of the old casera and immediately turn left to descend through the woods to the Prampera stream, in the hamlet of Castelaz. From there, take the road to Val Pramper that goes up to the Pian de la Fopa car park.

The old shepherds' entrance to Forno di Zoldo

This classic ascent along the historic mule track, built long before the very short via ferrata, still leads to the Spiz pastures. It is very easy to follow and recommended for everyone. Follow the mule track CAI 534 from the houses in Baron, a hamlet of Forno di Zoldo, beyond the Maè stream, which climbs through the woods and offers beautiful views of the villages in the valley. After a first stretch through enchanting woods, you will come to the Casera di Mezzodì and its beautiful view of the Pelmo. Continue south, again through beech woods. Follow a long, slightly uphill crossing until you reach a steep, winding valley. At the top is the Sora 'l Sass plateau. The descent to the refuge is rather quick (2 hours).

Sunrise on the Pelmo, as seen from the path to the Rifugio Angelini

The refuge and the peaks of San Sebastiano

CASERA DI COL MARSANG

The enchanting nature of Spiz di Mezzodì

Starting point: *Forno di Zoldo, hamlet of Le Boccole (806 metres), a few kilometres downstream from the village. Park near the campsite*
GPS: *46.339928 12.205273*
Time: *3 hours*
Difficulty: *Easy, for all hikers*
Elevation gain: *500 metres*
Trail markers: *Good*
Cartography: *Tabacco 1:25.000, sheet 025*

Nestled in the woods, on the eastern slopes of the Spiz di Mezzodì, the small Casera di Col Marsang offers a hike of rare intensity in enchanting nature. This authentic paradise is covered with beech trees (it is no coincidence the name Marsang refers to the blade used to cut wood), with wilder and steeper spots, and remarkable panoramic openings toward the Pelmo and Bosconero mountain ranges. The old access path to the casera, which already existed on the 1833 Topographical Map of Lombardy-Venetia, has been used by generations of woodcutters, coal merchants, shepherds and hunters. It is still well maintained, thanks to the dedication of the inhabitants of the Campo di Zoldo valley, allowing hikers to enjoy a beautiful, easy and evocative walk with complete peace of mind.

From the car park near the campsite, take the dirt road leading to the nearby quarry. Walk until you reach the entrance to a power station. The CAI 531 path starts on the left and leads to the Casera di Col Marsang (1,290 metres). First climb through the forest in steep zigzags until you reach the crossroads with a sign. Ignore the path that goes right toward Baron and Forno di Zoldo, and turn left, quickly crossing the mouth of the Val di Doa. The path runs for a long time, slightly uphill, along the entire densely wooded hillside, offering beautiful openings toward the Pelmo, until it climbs more steeply to reach the charming clearing and its small mountain hut (1.5 hours).

Spectacular panoramic views from the lookout point of the Pelos pass

Those who do not wish to stop at the casera can continue to the Pelos pass, which was already one of the most beautiful lookout points back in 1884. Follow the path to the Rifugio Angelini. The panoramic view of the mountains of Val di Zoldo is spectacular from the ridge next to the Forcella di Col Pelos (1,900 metres). The climb is rather steep but easy along the excellent CAI 532 trail and takes about 2 hours.

The Casera di Col Marsang in autumn

The Bosconero at sunrise, seen from the casera

COLCERVER AND ITS LAKE ⑭

The abandoned village of Val di Zoldo and its water mirror

Starting point: *Pralongo (1,000 metres), a hamlet of Forno di Zoldo*
GPS: *46.335982 12.155029*
Time: *3.5 hours*
Difficulty: *Easy, for all hikers*
Elevation gain: *350 metres*
Trail markers: *Good*
Cartography: *Tabacco 1:25.000, sheet 025*

Colcerver is a small hamlet in the Zoldo region. Its first inhabitants arrived in the 16th century, but now it is almost completely abandoned. There are a few old houses built of local stone, wooden barns with cut-out windows, courtyards and a pretty little church dating from the 18th century.

The roofs and walls of these buildings stand out against the winding ridge of the Spiz di Mezzodì, offering a charmingly harmonious picture. Strolling through the narrow streets and squares of the village is like stepping into the past, as it seems to have remained virtually unchanged over time. Only a handful of old people choose this life of solitude and silence, and some of the houses only wake up in summer. Only recently has the village been able to benefit from renovations, inspired by the children of emigrants who enjoy the tranquillity the village has to offer and try to keep the heritage of past generations alive.

It is possible to combine a visit to the village with a wonderful walk through the forest to the small El Vach lake: a deep blue mirror amid beech trees fed by a powerful waterfall gushing out of the rocky walls upstream. The waterfall can also be reached via a small detour.

From Pralongo, follow the signs for the Casera del Pian and park in the meadows south of the village. Continue on foot along the asphalt road that leads to the casera, which is now an excellent and much appreciated agriturism open all year round. It is also possible to climb up to the casera along a small forest path on the opposite bank of the stream, especially as there are cars on the asphalt road. From the casera, continue up, following the many signs for El Vach lake, on a path that winds through a magnificent beech wood with panoramic views of the Pelmo. Once you have reached the small water mirror, and possibly the waterfall that can be seen in the distance, on the Crepe di Rondoi, continue by following the signs for Colcerver. You will walk through lush woods sloping down before arriving at a pretty square with a fountain, surrounded by beautiful old barns. Walk between the old houses alongside the small church until the signpost for the way back to Pralongo. The path climbs steeply up the wooded slopes to the houses of Pralongo, near the car park.

Between the barns of Colcerver and the towers of Spiz di Mezzodì

CASTELLO DI MOSCHESIN

On the terrace of a dolomite castle with a view of the sea

Starting point: *The bridge over the Ru de Caleda (1,500 metres), a little below the Duran pass on the Agordo side*
GPS: *46.314269 12.099842*
Time: *7 hours*
Difficulty: *This is a strenuous hike, with some short grade II and lower climbing passages. The terrain is rather crumbly and requires sure-footedness and the use of a helmet. We recommend being accompanied by an expert or an alpine guide*
Elevation gain: *1,000 metres*
Trail markers: *This is a discreet trail with numerous cairns and a few faded red marks to help with orientation*
Cartography: *Tabacco 1:25.000, sheet 025*

The Castello di Moschesin ('Moschesin Castle') is one of the most important mountains in the Tamer e San Sebastiano group. Its recognisable profile is reminiscent of a solitary medieval fortress surrounded by towers and small buttresses.

The isolated summit offers one of the most complete circular views of the Southern Dolomites, in particular toward the Spiz di Mezzodì, Pramper, Talvena, Monti del Sole and Pale di San Martino. In the distance, the Adriatic coastline, the islands of the Venetian lagoon and even its bell towers are clearly visible.

The charm of this mountain also lies in the untouched nature that surrounds it: alpine meadows meet steep, craggy slopes. The normal route was mapped out as early as 1885 by a topographer accompanied by a local guide, while its vast eastern walls have been climbed up to grade V. The ascent on the topographer's trail is an excellent opportunity

for those who wish to try out steep, almost virgin terrain, with some easy but particularly satisfying climbing.

From the bridge over the Ru di Caleda, a little downstream from the Duran pass on the Agordo side, follow the Alta Via no. 1 all the way up the wooded Forcella Dagarei. After a first section of ascents and descents, exit onto scree with large rocks at the foot of Tamer Davanti and Tamer Grande, from where the Malga La Roa can also be seen in a clearing in the woods below. When you reach the scree slope below the Forcella Larga, which is clearly visible between the Cima delle Forcellette and the Castello di Moschesin, leave the marked path and take an excellent track on the left, marked by cairns, which zigzags up the slope. As you approach the rocks of the Cima di Forcella Stretta, the track becomes even more steep and is made up mostly of scree. You must stay on the right edge of the gravel flow, leaning as best you can on the rocky walls to reach the top of this difficult corridor. The path fans out and gives way to notches on a slope of meadow and gravel that quickly leads to the Forcella Larga (2,185 metres), which is characterised by large rocks on the meadows. This is certainly one of the most picturesque places of the Belluno Dolomites and offers a few detours, especially in the Van della Gardesana, overlooking the forests of the Pramper valley. The path to the Castello di Moschesin starts immediately to the right of the crossroads, where an excellent track starts just behind the maze of large rocks. The path climbs up on a ledge that skirts the eastern slopes of the Cima di Forcella Stretta. Beyond a ridge, the terrain will become rough and steep. You will have to climb up and down a few times, leaning against the walls. Follow the few red marks on the rock to the large, broken wall of Castello, which you will reach after descending over gravel and a tiring climb back up a loose slope. The track leads to the foot of the rocks, where you will find a vertical hinged chimney. Climb the chimney, which has many footholds, to flat, gravel terrain. Once you have crossed it along a thin track, another rocky ledge must be climbed, again through a chimney that has an exposed grade II exit. There are no further difficulties after this passage and the summit can be easily reached (2,499 metres, 4 hours).

Castello di Moschesin as seen from the Pramper

THE MENADAR PASS

An unassuming mountain pass and an unexpected panoramic view

Starting point: *The bridge on Ru de Caleda, a little before the Duran pass on the Agordo side*
GPS: *46.314269 12.099842*
Time: *2 hours*
Difficulty: *Short and easy hike accessible to everyone*
Elevation gain: *1,550 metres*
Trail markers: *Good*

The Menadar pass is a small hill on the Agordo side of the Tamer mountains, which offers unobstructed views of the Moiazza, San Sebastiano and Tamer mountain ranges, as well as of the Tavelna and the entire Agordo basin and its mountains. It is only at its highest point that this modest-looking, wood-covered dome will reveal an incredibly

unexpected viewpoint. The short walk from the road to the Duran pass to reach it and its ideal position in relation to the afternoon sun make it a very popular destination at sunset, where the colours of the alpenglow can be fully appreciated.

From the car park on the road to the Duran pass (1,500 metres), follow the Alta Via delle Dolomiti no. 1 through sparse forests, with beautiful views of the Moiazza rising to the north. When you reach the Forcella Dagarei, surrounded by fir trees, leave the main CAI 543 trail and turn right (sign) to climb the Menadar pass (1,737 metres, about 1 hour). Near the summit, the vegetation becomes sparse, offering a surprisingly wide panoramic view

The Casera della Roa: an afternoon hike

In the heart of the Tamer and Castello di Moschesin mountains, the Casera della Roa is located in an ancient pasture, between dense forests at an altitude of 1,436 metres. It is a beautiful destination for an afternoon hike, when the sun illuminates the beautiful surrounding rock faces.

It can be reached in about an hour and a quarter along the CAI 544 trail from the small car park on the road between Agordo and the Duran pass, in the hamlet of Cesurette. It is possible to combine the climb to the Menadar pass with the climb to the Casera.

On the Menadar pass, looking out to the Castello di Moschesin

THE CANYON OF VAL DI PIERO ⑰

Prince Amedeo's cave and waterfall

Starting point: *The hamlet of La Stanga on the Statale Agordina*
GPS: *46.210679 12.129729*
Time: *About 1 hour return*
Difficulty: *This is an easy hike that should not be attempted in times of heavy rain because of the risk of dangerous flooding*
Elevation gain: *50 metres*
Trail markers: *None*
Cartography: *Tabacco 1:25.000, sheet 024*

The Cascata del Principio Amedeo ('Prince Amedeo's Waterfall') was discovered by chance around 1860, during a disastrous flood caused when the Val di Piero mountain stream burst its banks. The curiosity of the workmen in charge of repairing the road to Agordo, which was overrun with debris, was sparked by this canyon, which until then was largely a mystery, almost feared by the inhabitants.

This is how the powerful water jet was discovered, gushing out of what appears to be a hole in the ceiling of a dark and gigantic cave, dug tens of metres into the vertical rock.

In fact, the erosion of the water on the double bend of a long gorge of about 400 metres only makes it look like a cave. The passing of water has excavated a portion of the rock that appears narrower near the ceiling than at the bottom, giving the impression it is surrounded by the mountain.

A few years after its discovery, Prince Amedeo of Savoy wanted to visit the gorge to admire the cave and the waterfall, which were then renamed after the famous visitor. Since then, very little attention has been paid to this impressive place, and it remains forgotten even though it is close to the busy road to Agordo.

This hike is unique. It is best to wear water shoes when planning it, as it is almost impossible to reach the cave and the base of the waterfall without having to walk in the cold water of the river at some points. On some sections, the high vertical walls of the canyon are only a few metres wide, so there are no banks to reach a dry section. There are some fun rock-climbing passages, fords, jumps and footbridges that alternate pleasantly, and help to relieve tension that can easily be felt when the walls close in on all sides and the roar of the powerful water jet can be heard nearby.

The Val di Piero gorge cuts through the rocky walls that overlook the Agordo road all the way to the Val Cordevale and the hamlet of La Stanga, where there is a famous restaurant. There is a sign indicating you should cross the bridge over the Val de Piero, but that is the only information. It is best to park in an open space right next to the bridge. Access to the bottom of the canyon is on the right-hand side, where a small path descends between the trees and leads to the shore. The hike is obviously conditioned by the level of the water, but it is impossible to take the wrong path.

In the Val di Piero canyon

Val di Piero: one of the last paradises in the Dolomites

The canyon is only the last section of Val di Piero, one of the wildest and most impressive valleys of the Schiara group. Its steep configuration does not allow the sun to shine through. Only a daring path (partially equipped) leads up its slopes and precipices to the Forcella Oderz, then down to the VII Alpini refuge.

Very few people know that, toward the middle of the valley, it is possible to admire the western wall of the Burel (2,281 metres), the second highest mountain in the Dolomites after the Agner, which seems to reach for the sky from the thick forest that rests at its foot. The writer Dino Buzzati, a native of Belluno and a connoisseur of these valleys, was so captivated by them that they are the inspiration behind the archetypal imaginary and unreal places in his 1942 story, *The Slaying of the Dragon*.

Unfortunately, the visit to the rest of Val di Piero is difficult and challenging. It is all the more difficult because the valley is infested with ticks, which can cause several diseases in humans. This discourages the modern hiker, but it is also what ensures that this rare paradise in the Dolomites remains isolated and wild.

PALA ALTA

The legend of Franco Miotto and chamois ledges

Starting point: On the road that connects Belluno to Sospirolo, reach the hamlet of Barp in Val Gresal. Follow the signs to Pian dei Gastaldi, drive up on the right bank to an open space where the road ends and becomes a mule track. Park there
GPS: 46.170602 12.146483
Time: 5.5 hours
Difficulty: This is a tiring hike suitable for experts. A steel cable helps facilitate a short section near the summit. Because the trail is constantly exposed in the middle of the day and its starting point is at a low altitude, it is recommended to do this hike at the end of autumn
Elevation gain: 1,050 metres
Trail markers: Good
Cartography: Tabacco 1:25.000, sheet 024

Franco Miotto was a mountaineer from Belluno who died in 2020 at the age of 88. He spent time in the harsh mountains of Belluno with his father, a passionate hunter, since he was a child, and learnt to

navigate safely along the passages where only chamois can pass. He too became a hunter and was one of the most sought-after poachers in the province. His escapes along impassable passages to elude the forest guards are now legendary. It is said he even managed to climb a grade IV wall with boots, a rifle and a chamois on his shoulders! His mountaineering career only began when he was 40 years old. His first major ascent was on the grade VI route of the north face of the Pala Alta. Then, with Riccardo Bee, he climbed the Italian-Polish route on the Burel, his favourite mountain, in early winter. Completed in four days, it included a number of dangerous obstacles in freezing temperatures. Dozens of other extreme climbs followed, on the Schiara, Monti del Sole, Pizzocco and the Pale di San Lucano. The extreme climbs culminated in a resounding success in 1982, when Miotto created three winter routes on the northern walls of the Nudo pass, with Benito Saviane and the young Mauro Corona. After having trekked across hundreds of routes as a hunter, Miotto also made his way across some extremely difficult paths: the steep ledges on which the chamois move in the most inaccessible areas of the province's mountains.

The ascent to the Pala Alta, an imposing peak near Belluno, marks the beginning of one of these itineraries and makes it possible to get up close and personal with the environment of the chamois in these wild areas of the Belluno Dolomites National Park. Even if the southern side, where the ascent takes place, does not have the typical appearance of the Dolomites, it offers unique, if not exclusive, views of the areas where Miotto walked and, above all, of his favourite peak: the Burel, the gigantic pillar of the Schiara, with its immense western wall overlooking Val di Piero.

From the car park, at about 900 metres, climb toward the head of the valley, following the sign for the summit. Ignore the drop-off on the left for the small church of San Giorgio and continue along the steep path to quickly reach the Forcella San Giorgio (1,304 metres). Stay on the slope overlooking Belluno and continue through a sparse forest, then climb the grassy slope and overcome some easy, rocky jumps. Enter a corridor topped by an original overhanging rock. Still on a narrow path, climb a steep slope to reach the eastern part of the Schiara group. Continue on a south-facing escarpment to a panoramic pulpit surrounded by mugo pines, where the Burel, the Pale del Balcon and the Schiara appear in all their glory. Keep to the left of the massive tower known as the 'Bareta del Prete' until you reach the halfway point, where there is a sign indicating the start of the Viaz dalla Pala Alta al Monte Coro, which was laid out by Miotto himself. For the Pala Alta, follow the red markings on the left, which descend along a short, equipped rocky corridor, and climb the last cliff of grass and small stones to reach the summit (1,933 metres, 3 hours).

CIMA DE ZITÀ

*Remote glacial valleys on the Van de Zità mountain
pastures which are jewels of the Belluno Dolomites
National Park*

Starting point: *From Longarone, drive toward Forno di Zoldo for about
4 km, turn left and reach the small village of Soffranco. Continue along the
carriageway of Val del Grisol, as far as the Piera Bridge (667 metres), where
you can park (signs)*
GPS: *46.262222 12.215541*
Time: *8 to 9 hours. Given the considerable length of the hike, it is recommended
to do it over two days, with an overnight stay at the Rifugio Pian de Fontana,
an excellent stopping point in a rather isolated and wild area*
Difficulty: *This is an easy hike, but it is long and tiring. It requires good
training and good visibility to appreciate the vast spaces of the summits*
Elevation gain: *1,800 metres*
Trail markers: *Excellent on the paths, totally absent on the summits.
Orientation remains straightforward with good visibility*
Cartography: *Tabacco 1:25.000, sheet 025*

Van de Zità are two high mountain karstic cirques, the seat of ancient glaciers shaped over time by snow and meteoric waters. The name Zità comes from the shape of the peaks that delimit the cirques and recall a fortified citadel. They are one of the most remote and solitary places in the Schiara and Talvena group, with a typical landscape characterised by rising rocks, sinkholes, fields of grooves, rocky debris and moraine.

The cirques are divided into two distinct valleys (Van de Fora and Van de Entro), between which stands a rocky ridge curiously named Le Preson, due to the presence of many cavities in its limestone walls that look like prison cells. In addition to the rocks, this area is dominated by high-altitude meadows. In fact, they are the most extensive in the Belluno Dolomites National Park. They descend all the way to the ancient pastures of the Pian de Fontana refuge and the Casera dei Ronch. The landscapes toward the Talvena and Schiara crests are unquestionably charming, especially at midday when they extend as far as the one-of-a-kind obelisk of the Gusela del Vescovà. Although the Alta Via delle Dolomiti no. 1 passes through Van de Zità, the area remains unknown

to most people, despite offering a number of spots worth exploring in a setting of exceptional value. In particular, it is easy to climb the splendid Cima di Zità Sud, the North Cima (along a more demanding route that can only be found on site) or the easy but unknown Cima della Campana. This last summit is located at an altitude not marked on maps, and offers a surprising view of the Costa dei Nass valley, a deep and very impressive groove reminiscent of Himalayan tones, as some climbers of various nationalities have observed.

From the bridge, follow the signs for the Rifugio Pian de Fontana and continue on the road to the Ross Bridge (737 metres). On the other side of the bridge, the road becomes a mule track that climbs steeply and in many twists and turns into Val dei Ross. In the upper part of the valley, pass to the left side to reach the Casera dei Ronch, on the edge of a dense forest. Continue along the wide, almost flat path until you reach a small valley where the mountain stream flows down from Van de Zità, then climb up the right-hand side. Ignore the path to Forcella La Varetta on the left and pass the last steep wooded slope before the large pasture on the plateau where the Rifugio Pian de Fontana (1,632 metres, 2.5 hours) stands. Continue on the Alta Via directly to Rifugio Pramperet, going beyond the steep moraine threshold that surrounds Van de Zità. The path runs along the hole-poked slopes of Le Preson. It is therefore on the left and stretches into the exceptional setting of Van de Fora. Approach the Forcella dei Erbandoi, cross first under the Cima

Sud de Zità, then under the Cima Nord, to reach the Forcella Sud de Zità pass (2,351 metres, 2 hours from the refuge), where you can appreciate an exceptional panoramic view. Leave the Alta Via, which descends toward Pramperet, and head toward the Cima Sud (2,450 metres), which can be visited in a few minutes after climbing the scree ridge and from which you can admire the splendid scenery of the Van, the Talvena and the Schiara mountains. To reach the Cima Nord (2,465 metres), the highest and most panoramic summit, you have to retrace your steps to the south and continue on the steep scree slopes to the fork at its base. Follow the steep ridge, which requires some easy climbing, and you will reach the summit (the last section is for experienced hikers only). To return to the valley, we recommend the Le Preson tour via Van de Entro. Start by going down into the valley along the path until you spot a faint trail over the meadows. This is on the left of the grassy back of Le Preson and enters the solemn valley above Van de Entro. Before descending, take the time to stroll along the Cima della Campana, whose cross stands on the grassy dome that marks the edge of the ridge on the left. This dome can be reached after an exciting climb up the flowery slopes, where you will discover a small capital bearing an inscription and a bell, not to mention the exceptional view of the opposite slope. Head back to the path and continue the descent across the dreamy scenery. Visit the real Van de Entro, a circular basin shaped by the ancient glacier. At the bottom of the moraine sill, keep to the left, which will lead you to a path that heads up, just before the steep section to the Rifugio Pian de Fontana

The grassy Cima della Campana and the Van de Zità

BUS DEL BUSON

A fossil stream at the foot of Gusela del Vescovà

Starting point: *Case Bortot (694 metres), accessible from Bolzano Bellunese, a hamlet in Belluno, along the asphalt road (park just before the hamlet)*
GPS: *46.183076 12.195515*
Time: *2 hours*
Difficulty: *This is an easy hike, but the path is steep*
Elevation gain: *150 metres*
Trail markers: *Good*
Cartography: *Tabacco 1:25.000, sheet 024*

The Bus del Buson is a relict canyon on the slopes of the Schiara, just above the town of Belluno, carved out about 15,000 years ago by the Ardo mountain stream. Its high, stratified limestone walls were shaped by the strength of the water before it was diverted by what was probably a landslide upstream and which explains why the canyon is now easily accessible along its entire length, unlike the neighbouring gorges, which are only accessible to those with a high level of canyoning expertise.

In some sections, the walls are so close together that only one person can pass through at a time, and the little light that filters through, together with the typical damp and cold microclimate, has given rise to a host of unique endemic flora. Where the walls of the canyon recede, magnificent spaces offering a unique acoustic open up, so much so that in summer they become the natural stage for a musical performance. The hike consists of a recently laid out loop with signs. The short and charming hike can be combined with a walk to Ponte del Mariano, or to the VII Alpini refuge on the Alta Via delle Dolomiti no. 1. In fact, the very first Alta Via, inaugurated in 1966, ends at Case Bortot.

Piero Rossi, the man behind the creation of the route from Lake Braies to Belluno that is appreciated by thousands of people from all over the world, was himself from Belluno. He was also behind the monumental guide to the Schiara which, together with the elegant Gusela del Vescovà, a 40-metre obelisk slightly below the main summit, watches over the town of Belluno. You can admire it perfectly in the distance as you walk along the first stretch that leads directly to Lake Braies, after visiting the canyon.

In the Bus del Buson ▶

From the car park, walk along the CAI 501 trail to the VII Alpini refuge. After a few minutes you will see a sign on the right indicating the direction to Bus del Buson. Leave the Alta Via and descend steeply through the woods, being careful, especially if the ground is slippery. Continue along a light rock face until you reach the entrance to the canyon, which is an impressive and fascinating lair that lets in very little light and where a cold breeze often

blows. Continue slightly downhill to the bottom of a stone amphitheatre where the canopy seems to close in on the trees. Climb up, between the limestone stratifications, to emerge again into the woods. The path climbs back to the road a few hundred metres upstream from where you left it. For Case Bortot, go down to the left, and to continue toward the Rifugio VII Alpini, turn right.

THE CAJADA FOREST

The enchanting forest of the Belluno Dolomites National Park

Starting point: *From Faè di Longarone, follow the signs and a rather steep asphalt road up to Pian delle Stele and the Casera Cajada. It is possible to park right before the casera, in the large open space. Drive carefully as the road is steep and narrow with only a few sections with safety barriers*
GPS: *46.240516 12.246804*
Time: *4 hours*
Difficulty: *Easy, for all hikers*
Elevation gain: *300 metres*
Trail markers: *Good*
Cartography: *Tabacco 1:25.000, sheet 024*

The Cajada forest was formed on the remains of an ancient landslide that levelled out when the Piave glacier retreated. It is surrounded by the eastern slopes of the Schiara group. This splendid forest of mixed wood was exploited for centuries by the Republic of Venice, which mainly used its precious wood for the construction of ships. The presence of exceptionally large red and white fir trees is one of the characteristics of the lower part of the forest, which stretches out, peaceful and almost flat, while birches, hornbeams, beeches and larches dominate the wilder upper part of the surrounding peaks. In the heart of the forest there are pleasant clearings with a few private buildings and some old *casere* (huts), which were used for summer pastures. The peace of the forest is an inviting call to take long, relaxing walks, which

are particularly pleasant in autumn, when this magical natural basin explodes in a thousand shades of red and yellow, making it one of the most beautiful destinations in the park.

From the car park, continue along the dirt road to reach the Pian delle Stele prairie, near Cimon and the Cime di Cajada, to the casera of the same name (1,157 metres). A tombstone commemorates the death of three inhabitants of the valley killed during a raid in 1944 during the Second World War, while the ancient fountain bears the date 1870. The charm of the place will undoubtedly invite you to take a few detours between the small huts scattered on the edge of a spruce wood. From the casera, continue on the asphalt road and cross the thick forest until the crossroads to the VII Alpini refuge. Turn left toward Casera Palughet and climb slightly up to the small clearing on Col dei Broli, where an information board indicates the nearby monumental white fir tree called La Regina di Cajada ('The Queen of Cajada'), one of the most ancient trees of the Veneto region. Continue along the road which alternates between ascents and descents and exit at the Igoi pass, another remarkable panoramic breakthrough toward the walls of Monte Pelf and the jagged-

looking Cime di Cajada. A little further on, the road descends again and leads to another interesting spot of rare beauty where the Casera Palughet (1,257 metres) is located (1 hour from Cajada). The name of the casera is linked to the pasture visible just opposite, a marshy basin ('palude' in Italian) between thick forests, where water tends to stagnate and frequently forms patches of condensation on cold days. Seen from above, the basin looks like a steaming cauldron. From the casera, take the forest road around the right side of the pasture and exit on the edge of the huge landslide that stretches from the edge of the forest toward Val Desedan and the Piave. The route continues on the dirt road that climbs over the modestly high slopes of the Saline above the forest and then climbs more steeply to offer a surprising view at Casera Becola (1,428 metres, 45 minutes from Palughet). From there you can see all the Dolomites of Oltrepiave, the Col Nudo and even the peaks of the Comelico. From the small casera, return to the edge of the scree. You'll see a small path on the right that goes around the right side of the Palughet basin and allows you to return to the Col d'Igoi via a shortcut. Return to the car park by taking the path you took on the way up. There are many possible detours to discover all the interesting places along the way.

PESCORS

The rugged beauty of the Dolomites of Belluno

Starting point: *Drive up to the Casera Cajada. You can continue by car until the small car park near the crossroads to the VII Alpini refuge*
GPS: *46.238689 12.239470*
Time: *4.5 hours*
Difficulty: *This is an easy hike, but it goes along steep and not very visible paths*
Elevation gain: *600 metres*
Trail markers: *Good*
Cartography: *Tabacco 1:25.000, sheet 024*

Pescors is the easternmost area of the Schiara massif, where the mountains of the Dolomites merge with the wild, almost pre-Alpine environment of the Cajada peaks. The alternation of rocky walls and dense vegetation, and the strange shapes of the towers mixed with the delicate alpine meadows above the enchanting forests, give this jewel of the Belluno Dolomites a very special quality.

This is where the idea of 'rugged beauty', as it was meant in 19th-century Romantic literature and painting, is fully expressed.

The elegant shapes of the Dolomites emerge from the dense forest, and the view disappears between the cliffs and the bold lines of the chamois ridges. The climb up the ridge next to the imposing Pescors tower, under the walls of Monte Pelf, offers an original and little-known hike that unveils an enchanting, unspoilt and solitary world, difficult to imagine in a place so close to Longarone and the Piave valley.

From the small car park, continue along the forest road toward the Rifugio VII Alpini and enter the Cajada forest. After a first section that is almost flat, the road turns into a path and climbs steeply among the beech trees, which are particularly beautiful in autumn. Once you have passed the stream, go up the wooded slope immediately to the right, where there is an old metal signpost that served as a beacon. Continue up tight twists and turns in the woods to reach a clearing and the remains of the Casera Caneva, surrounded by the superb rock curtains of the eastern wall of the Pelf. Leave the main signpost that turns left toward the refuge, and find a small signpost numbered CAI 527 that leads off to the right. Enter the forest on a path that is not very visible and quickly crosses a pebble beach from which the Torre di Pescors can already be seen. Further on, the path will improve and you'll notice it is marked by stakes planted in the high meadows all the way until it reaches a pretty clearing. The path climbs steeply up to the rocky walls that protrude from the towers which make up the Cime di Cajada, where the chamois find shelter. The path climbs along a steep, grassy corridor, at

the top of which you will reach the Forcella di Col Torond (1,750 metres, 1.5 hours). From there, it won't be long until you reach the small summit immediately to the right, with a panoramic view of the Cajada basin. Back at the fork, cross the Torond pass at high altitude and you will reach another saddle: this is the true passage of the ridge between the Cajada and Val del Grisol near Soffranco, in Val Zoldana. Descend a little to the north and, for wider panoramic views of the Torre di Pescors and the Northern Dolomites,

leave the track and descend to another unsignposted track (not very visible but easy to spot) that goes around the Cime di Cajada at altitude. This track is not signposted and is reserved for those who know the area well. Follow a section to admire the unusual beauty of the Cirque del Fontanon, on the northern side of the Pelf, the Torre di Pescors, flanked by other smaller pinnacles, and the giant mountains of the Cadore region (Antelao, Pelmo, Bosconero, Sorapiss) that rise to the north (2.5 hours).

CIMON DI CAJADA

An unmissable destination for hikers who love wild and secluded places

Starting point: *See previous hike*
GPS: *46.240516 12.246804*
Time: *4.5 hours*
Difficulty: *Easy until Selle del Gravedel, then tiring along the steep meadow along a rather narrow trail (for experts)*
Elevation gain: *700 metres*
Trail markers: *Good until Selle del Gravedel, absent thereafter*
Cartography: *Tabacco 1:25.000, sheet 024*

W ith its vertical wall that looks like organ pipes alternating with grassy corridors and cross-sectional ledges, the Cimon towers above the forest basin. The slender shape of the imposing rocky pedestal gradually blends in with grassy plains and sparse woods at the summit. Many isolated towers rise from the thick forests like enigmatic and ominous figures watching over the peacefulness of one of the least frequented areas of the Dolomites.

The beauty of this mountain is even more striking when you discover it was exploited for decades by lumberjacks and hunters, many of whom left visible traces. These traces are evidence of the very first,

and all the more daring, attempts at mountaineering that occurred on very dangerous, steep slopes for subsistence purposes. Isolated from the other peaks of the Schiarra group, Cimon offers a magnificent view of the Piave valley and the Dolomites. With the superb scenery that accompanies the ascent, this hike is an immersion in one of the most beautiful natural landscapes around, particularly when decked out in its autumn colours. A must for those who love wild and solitary places!

From the Casera di Cajada, climb north along a forest road and take a path in the forest above the Pian delle Stele (there is a signpost near the casera: marker CAI 509). The path becomes progressively steeper and follows a narrow valley surrounded by bold and original rock towers. After reaching an excellent viewpoint overlooking the Cajada basin near a grassy plateau, carry on across and up, between sparse trees, to reach the Selle del Gravedel ridge (1,713 metres). Leave the marked path that descends to the Casera del Gravedel and take to the ridge that leads to the Cimon. If you want to stop climbing and still enjoy the view, just before the pass, take a track on the left along the ridge that will lead to a panoramic dome (1,756 metres) between bushes and trees. For the Cimon, follow the ridge, which has steep sections, including across meadows, as the track passes over some jumps and narrow sections. After a mainly downhill section, you will reach a trench-like saddle. The climb becomes steeper, and it is advisable to go left to take advantage of some sections where the mountain is not so difficult and steep. Once out of the woods, the hike ends on the grassy dome where the large cross announces the summit

Olt de Gostin: a perfectly circular portal 50 metres above the floor

The Olt de Gostin is a remarkable geological phenomenon on the slopes of the Cimon di Cajada. The perfectly circular opening, which is more than 50 metres high, was created over thousands of years by the erosion of the waters of the Gostin valley. This 'eye of the Dolomites' can be seen from the road toward the Cajada, after passing the only house on the left as you climb, at an esplanade near a sharp bend on the right. The view is excellent and there is a path leading up through steeply sloping woods (about an hour's walk). A little further on, you can admire the Cascatella di Gostin ('Gostin waterfall'), which crosses the road in a striking, rocky bulge.

CUNA DEL CRIDOLA

At the heart of the enchanted castle of Cridola

Starting point: *From Lorenzago di Cadore, drive up to Passo Mauria. After about 2 km, park on the right at the indicated point (987 metres)*
GPS: *46.468108 12.468681*
Time: *6.5 hours*
Difficulty: *This hike is easy, but it is long and strenuous*
Elevation gain: *1,150 metres*
Trail markers: *Good*
Cartography: *Tabacco 1:25.000, sheet 002*

Cuna is a basin suspended at the head of Val Cridola, a grandiose furrow on the northern slope of the Cridola group, and a majestic backdrop for the villages of central Cadore. The only meadows in the entire valley are at the bottom of this mountain basin, and they offer an idyllic oasis of greenery and flowers between the scree and large rocks that tumble down from the threatening walls of Monti Tor, Monte Vallonut and the towers and castle of Cridola.

Blocked on three sides by imposing formations, the only place to look is to the north, where the high peaks of Cadore, including the Tre Cime di Lavaredo, can be seen.

Set in the heart of the meadows since 1978 is the Bivacco Vaccari, a typical half-barrel made of sheet metal that serves as a stopping point for mountaineers and hikers. Even the simple climb up the long Val Cridola is a peaceful hike with little traffic, revealing a charming and unspoilt corner of Cadore.

From the car park, descend along the CAI 340 forest road which passes by the Fienili Campo (barns) and the old sawmill at the bottom of the Cridola Valley. From there, you'll have a magnificent view of the entire valley. Continue along the road until it stops near the Sorgenti del Cridola ('Cridola springs'). Legend has it that if hikers drink the springs' waters, they become eternally enslaved to the mountain! Once you have crossed the mountain stream, you will make your way along the endless river of scree that flows between the surrounding high rocky slopes. Continue past the large wall of the Cridola and pass to the left of the large rockslides. Beyond the last spring before the bivouac, the Olivato trail connects to the path on the left. This is the beginning of the steep, grassy slope that leads to the Cuna (2,050 metres, 3.5 hours) in a splendid setting.

Forca del Cridola: in the midst of rock castles

Those who still have energy to burn can climb to the Forca del Cridola pass (2,176 metres), on the border between the regions of Veneto and Friuli. There you can admire the great walls that surround the Cuna and enjoy the unprecedented views of the opposite peaks of the Carnia. The detour is marked by a CAI 340 marker, first between large rocks that block the Cuna and then over scree that requires some effort to climb (45 minutes from the bivouac).

Climbing up the Cuna scree toward the Forca del Cridola

Bivacco Vaccari and the Cridola

CRODON DI SCODAVACCA

A fantastic viewpoint of the Oltrepiave Dolomites

Starting point: *Rifugio Cercenà (1,051 metres), accessible from Domegge along the steep asphalt road that leads directly to the Rifugio Padova*
GPS: *46.433098 12.435010*
Time: *8 hours*
Difficulty: *This is a long and very tiring hike across very steep scree at the top, but it is without difficulty. Less experienced hikers can stop at the Bivacchi Montanel*
Elevation gain: *1,350 metres*
Trail markers: *Excellent until the bivouac, sporadic after. A good sense of direction is essential on the last section*
Cartography: *Tabacco 1:25.000, sheet 021*
Accommodation: *Bivacchi Montanel. The largest baita (typical chalet) is usually closed, but the keys can be requested from the CAI office in Domegge. The second one is always open, with four beds and some blankets*

Crodon di Scodavacca offers enchanting views of the castle-like Cridola bordered with its towers and, above all, of the entire ridge of the Spalti di Toro-Monfalconi mountain range with its amazing series of towers, peaks, screes and rock faces rising up just opposite. This unusual viewpoint has little traffic and is still a favourite spot among chamois: only a few tireless hikers dare to venture onto these steep slopes to discover their privileged landscapes.

At the foot of the mountain lies a charming, rocky cirque called Cadin di Montanel, a genuine oasis of flat greenery in the middle of

desert of rocks and scree, which is in itself a reward for the difficult climb. There are two small wooden bivouacs there. For those who wish to stop and admire the spectacular sunset on a clear day, they are a perfect break from the long climb.

From the refuge, follow the CAI 345 trail that climbs through thick woodland to the Dalego barns, which stand in a picturesque clearing. From this scenic spot, the path turns right on a rather steep slope and quickly gains altitude, until it goes around the Col de l'Elma and up Val Montanel. Once you reach a wooded area with a view of the Talagona valley, continue through the mugo pines, pass a spring and, after a final effort on steep ground, reach the clearing where the two Montanel bivouacs are located (2,048 metres, 2.5 hours). From the bivouacs, follow the signposted track that goes up the Cadin di Montanel directly toward the mountain of the same name, in a superb setting typical of the Dolomites, until you reach the scree with pebbles rolling down from the surrounding peaks. On the right, the corridor that leads to the Forcella del Frodon di Scodavacca is clearly visible. It is the only passage to the top that is otherwise entirely inaccessible due to the walls. Leave the marked path and climb up the steep and unstable scree (where you will need a certain amount of determination), using the few tracks to reach the narrow pass. Climb to the right over unstable rocks and gravel to reach the summit in a short time (2,389 metres, 1.5 hours from the bivouacs). At the top, it is advisable to push on, carefully, to the slender ridge that towers above the Talagona valley and the Rifugio Padova, which can be spotted down below.

The Oltrepiave Dolomites from the Crodon di Scodavacca. In the meadow below, the Rifugio Padova

THE MARCHI-GRANZOTTO BIVOUAC

The enchanting Monfalcon di Forni valley

Starting point: *From Cimolais, drive up the entire Val Cimoliana (13 km), until the parking of the Rifugio Pordenone in Pian Meluzzo (1,150 metres). There is normally a toll booth just after Cimolais to access the Friulian Dolomites Natural Park. It is best to ask at the refuge how practicable the road is, as it is subject to frequent landslides*
GPS: *46.378762 12.490584*
Time: *7 hours*
Difficulty: *Easy but long and strenuous hike*
Elevation gain: *1,200 metres*
Trail markers: *Good*
Cartography: *Tabacco 1:25.000, sheet 021*

T he Marchi-Granzotto bivouac is located at 2,170 metres, at the head of the Monfalcon di Forni valley, one of the natural monuments of the Oltrepiave Dolomites. Its upper part is a vast basin covered with rocky scree and alpine meadows, surrounded by a labyrinth of towers, points, portals and rocky corridors. The refuge, with its functional half-barrel structure, contains 12 beds and rests on greenery just below the Forcella Monfalcon di Formi, between the threatening walls of the Monfalcon di Cimoliana and the Monfalcon di Forni. There are many ways to reach the bivouac, all of which are equally interesting for their exceptional, unspoilt settings. From the Cimoliana valley, within the Friulian Dolomites Natural Park, you can combine the climb to the Monfalcon di Forni valley with the equally interesting descent into the Monfalcon di Cimoliana valley. Those who wish to reach it from the Veneto region can drive up from Domegge di Cadore to the Padova refuge and climb the entire Val d'Arade.

From Pian Meluzzo, follow the signs and enter the Meluzzo valley along the CAI 361 road, which begins by crossing the vast meadow where the Casera Meluzzo is located. Beyond the pasture and surrounded by high, rocky peaks, the path crosses a flat area covered in gravel and tall mugo pines and runs over torrents of scree. At the entrance to the Postegae valley, ignore the junction for Forcella Pramaggiore and continue on a moderate slope over sections of loose rock beside the Rio Valbinon, which you will walk alongside for a long time. When you reach the clearing where the Cason dei Pradi stands (1,363 metres), leave the direct path for Valbinon and turn left to climb a challenging slope through the woods. After passing a steep stretch from right to left, exit onto the Monfalcon di Forni valley, amid meadows, terraces, streams and rocky screes. Continue with a moderate ascent and enjoy the pleasant stroll in the gentle, charming surroundings until you reach the bivouac above rocky, flat terrain that divides the head of the valley (4 hours). On the way back, continue following the CAI 359 markers, climbing to the Forcella Monfalcon di Forni (2,309 metres). A little below, you can cross at high altitude over the valley to Forcella del Leone and its gravel ground (at 2,290 metres, also accessible directly from the bivouac via scree). There, under the spectacular vertical wall of Monfalcon di Cimoliana, where a gigantic rock portal has been formed, you can begin the easy and bucolic descent of the entire Monfalcon di Cimoliana valley. As beautiful as the previous one, it will lead you back to Pian Meluzzo. Before reaching Pian Meluzzo, the CAI 349 marker points to the right and enters the forest. After a short crossing, you will reach the Rifugio Pordenone (1,249 metres) and the car park.

The bivouac and the Monfalcon di Cimoliana

The Monfalcon di Forni valley, as seen from the Forcella of the same name. In the centre of the picture is the bivouac. In the background, the peaks of Pramaggiore in the Friulian Dolomites Natural Park

27

CIMA DI SAN LORENZO

Feel like a pioneer on the ridges of the Cadin valley

Starting point: *From Domegge di Cadore, drive down to the lake at the heart of Cadore and cross it on the small bridge. From there, drive up Val Talagona along the steep and narrow asphalt road until the small parking near the Rifugio Padova (1,278 metres). In summer, it is only possible to go up in the morning and down in the afternoon*
GPS: *46.413715 12.461362*
Time: *7 hours*
Difficulty: *Long and strenuous hike, only for expert hikers. There is a short Grade I exposed section at the summit. This hike should only be attempted when conditions offer excellent visibility*
Elevation gain: *1,100 metres*
Trail markers: *Excellent until the threshold of the Cadin valley, but totally absent after*
Cartography: *Tabacco 1:25.000, sheet 021*

The summit of San Lorenzo is between the Spalti di Toro, in the middle of innumerable towers and forks that make this very long, extravagant ridge so characteristic. It has a privileged position in a corner at the southern head of the beautiful and little-known Cadin valley, one of the most secret places in Cadore.

Its summit and the extraordinary panorama it offers, both toward Cadore and the Oltrepiave Dolomites, have yet to be discovered and, above all, conquered. One step at a time, the terrain to climb to reach the summit is made up of gravel, with no paths. Also, the small final wall has a few short, exposed sections on broken rock. Finding your way to the top is nevertheless rather simple, as long as an unusual adventure on rocky scree does not discourage you. San Lorenzo is a mountain for those who want to test their limits in the wilderness!

The first ascent was made in 1903 by the Austrian duo Domenigg and von Saar, the same two climbers who first reached the summit of the much more famous Campanile di Val Montanaia.

From the car park at the refuge, take the CAI 357 trail that runs alongside a marquee and climbs through the woods to the lower threshold of Val Cadin. After an initial section in the forest, take a steeper ridge on gravel amid mugo pines to reach a delightful plateau at the bottom of Val Cadin. A signpost indicates the direction of Forcella Segnata and Val Cadin. Turn right toward the head of the valley, leaving the CAI signpost and follow the red marks indicating the direction to an obvious track (which leads to the start of the beautiful and clearly visible Campanile Toro). Soon, you will leave the vegetation and reach a scree section. The Forcella San Lorenzo, though not yet visible, is on the right of the tower of the same name. Cross the entire stream of stones that flows from the walls halfway up the slope and head toward the head of the valley, which is closed off by some beautiful, jagged peaks that form a semicircle. Ignore the faint traces that go up the corridors at the base of Campanile Toro and continue to the rocky walls of the Cima Talagona. Turn left and climb another unstable and challenging scree section toward the base of the Torre di San Lorenzo, which is strangely shaped like a fiasco (an Italian bottle usually with a rounded bottom covered with a close-fitting straw basket). To the right of the walls of the Torre di San Lorenzo, a steep corridor rises and ends in a narrow gully. At first glance it will seem impassable, but it is easy to climb up on the crumbly rock debris to the summit, where the small opening of the Forcella San Lorenzo (2,240 metres) appears. On the opposite slope, the Cimoliana valley opens up, with the remarkable Pramaggiore group to be admired. From the ridge, go immediately to the right along the tracks on the grass and rock, and then onto a small, exposed wall above Val Cadin. After a few stretches requiring particular caution, leaning carefully on the broken rocks, climb to the magnificent summit terrace (2,363 metres, 4 hours).

View from the summit, toward the Val Cimoliana, the Pramaggiore and the Vacalizza group

28

CASERA DI VEDORCIA

Between the towers of a castle-like mountain

Starting point: From Domegge di Cadore, drive down to the lake at the heart of Cadore and cross it on the small bridge. From there, drive up Val Talagona along the steep and narrow asphalt road until the small parking in the hamlet of Antarigole (1,105 metres). In summer, it is only possible to go up in the morning and down in the afternoon
GPS: 46.422390 12.440713
Time: 5 hours
Difficulty: Easy, for all hikers
Elevation gain: 700 metres
Trail makers: Good
Cartography: Tabacco 1:25.000, sheet 021

The Casera di Vedorcia overlooks the picturesque ridge formed by the Cridola, the Monfalconi and the Spalti di Toro. With their peculiar shape, these mountains compete with the Cadini di Misurina for the title of best castle in the Dolomites.

At sunset, the peaks light up with the alpenglow and contribute to making this lost place in the Dolomites of Oltrepiave, which until a few decades ago was totally ignored and isolated, increasingly popular.

The casera is surrounded by numerous private barns typical of the area and, in summer, the nearby Rifugio Tita Barba is an excellent stopping point that offers a warm and relaxing welcome.

The access to Vedorcia from Val Talagona through the Fosso degli Elmi, itself a delicate setting of ponds, waterfalls, flowers and moss cushions, is one of the most romantic stretches of Cadore.

From the sign at the car park, go down to the CAI 350 trail and cross the small wooden bridge over the Pra di Toro stream. Climb through the forest, passing by some beautiful waterfalls. Ignore the fork in the road to the Rifugio Padova (next to some splendid waterfalls) and go to the Casera Valle (1,360 metres), which you'll find in a small clearing that offers a magnificent view of the Cadin peaks. At the crossroads near the casera, follow the CAI 352 sign, which climbs gently along the Fosso degli Elmi, where you can admire the many emerald-coloured ponds and beautiful rivers. The path enters a sparse forest and becomes steeper, but it remains perfectly visible. After the forest, it enters an area of rocky scree on the side of the river and stretches to the vast grassy plains below the Cime Cadin and around the Forcella Spè. There, you'll find a crossroads with signs. Turn right (here you can take a quick detour to the fork, 2,049 metres), where the panoramic view is worth the detour. Continue along a long, flat stretch under the Costa Vedorcia, passing by tabià (typical cottages) nestled in the woods. The mule track leads to the Rifugio Tita Barba (signpost) or, if you descend a little further to the right, directly to the Casera di Vedorcia (1,704 metres). Take the pleasant CAI 350 path to return to the valley. From the casera, it will lead you to the Casera Valle more quickly.

The Castello di Vedorcia and the Cime Cadin on the way up to Vedorcia

Casera Vedorcia and the Oltrepiave Dolomites

THE CASERA VALBINON REFUGE

An alpine refuge from another time set in the middle of the ancient mountain pastures of Forni di Sopra

Starting point: *From Cimolais, drive up the entire Val Cimoliana (13 km) until the parking of the Rifugio Pordenone in Pian Meluzzo (1,150 metres). There is normally a toll booth just after Cimolais to access the Friulian Dolomites Natural Park. It is best to ask at the refuge how practicable the road is, as it is subject to frequent landslides*
GPS: *46.378762 12.490584*
Time: *5.5 hours. Even if the hike is not particularly long, we recommend spending the night at the refuge, to appreciate its no-frills hospitality, similar to the very first refuges built in the Dolomites in the early 18th century*
Difficulty: *Easy, for all hikers*
Elevation gain: *650 metres*
Trail markers: *Good*
Cartography: *Tabacco 1:25.000, sheet 021*

The Casera Valbinon refuge is at an altitude of 1,778 metres, at the head of Val Cimoliana, between the Crodon di Brica ridge and the Cime Urtisiel, in the Pramaggiore group. Its views of the Monfalconi and Spalti di Toro peaks are splendid, as are the immense green forests at the bottom of the valley. The name Valbinon (from the word 'albeo', meaning clear, white) can be found in ancient documents dating to around 1575, when the inhabitants of Cimolais and Forni di Sopra were fighting over the area's large pastures. The latter finally used them until the Second World War. Abandoned and neglected since, the stables collapsed in the 1960s. Only the main casera continued to provide a spartan shelter for the very few hikers who ventured there.

It was only in 1997, thanks to the intervention of the Friulian Dolomites Natural Park, that the building was completely restored and converted into an alpine refuge, stripped back to the essentials, as it once was. The refuge is now run in the summer by young people from Forni di Sopra, whose simple and friendly welcome is very similar to that of the first Dolomite shelters built for mountaineers. The refuge is also an enlightening model of how to make the most of an ancient pastoral site without denaturing it, unlike the current trend toward mass tourism and hotels even in the high mountains. Keep in mind that there are no roads or cable cars for transporting food and equipment, so everything is brought in by helicopter on a few rare occasions during the high season.

From Pian Meluzzo, follow the signs into the Meluzzo valley on the small CAI 361 road that crosses the entire vast meadow on which the Casera Meluzzo is located. After the pasture, surrounded by high, rocky peaks, the path enters a flat area covered in gravel and overgrown with very large mugo pines, before it runs over torrents of scree. Once at the entrance to Val Postegae, ignore the crossroads for Forcella Pramaggiore and continue on a moderate slope over strips of detrital terrain next to the Rio Valbinon. Follow it for a while. When you reach the clearing that is home to the Cason dei Pecoli, leave the path leading directly to Val di Brica and the one for the Bivacco Marchi-Granzotto and enter the Valbinon. The track climbs for a long time through a sparse forest and suddenly leads to the fabulous alpine pasture where the refuge is located (just under 3 hours).

Camporosso

Camporosso is a large, flowery meadow whose relief has been smoothed out by water basins and peat bogs. It is located between beautiful, steep peaks and extends a little upstream from the refuge. On a hill covered by a blanket of greenery is the small Cason di Camporosso (1,945 metres), which used to be a spartan shepherds' shelter made of tree trunks.

It can be reached by hiking toward the Lavinal pass in less than an hour. It is also possible to reach the Forcella Val di Brica from the edge of the Camporosso, which houses a frail, twisted monolith called 'La Fantulina', meaning 'doll' in the local dialect due to its uncanny resemblance.

The Rifugio Casera Valbinon and the peaks of the Monfalconi

The meadows of the Casera Meluzzo on the way up to the refuge

CASERA BREGOLINA GRANDE

The legendary plateaus between Claut and Cimolais

Starting point: *From Cimolais, drive up the entire Val Cimoliana (13 km), until the parking of the Rifugio Pordenone in Pian Meluzzo (1,150 metres). There is normally a toll booth just after Cimolais to access the Friulian Dolomites Natural Park. It is best to ask at the refuge how practicable the road is, as it is subject to frequent landslides*
GPS: *46.378762 12.490584*
Time: *6 hours*
Difficulty: *Easy, for all hikers*
Elevation gain: *950 metres, with positive and negative elevation*
Trail markers: *Good*
Cartography: *Tabacco 1:25.000, sheet 021*

Offering a view of the solitary peaks of Monte Turlon, the Pale Candele and the imposing Cima dei Preti, Casera Bregolina Grande, or Casera de Cimolais, stands on an idyllic, panoramic meadow under Monte Ferrara, in the Pramaggiore group.

It is in one of the most isolated and wild areas of the Friulian Dolomites Natural Park. The only easy and safe routes are those that wind around the ancient casere, as the summits are difficult, if not impossible, to reach.

Thanks to the surrounding wilderness, the open spaces around the Casera Bregolina Grande are among the calmest and brightest in the area.

After enjoying a meal in the park, the casera is an excellent high mountain stopover, with a few beds, a stove and a small fireplace. It can be reached after a wonderful walk starting from the Cimoliana valley. Along the walk you will discover the impressive detrital valley of Ciol de Mont, the Casera Roncada and the magnificent high-altitude meadows near the Forcella Savalons, with their incomparable panoramic view of the entire ridge that runs from the Cima dei Preti to the Cridola.

It is impossible not to mention the Campanile di Val Montanaia, which stands isolated in the centre of the valley of the same name. It is a singular vision that justifies the excursion in itself.

From the car park, climb through a grove that quickly leads to the vast detrital plains of the Ciol de Mont, a canyon that is fairly wide and flat at the start. The CAI 370 trail leads up the valley until it reaches a torrent on the left side of the mountain. There, leave the bottom of the valley and turn right on a steep slope leading into the woods of Col Roncada. Near the Torri Postegae, climb to the first pastures of Roncada and pass by the Casera Roncada (1,781 metres) after a steep passage through the woods. From the small clearing with the wooden hut, enter the forest and continue for a long time, slightly uphill, until you reach a grassy area that offers a magnificent view. You'll have reached the wonderful upper Roncada plateau, characterised by its marshy pools. Cross this first plateau and climb to the Forcella della Lama. Cross the old Pian della Casera mountain pasture (of which no trace remains) and climb to Forcella Savalons (1,976 metres), which stands out because of its wooden cross in sandy, flat terrain. With the fork behind you, descend on the southern slopes of Monte Ferrara to reach the meadows, where you will find the Casera Bregolina Grande (1,858 metres, 3 hours).

◀ The Campanile di Montanaia rising above the woods near Forcella Savalons

CASERA DEL CAVALET

The legendary alpine pasture of the Dolomites

Starting point: From Domegge di Cadore, drive down to the lake at the heart of Cadore and cross it on the small bridge. From there, drive up Val Talagona along the steep and narrow asphalt road until the small parking in the little village of Antarigole (1,105 metres). In summer, it is only possible to go up in the morning and down in the afternoon
GPS: 46.422390 12.440713
Time: 8 hours
Difficulty: Long and strenuous hike that does not present any difficulty, except for a short, steep section just before the Forcella per Vedorcia
Elevation gain: 1,200 metres
Trail markers: Good
Cartography: Tabacco 1:25.000, sheet 023

The Cavalet is an extraordinary alpine basin and its age-old casera (mountain hut) still rests there, alone and well hidden, between the northern peaks of the Cima dei Preti. According to all those who love unusual and little-known places, Cavalet is one of the most beautiful places in the Dolomites.

The alpine pasture was abandoned decades ago, but the casera still manages to withstand the passing of time thanks to conservation carried out by the authorities of the Friulian Dolomites National Park. The main buildings are always locked, but it is possible to request the key from the municipality of Pieve di Cadore or from the local CAI office. As an emergency, however, one bare room always remains open.

The minimal accommodation and the long and difficult access to the pasture, combined with the soft beauty of the meadows, are what make this place feel exclusive, as if it were a testing summit intended to deter

groups of tourists who besiege the more fashionable places in summer. The setting for this long hike to the alpine pasture has remained exceptionally wild and offers total immersion in the surrounding nature.

From the signs at the car park, head to the CAI 350 trail and cross the Pra di Toro stream on a small wooden bridge. Go up through the forest, passing some beautiful waterfalls. Ignore the crossroads at the Rifugio Padova (next to splendid waterfalls) and go to Casera Valle (1,360 metres), which is in a small clearing with a beautiful view of the Cadin peaks. At the crossroads near the casera, follow the CAI 350 marker along a path that becomes steeper and steeper, until you reach the pastures of the Casera Vedorcia (1,704 metres). Continue toward the Rifugio Tita Barba, but just before reaching it, near the characteristic tabià (mountain chalets), turn left onto a small forest road that stretches almost flat toward the south and crosses

*clearings in the forest (this path is marked CAI 350 on the Tabacco map).
After crossing a stream bed and tackling a steep climb, take the road that
comes directly from the Rifugio Tita Barba and leads, a little further on,
to a crossroads with a sign near the Pian dei Lares (2,049 metres). Turn
right and climb with a final effort over rough and crumbly terrain to the
Forcella dei Lares, which overlooks the Val d'Anfela. Embark on a long
crossing almost to the head of the valley, roughly on the slopes of the Cima
Spe and the Cima dei Lares. Once you arrive at the end, enter a corridor
of crumbly terrain that gives access to a scree slope beyond which you will
reach the Forcella per Vedorcia (2,234 metres). The rocky landscape turns
into high mountain meadows and descends to the Cavalet basin. Make your
way to the casera (1,995 metres) at the bottom of the alpine pasture, being
careful to follow the path that tends to disappear in the grass (follow the
stakes, 4.5 hours from Antarigole).*

SASSO DI MEZZODÌ

One of the first alpine wilderness areas recognised at a European level

Starting point: *Macchietto di Cadore (532 metres)*
GPS: *46.368846 12.354349*
Time: *8.5 hours*
Difficulty: *This is a long and very strenuous hike on a steep path with a few delicate and exposed sections in the upper part. This hike is for experienced and trained hikers. Do not take the indistinct track beyond Casera dell'Alberghet. It is recommended to do this hike at the end of autumn in cold and dry weather*
Elevation gain: *1,550 metres*
Trail markers: *Minimal, with a few red markers and stone cairns after the casera*
Cartography: *Tabacco 1:25.000, sheet 021*

V al Montina is one of the first alpine wilderness areas of European importance. It has remained untouched by nature and is rich in biodiversity.

Although it borders the Statale d'Alemagna, a busy road at the foot of the colossal Duranno and Cima dei Preti mountains, it lies completely off the beaten track due to its difficult access and the fact it was completely abandoned by humankind at the end of the 17th century.

There are very few tracks that remain, and they correspond to the old trails left by hunters and shepherds. Today, these activities can only be found along the very long paths to the Bivacco Baroni and the Casera dell'Alberghet.

Only the Casera Val Montina, in a clearing in the middle of the woods at the bottom of the valley, offers a short and pleasant introductory

walk along thematic paths. Beyond these paths lies a terrestrial paradise which is home to many species of animal and which, thanks to the fact the Alpine microclimate has not been affected by pollution or human activities, is home to some exclusive endemic varieties, including certain plants normally found only in the Arctic.

The hike to the Sasso di Mezzodì, an imposing pillar whose walls fall steeply to the road, is one of the few that can be safely undertaken to a valley peak, although it requires effort and vigilance. This unique high point offers an exceptional and often overlooked panoramic view over the entire valley. The views of the gigantic walls of the Duranno and the Cima dei Preti, the two highest mountains in the Oltrepiave Dolomites, as well as the Bosconero, the Tofane, the Antelao and the Marmarole, right up to the borders of the Comelico, are no less breathtaking.

From the church of the Madonna della Salute in Macchietto, follow the signs for the Bivacco Baroni and the Casera Val Montina, then cross the Piave on a metal bridge. Beyond the bridge, follow the path to the Casera Val Montina for a short distance, soon turning right at the sign. Climb steeply up the wooded slope until you reach a crossroads. Leave the track that leads left to the Casera Val Montina and the path that goes straight on toward the Bivacco Baroni. Instead, turn right (be careful, there are no signs) and climb the wooded slope between the Piave valley and the Terzacroda valley. The path stretches for a long time in tiring twists and turns until it reaches the ruins of Casera Pra Federa, where the gradient becomes less steep and a long crossing on the slopes of Monte Val della Cima begins. A little further on, the path turns to the left for the Sasso di Mezzodì (signposted). If you wish to reach the Casera dell'Alberghet, continue on the signposted path for about ten minutes. From the signpost, go up through the woods on very steep slopes, where the track is often only faintly visible in the undergrowth. Continue for a little while and resume the climb up a steep hillside among mugo pines. The path passes by an almost vertical gravel corridor and near a large rock at the top of the slope, where a red arrow points to the right. Before following the signposted path that passes under the large rock, notice the faint track between the mugo pines which turns right (stone cairn). This track allows you to climb directly, but with a lot of effort, through the pines. You will then emerge above the rocky section, having avoided the difficulties (the alternative is to follow the red marks that lead past a very steep rocky slab and a 10-metre-long, exposed, grade I section). A little further on, you will finally reach the ridge, where you can see the summit and its large cross. Stay to the left, as the slopes offer moderate exposure due to the vegetation, and climb a hill through a scree corridor (this is a tricky passage). Beyond, you will reach a clearing among the mugo pines, where the track tends to get lost. Follow it carefully to reach the final ridge and the isolated summit with its cross (2,035 metres, 5 hours from Macchietto).

RIFUGIO CAVA DI MONTE BUSCADA

A playground of ammonites, knots and pulleys

Starting point: *From Erto, drive up along the Val Zemola road (signs for the refuges) and pass the Capitello di San Liberale. Park near the last bend to the right, at an altitude of about 1,000 metres, where there is room for a few cars*
GPS: *46.283329 12.367361*
Time: *4 hours*
Difficulty: *Easy hike*
Elevation gain: *750 metres*
Trail markers: *Sufficient*
Cartography: *Tabacco 1:25.000, sheet 021*

The Rifugio Cava di Monte Buscada ('Quarry of Monte Buscada') is at an altitude of 1,758 metres in Val Zemola, on meadows dominated by the Monte Buscada and the Palazza mountains. For decades, the building that now houses the refuge was used for the quarry where the precious marble of the Erto region was extracted: Ramello Ammonitico Rosso, named after its red colour and the traces of ammonite it contains. In the 1970s, the famous writer, mountaineer and sculptor Mauro Corona worked there as a simple stonemason, as did the current manager of the refuge. The latter recently restored the building, opened an open-air museum on industrial archaeology, and created a geo-palaeontological park nearby.

The refuge is located in one of the most picturesque and panoramic areas of Val Zemola, a jewel of the Friulian Dolomites Natural Park, which now has a vast network of paths linking the *casere* (typical old chalets), refuges and peaks. Direct access to the refuge from the Casera Mela car park is certainly quick and easy, but we suggest a comprehensive and more interesting hike, with better views, along an ancient path that begins a little above Erto and was once used by the quarrymen of the area.

From the car park near the bend in the road, continue along the asphalt road of the Zemola valley until you reach a small chapel on the edge of the precipice created by the Zemola stream, which rushes down with impressive strength. On the wooded hillside just above, there is a water source for the aqueduct and the start of two paths, including the one that leads directly to the Rifugio Cava Buscada (be aware that there is no sign). After climbing the concrete steps, the path splits. Go right and up the entire hillside that descends from the heights of Monte Borgà, following the red markers along this beautiful track. The track climbs and offers magnificent views of the Vajont valley and the Nudo pass, which emerges beyond the remains of the lake, before joining the CAI 381 trail from the centre of Erto. Follow it to the right for a long stretch over the alpine meadows of Monte Borgà. There, you can take a nice detour to the nearby Forcella Borgà. On the pass, admire the impressive stratifications of Monte Borgà and the vast panoramas that open up beyond the Piave valley. Once you reach the Rifugio Cava Buscada (2 hours), it is possible to visit the quarry along a dedicated route and continue along a forest road that goes slightly down the slopes of Monte Buscada. After passing a gallery dug into the back of the mountain, you will come to a crossroads for the Casera Bedin, where we recommend stopping to enjoy the superb view of Monte Duranno and the entire Val Zemola (20 minutes from the crossroads). From the crossroads, return to the bottom of the valley along the forest road that passes by Casera Mela, which has now been converted into an agritourism service, and descend again to return to Erto along a road also used by cars.

The Rifugio Cava di Monte Buscada

THE 'BOOKS' OF SAN DANIELE

The stone library of Monte Borgà

Starting point: From Erto, drive up the road of Val Zemola (signs for the refuges) and go beyond Capitello di San Liberale. Park near the last bend to the left, at an altitude of about 1,000 metres, where there is space for a few cars
GPS: 46.283329 12.367361
Time: 7 hours
Difficulty: This is an easy hike, but the terrain is particularly steep. It is recommended to have good footing and good training
Elevation gain: 1,250 metres
Trail markers: Good
Cartography: Tabacco 1:25.000, sheet 021

The Libri di San Daniele ('Books of Saint Daniel') are huge slabs of stratified rock, piled haphazardly on top of each other and forming book-like stone slabs. The name of the place refers to an ancient, popular legend according to which Saint Daniel, protector of travellers, transported an old library to a remote part of the mountain to save it from fires and the wickedness of men, preserving the knowledge and wisdom on massive slabs of stone. It is believed there was an earthquake that knocked over the rocks, and as a result, the slabs of stone look like books stacked loosely together. In addition to the splendid views of the site, the slabs are an interesting stop for those who climb from Erto in the Vajont valley to Monte Borgà through the meadows just below the

ridge between Monte Sterpezza and Monte Piave. Beyond the Vajont valley is the ghostly and tragic M-shaped scar on the side of Monte Toc, the result of the landslide on 9 October 1963 which caused the artificial lake to overflow, destroying Erto, Longarone and its hamlets.

From the small car park along the road, turn left onto the Troi dal Sciarbon ('Coal Trail'), which climbs through dense forests and heads south-west to join another track that leads directly to the last houses in Erto. Continue on a steep climb over fossil-bearing rocks to reach the meadows where the ruins of the Casera Tamer still stand. Continue north, still on steep slopes, between scree and mugo pine forests, in a valley flanked by two characteristic towers, to reach the ruins of Casera Borgà. There are splendid views toward the Nudo pass and Monte Toc. After another strenuous climb, you will reach a grassy area between Monte Sterpezza and Monte Borgà. Take the CAI 393 trail from Casso to the Libri di San Daniele and Monte Piave. Before going to the Libri, it is worth visiting Monte Borgà (2,228 metres), the most important peak in the area, which offers one of the clearest views in the Oltrepiave Dolomites. From the flat area, head east to reach this panoramic peak through the meadows (3.5 hours). Retrace your steps, following the beautiful path through the high mountain meadows, just below the ridge and overlooking impressive cracks toward the Piave valley below. The book-like slabs are in a basin next to one of these cracks in the rock (30 minutes from the flat area below Monte Borgà).

MONTE MESSER

Harsh terrain between the Adriatic Sea and the Dolomites

Starting point: *From Chies d'Alpago, drive until the Rifugio Alpago then up the slope on the left until Casera Pian Formosa (1,204 metres) along an asphalt road that can be steep and narrow in parts (sign). Located on a magnificent sloping ledge surrounded by forests, the casera is an excellent agritourism site*
GPS: *46.167149 12.434249*
Time: *5 hours*
Difficulty: *Easy hike until Forcella Antander, but good footing is required after*
Elevation gain: *1,050 metres*
Trail markers: *Good*
Cartography: *Tabacco 1:25.000, sheet 012*

Monte Messer is one of the main peaks of the ridge that runs from Col Nudo to Monte Cavallo. It is a limestone mountain chain stretching for over 14 km and dominating the villages of the Alpago and the lower slopes of Friuli. The endless views to the north of the full extent of the Dolomites and the Po plain stretching as far as the Adriatic Sea to the south are the special features of these mountains that are rugged near the ridges yet bucolic and densely forested.

The Messer stands tall in the middle of the mountain range, making it possible to appreciate the full extent and perfect harmony of the landscape, thanks to an infinite number of plains that fade into the distance. The Messer does not have the typical features that make the neighbouring Dolomites so characteristic, but it does nonetheless offer a precious, almost untouched landscape.

The villages scattered throughout the commune of Alpago also boast many traditions linked to the alpine pastures, and there are many typical chalets and agritourism farms where you can enjoy local delicacies.

From the Pian Formosa hill, follow the CAI 979 sign for the Bivacco Toffolon that will quickly take you to the moraine that gives access to the Antander valley. For a short stretch, ignore the signs indicating you should climb. Continue on the small, clearly visible road that rises less steeply and passes by a monumental beech tree near a casera in the middle of the meadows. After passing the beech tree, climb to a panoramic point from which you can see all the peaks of the Alpago and the Dolomites. Continue to join the CAI trail that you abandoned earlier. The slopes will start to become increasingly steep, and you will have to climb the moraine threshold that leads to the scree under Monte Messer, in an extremely picturesque environment. Climbing up the rocky debris, you will reach grassy areas that stretch to a hill where the valley splits in two. The signpost leads to the right, passing under the Noni del Messer and then near the limestone walls. After passing a last mound, you can reach the clearing of the Bivacco Toffolon (1,993 metres) and the nearby Forcella Antander (2,018 metres, 2 hours). This pass sits on the ridge on the border between the regions of Veneto and Friuli. It is also an exceptional viewpoint overlooking the Friulian Dolomites. You can clearly see the Campanile di Val Montanaia in the centre of the valley of the same name. From Forcella Antander, continue south-east along the ridge, following a narrow, signposted path that gradually climbs in a series of twists and turns until it reaches the rocky back of Monte Messer. The trail continues below the ridge on the side of the Antander valley and climbs through some slightly exposed areas. These passages are rather easy, but you have to be careful with the rocky jumps on the right. On an ever more scenic path at high altitude, climb to the summit ridge, from where you can reach the summit itself, at 2,230 metres (less than an hour from Bivacco Toffolon).

Arriving at the summit of the Messer, with the Dolomites in the background

VAL SALATIS

36

*A classic example of a glacial valley and an
exceptional viewpoint*

Starting point: *From Tambre d'Alpago, drive to Pianon and then Malga Cate
(1,054 metres)*
GPS: *46.160603 12.443053*
Time: *7 hours; we recommend doing the hike over two days, staying the night at
the Rifugio Semenza*
Difficulty: *Easy, for all hikers, but relatively long. The climb to the Cimon del
Cavallo is reserved for experienced hikers*
Elevation gain: *1,100 metres*
Trail markers: *Excellent*
Cartography: *Tabacco 1:25.000, sheet 012*

V al Salatis is a vast basin of glacial origin between the peaks of the Col Nudo group and Monte Cavallo. It marks a clear separation in the geological and morphological structure between the two peaks. Slabs of dolomitic rock culminate on the gigantic northern slopes of the Crep Nudo and Col Nudo on the north side of the valley, while the south is dominated by karstic domes covered with forests and alpine meadows that descend from the Cimon del Cavallo.

The very long valley begins with the peaceful villages of the Alpago and seems to be from an almost pre-Alpine area. Moulded in the shape of a horseshoe by the ancient glaciers, it opens out in a fan shape near the peaks and the Forcella Lastè. In this last section, it takes on the appropriate name of Val Sperlonga, in reference to its appearance resembling a long cave ('lunga spelonca' in Italian). At the head of the valley is the Semenza refuge, the only manned stopping point in this extensive mountain range.

Located halfway up the mountain, the refuge is an excellent base for an overnight stay in the mountains and for climbing the Cimon del Cavallo, which is the highest peak in the area. The summit is also an exceptional viewpoint, as it is the first alpine elevation overlooking the Po valley and the Adriatic Sea.

From the car park of the alpine pasture, follow the asphalt road and then the shortcuts marked with the CAI 924 marker to venture up the slopes of Monte Messer until the almost flat upper part of Val Salatis. After passing the Stalla Campitello, you will reach the tiny Casera Pian delle Stele (1,421 metres), where the road ends (1 hour). Continue on a path through a truly enchanting beech wood until you reach a signposted crossroads. Do not turn right toward the Rifugio Semenza (this is the way back), but instead go left to quickly reach the undulating terrain at the foot of the scree slopes of Monte Sestier. Gradually climb the spectacular Forcella Sestier in a magnificent setting. On the opposite slope, enjoy the view of the Carnic and Julian Alps and the Barcis lake. The path then joins the Alta Via no. 7, which runs along the entire ridge of the group and follows it over the panoramic ridge

In winter, on the ridge between Forcella Sestier and Forcella Caulana. In the background, the summit of Lastè

to the Forcella Caulana (1,960 metres). From this pass (1.5 hours from Casera Pian delle Stele) you can see the Po valley, the Adriatic Sea and, in good weather, the coast of Istria. Cross under the Cima di Valgrande, passing through the Forcella of the same name. Go around the entire head of Val Sperlonga, following the CAI 925 signs. The crossing ends at the red Bivacco Lastè, on the Forcella of the same name. Just after the pass, on the southern slope, is the Rifugio Semenza (2,020 metres, 1 hour from Forcella Caulana). After a break, return to the Forcella and descend, again on the CAI 924 trail, into the magical rocky and glacial scenery of the Sperlonga valley, where the snow lasts until early summer. Descend to the basin at the bottom of the valley and exit to the left along some counter-slopes to return to the Casera Pian delle Stele.

Cima Lastè (2,247 metres) and Cimon del Cavallo (2,251 metres): an exceptional panorama

Cima Lastè is at the top of a grassy ridge that can be easily climbed and runs east from Forcella Lastè. Next to it is Cimon del Cavallo but, as it is surrounded by rocks at the top, it can only be reached after a short climb with metal cables. If the first one is recommended for everyone (and already offers an exceptional view), the second one requires a bit of confidence on the exposed rock, even if there are no particular difficulties. Both can be achieved in a loop of about 1 hour, always following the Alta Via no 7.

Sunset in the Dolomites, near Forcella Lastè

ANDER DELLE MATE

37

The enigmatic karstic eye of the Cansiglio forest

Starting point: *Pian Canaie, accessible by car from Tambre d'Alpago passing through Sant'Anna e Vivaio*
GPS: *46.115201 12.434857*
Time: *5 hours*
Difficulty: *Easy, but a sense of direction is required in the woods (follow the signs carefully)*
Elevation gain: *300 metres*
Trail markers: *Good*
Cartography: *Tabacco 1:25.000, sheet 012*

Just below the popular Forcella Palantina, so well hidden that it is almost invisible, is a large cave with a rugged floor called Ander delle Mate. The origin of this name is rather vague, but it seems to refer to women (*mater* means 'mother' in Latin) or a place used by witches. It is one of the most mysterious places in the Cansiglio forest. Said to be charged with sacred energy, it was appreciated by the ancient inhabitants of the plains at the edge of the woods and on the bare grassy slopes as a place to perform magic rites. With its door open to the sky, like the eye of a giant, it is believed the karstic cave was formed after the limestone floor of the mountain collapsed. The entrance is hidden by the grass of the surrounding meadows, then the walls sink down, letting the light in from above. The water that filters through there reappears downstream in the Friulian plain, after a long journey deep in the heart of the karstic layers, which are still the object of speleological explorations. Reaching this lair on an autumn day, with clouds possibly gathering around the mountain peaks, is undoubtedly the best way to appreciate the scenery. This hike feels like a long walk in the heart of an enchanted forest, strewn with secluded, isolated navigation locks that breathe fresh air and where deer bellow at dusk.

From Pian Canaie, continue on the road to Campon until you see the forest path to the left and the CAI 983 markers. You'll arrive in one of the most precious and evocative areas of the Cansiglio, which alternates between flat surfaces and grandiose, dense forests. After a flat area with some clearings, the forest road becomes a path and begins to climb to another basin populated by fir trees, due to the particularly cold microclimate resulting from the effects of thermal inversion. Pass through a final gap that leads out of the vegetation. The trees give way to a tormented karstic landscape of meadows, sinkholes and wandering rocks. In the distance you'll notice the Dolomites stretching out, while to the south, the profile of the Adriatic coast and the bell towers of Venice are clearly visible. At a crossroads, leave the signs pointing to Piancavallo and the Rifugio Arneri and turn left toward the Forcella Palantina and the cave. Keep a close eye out for the entrance, which blends in with the landscape. The descent to the bottom of the cave must be made with care, especially if the rocks are wet.

◄ In the Ander delle Mate

Autumn in the Cansiglio forest

From the entrance of the cave in winter

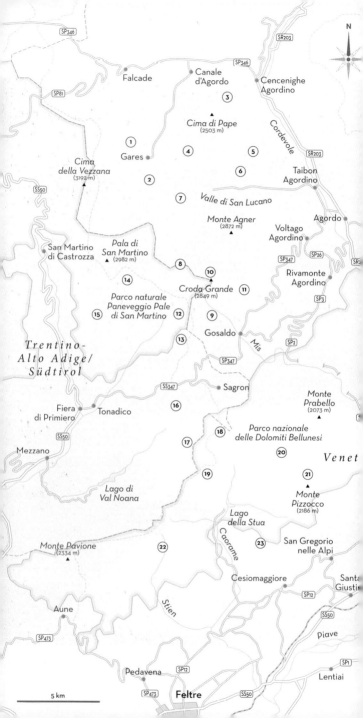

From Falcade to Feltre

MALGA STIA

An excursion on the alpine pastures of Gares

Starting point: *Gares (1,381 metres), accessible by car from Canale d'Agordo on the road between Cencenighe and Falcade*
GPS: *46.311362 11.882015*
Time: *3 hours*
Difficulty: *Easy, for all hikers*
Elevation gain: *400 metres*
Trail markers: *Excellent*
Cartography: *Tabacco 1:25.000, sheet 022*

A t an altitude of 1,785 metres, on the slopes of the Cimon della Stia, stands a volcanic outcrop covered with alpine meadows. On the long ridge that descends from the top of the Cima di Focobon to the Canale d'Agordo, the alpine pasture extends over a vast plain with a magnificent view of the Agner group, the Focobon group and, above the bubbling Comelle waterfall, the Pale di San Martino plateau.

As you climb toward the Forcella della Stia, the views become increasingly panoramic and extend across almost all the mountains of the Alto Agordino. The alpine hut has a large pasture with many animals and this excellent place for agritourism also sells local products. One of the stables has been converted into a small museum and a workshop for children. Recently, mountain bikers and, in winter, cross-country skiers and snowshoe enthusiasts, have also discovered this area.

From the car park at the Gares church, follow the forest road to the alpine hut on an obvious and somewhat monotonous path, at least as far as the meadows on the summits. An alternative is to follow the marked path, which is very steep but quicker and more direct and climbs from Val di Creta.

The superb view of Forcella della Stia

Forcella della Stia opens up between the Punta dei Mar and the Cimon della Stia mountains, linking Val Focobon to Val di Gares. The effort of climbing this very steep climb between the meadows and the slopes is worth your while and offers a superb view. Although it does not present any difficulty, the ascent can only be made on dry ground, as the path is quite uneven in its upper part.

From the alpine hut, head north-west through pastures, following the few markers among the huge rocks. Once you have climbed the whole Pian della Stia, enter a small, steep, grassy valley before reaching the fork (2,190 metres, 45 minutes from the alpine hut).

The village of Gares with the Malga Stia at the top

The Focobon mountain chain and the Mulaz, as seen from the Forcella della Stia

The Pale di San Lucano and the Agner, as seen from the Forcella della Stia

SASS NEGHER

The old mines of Gares

Starting point: Gares, accessible by car from Canale d'Agordo. Park near the Capanna Cima Comelle (1,333 metres)
GPS: 46.306196 11.882129
Time: 3 hours
Difficulty: Easy, for all hikers
Elevation gain: 450 metres
Trail markers: Excellent
Cartography: Tabacco 1:25.000, sheet 022

The mines of Gares were in operation from 1450 to 1748, during the time of the Republic of Venice. Copper, iron, lead and mercury ores were mainly extracted. The main galleries were built just below the Forcella Cesurette, on the slopes of the Sass Negher, a volcanic rock mass clearly visible from the village and near the Casera Valbona.

The entrances to the mines still exist, and there is still some old wooden scaffolding from the last mining period, but only experts can access them. The contrast between the dark rocks around the casera and the pale dolomite mountains that rise above the forests is beautiful.

From the car park, follow the signs and take the CAI 756 trail which quickly enters the woods and rises to a crossroads. Ignore the path to the left that heads toward Forcella Cesurette and turn right to continue up the slopes of Sass Negher, which rises on the right with its dark rocks. Cross the slopes of the mountain, where you can see the entrances to the mines at an altitude of around 1,880 metres. From there, you will be able to reach the beautiful Casera Valbona (1,783 metres, 1.5 hours).

Gares and its waterfall

The ancient village of Gares, at the top of the charming valley of the same name, owed its longest period of prosperity to its mining activity, which reached a peak in the 18th century under the Remondini family of Bassano. The family is credited with the construction of the village's church, which was dedicated to the Madonna della Neve in 1732 but was destroyed in 1944 with the rest of the village as reprisal by German soldiers.

We recommend climbing a little higher up to the powerful water jet of the Cascata delle Comelle, which collects the filtered waters of the Altipiano delle Pale plateau. It can be easily reached by following the paths for the Capanna Cima Comelle.

The Sass Negher from the meadows above the Casera Valbona

The Sass Negher and the Civetta from the meadows above the Casera Valbona

CAMPEDEL AND CAMPIGOL ON CIMA PAPE

Alpine pastures between volcanoes and dolomites

Starting point: *From Cencenighe Agordino, drive to the villages of Martin and then Bogo (1,194 metres), where you can park*
GPS: *46.345784 11.957160*
Time: *4 hours*
Difficulty: *Easy, for all hikers*
Elevation gain: *800 metres*
Trail markers: *Good*
Cartography: *Tabacco 1:25.000, sheet 022*

The names of these two ancient sites refer to the word 'campo' (meaning 'field' in Italian). The word refers to a small, grassy area in the middle of vast forests once used for haying or grazing. The sites are, in fact, the main alpine pastures of the hamlets above Cencenighe Agordino, clinging to the volcanic slopes of the Cima Pape. The Casera Campedel sits on the northern ridge of the Col del Boi and is ideally located to admire Monte Civetta. Also known as Malga del Vecio ('Vecio Alp'), it has not been climbed for decades, but still offers an emergency shelter for hikers. The Fienili Campigol ('Campigol Barns'), or La Busa, are a short distance away, on what is a beautiful, hanging meadow set in a bucolic basin. These splendid places, although easily accessible, are not usually targeted by mass tourism. They are therefore ideal for those seeking alternative walks, surrounded by silence and scenic settings yet to be discovered.

From the Bogo car park, follow the signs for the Cima Pape and climb steeply to the small village of Chioit, which is on a pass that extends over Val Cordevole. Once you have passed the few houses, continue through the woods to a crossroads with a sign. Leave the most direct path to the Cima Pape and turn right up the path in the forest that thins out as you climb. After a few clearings, you will come to the meadow where the Casera Campedel is located (1,818 metres, 1.5 hours). The surrounding area offers a magnificent view of the Cime d'Auta and the Marmolada to the north. From Campedel, go up through the clearing just above and continue the ascent toward the Cima Pape, bypassing the Col dei Boi to the south. A little further on, enter the Campigol basin (1,936 metres) with its ancient barns facing the imposing landscape of Monte Civetta and Val Cordevole (half an hour from Campedel). Those looking for more views can go over the meadows to the Col dei Boi (2,052 metres). With its summit split in two and free of vegetation, it offers even wider views.

The wide, panoramic view of Cima Pape

This is the highest peak of the great volcanic ridge of the same name, in the eastern part of the Pale di San Martino. The mountain stands out with its light-coloured dolomites surrounded by dark rocks and is famous for its grandiose panorama. On the summit is a large metal cross and a plaque commemorating Pope John Paul I, who was born Albino Luciani in Canale d'Agordo, just below the summit. Continuing beyond the Campigol, a rather strenuous path set mostly on very steep, grassy slopes will take you to the summit.

Mountain hut at Campigol, facing Val Cordevole and the Pale di San Lucano

CASERA AI DOFF

The spectacular alpine pasture of the San Lucano valley

Starting point: *Col di Prà (843 metres), in the San Lucano valley, accessible through Taibon Agordino on the asphalt road. Park near the last houses in the village*
GPS: *46.296679 11.926785*
Time: *6 hours. Because of how isolated and beautiful the alpine pasture is, we recommend spending the night at the casera, which is an excellent bivouac. Take a sleeping bag and food.*
Difficulty: *Easy, for all hikers*
Elevation gain: *1,000 metres*
Trail markers: *Excellent*
Cartography: *Tabacco 1:25.000, sheet 022*

The Casera ai Doff is on the meadows that form a ridge connecting the San Lucano valley to the Gares valley and dominated by the volcanic foothills of the Cima Pape. It is the most beautiful and largest alpine pasture in the enormous impluvium of the San Lucano valley, offering grandiose views of the rocky walls of the Agner, the peaks surrounding the Angheraz valley, and the Pale di San Lucano. This comfortable *casera* is the starting point for a beautiful hike from the Col de la Pra, passing by the Malgonera, another popular stopover at altitude. Historical records show that people have lived on the pastures since 1500 and they also documented the subsequent exploitation of the spruce forests for the production of coal once used for the smelting furnaces of Agordino. The area has recently been designated a 'site of Community importance' by the European Community and as a special protection area for the rare species of wildlife that thrive there.

From the car park, continue on the road that is closed to vehicles. Follow the signs and take the path that climbs through the woods, on the right side of the Bordina mountain stream. Higher up, take the picturesque forest road and enjoy the many waterfalls as it leads you to Pont (1,149 metres). Leave the road, cross a bridge and turn right onto the mule track CAI 764 for the Casera Malgonera. The first section is very steep on uneven ground and goes deeper into the forest. Continue until you reach the junction with the Gardes valley. Go straight through some clearings until you emerge from the vegetation at the edge of the very comfortable and well-equipped Casera Malgonera (2 hours). Leave the casera and walk up the steep meadows above. Head west along the CAI 762 trail that will take you around a few valleys and hills. The view of the northern slopes of the Agner and the Angheraz valley is fantastic. Shortly after, climb up to the old Doff pasture, and you will soon reach the alpine pasture (1,876 metres, 3 hours from the car park).

To Forcella Cesurette

It is possible to extend the excursion to the alpine pasture by continuing to Forcella Cesurette and Casera Campigat (1,801 metres). The hike is mainly along the green ridge that separates the San Lucano valley from the Gares valley, and it takes about 2 hours as you follow the CAI 762 signposts to the pass. From there, return to the Pra pass along the forestry–pastoral road that leads to the old Campigat alpine pasture and down into the valley via the Casera della Stua and the little village of Pont (another 2 hours).

The Agner, as seen from the Casera ai Doff

MONTE SAN LUCANO

A wild, vertical El Dorado in Italy's version of Yosemite valley

Starting point: *Pradimezzo (873 metres), a village of Cencenighe. Park a little before the last houses in the village*
GPS: *46.339168 11.969904*
Time: *8 hours. It is possible to do the hike over two days by spending the night at the Bivacco Bedin, near the Forcella della Besausega (see page 411)*
Difficulty: *This is a long and tiring hike, with signposts only up to the Forcella della Besausega. Beyond this point, the hike follows a faint track that requires good footing and excellent visibility. The technical difficulty is concentrated in a short, steep and exposed section on the rocks above the fork. Due to the particularities of the itinerary, we advise you to be accompanied by an alpine guide or an expert*
Elevation gain: *1,550 metres*
Trail markers: *Excellent until the fork, but totally absent after*
Cartography: *Tabacco 1:25.000, sheet 022*

Monte San Lucano is the highest peak of the Pale di San Lucano mountains and, together with the Agner, has made the San Lucano valley famous in the international alpine landscape as Italy's response to Yosemite valley.

In this environment of cyclopean walls and vertical abysses, Monte San Lucano is not only one of the few peaks reached simply by walking, but also the highest and most panoramic summit. None of the peaks of the Pale di San Lucano have been altered by paths, markers, signs or cables, making nature and adventure the main features of this hike.

On this mountain, you will feel like a pioneer as you discover surprising scenery, a mixture of high-altitude meadows, karstic glacial cirques, stretches of piled-up rocks and extraordinary views of peaks such as the colossal Agner, the highest wall in the Dolomites, the Terza Pala, the Torre and the Spiz di Lagunaz. All these mountains have their own mountaineering stories, which are now as legendary as the heroes who lived them.

From the car park, pass between the houses and turn right onto the steep CAI 764 trail, which climbs and crosses the landslide caused by the 1966 flood. Cross a steep gorge over a small bridge and advance into Val de Torcol through enchanting woods to reach the clearing where the abandoned casera of the same name is located. Cross the meadow and return to the woods on a less steep path, then continue in the area where there used to be pastures. After crossing two streams, you will come to the Casera d'Ambrusogn mountain pasture (1,700 metres) on the slopes of Monte San Lucano and the Cime d'Ambrusogn (2 hours). Go up through a sparse forest and rocky meadows on the slopes of the Cime d'Ambrusogn toward Bivacco Bedin, gaining altitude in an increasingly open and panoramic environment. When the path approaches the Forcella della Besausega (2,131 metres), leave the signposted path and take a grass track, which crosses to the right and leads to the pass. Notice how impressive the pass is if you lean over the opposite side (1 hour from the casera). 'Besausega' means 'witch' in the local dialect. The bewitching setting, especially if you dare to lean over the intimidating, and even frightening edge toward the south, explains the name well. From there, tackle the very steep, rocky strip that stretches above the meadows. Make sure to take advantage of the less exposed passages. There is a grade I section of about 30 metres, well equipped with flats that are nevertheless quite vertical. To pass this section, make sure to choose the most appropriate pathways and particularly those recommended by the old markers (there was once a marked path and a via ferrata crossing

◄ Agner and Pale di San Lucano, as seen from Monte San Lucano

the mountain, but they were dismantled in the 1990s). After this section, go up a meadow covered with scattered rocks on a slope that descends toward the fork. You'll be approaching the rocks of the Mul, the eastern sub-peak of San Lucano. Without climbing too high, at a cairn, take a grassy section that crosses roughly at altitude toward the south, in a clear and beautiful landscape. You will pass panoramic, flat terrain and come into view of the Campanile della Besausega and the summit plains of the Seconda Pala, from where the Agner is clearly visible. Continue along the fine, grassy ledge exposed over rocky jumps, until you reach the ridge that connects San Lucano to the Mul. There, in one of the most distinct yet hidden places in the Dolomites, you will have to start to tackle the back of the summit. Navigate between the rocks and turn right around the last rock of the sub-peak to emerge on the suspended terrace at the top of San Lucano (2,409 metres, 1.5 hours from the fork).

Bivacco Bedin: one of the most beautiful bivouacs in the Dolomites

Bivacco Bedin ('Bedin bivouac') stands at 2,210 metres above sea level on the flat, meadow-covered summit of the Prima Pala di San Lucano. It is justifiably considered one of the most beautiful bivouacs in the Dolomites. Its well-deserved fame is due to the exceptional environment around it and the structure of the building, which even has a comfortable veranda offering a breathtaking panorama. It can be reached in half an hour along a marked path after passing the Forcella della Besausega. The trail is safe, but slightly exposed over the chasms of the Boral de la Besausega. Taking advantage of a night at the bivouac means you can enjoy the early morning light as you make the ascent to San Lucano.

A few steps from the summit, toward the Civetta

CIMA DI VAN DEL PEZ

Following a chamois trail

Starting point: *Col di Prà (843 metres), in the San Lucano valley, accessible by car from Taibon Agordino along the asphalt road. Park near the last few houses in the village*
GPS: *46.296679 11.926785*
Time: *7.5 hours*
Difficulty: *This hike does not present any difficulties but is recommended for qualified and resistant hikers as it requires good orientation and excellent visibility. Good stability is essential on the very steep meadows*
Elevation gain: *1,400 metres*
Trail markers: *Sufficient until Forcella di Gardes (even if the high grass around the pass makes it hard to see the path), but then absent, except for a few stone cairns, until the summit*
Cartography: *Tabacco 1:25.000, sheet 022*

The summit of the Van del Pez, or Quarta Pala di San Lucano, dominates the San Lucano valley with its 1,400-metre-high rock face. Together with those of the Torre, the Spiz di Lagunaz and the Terza Pala di San Lucano, Van del Pez overlooks the Boral di Lagunaz. In the local dialect, 'boraz' refers to a narrow, steep and frightening place, which lends itself well to the environment here, where the classic, postcard-worthy scenery of the Dolomites is set aside to give way to much more powerful and impressive landscapes.

Just like on the western dihedral of the Spiz di Lagunaz or on the pillars of the Quarta Pala, difficult tracks which have since become legendary were carved in these walls, amid the complete and deliberately sought silence of the mountains. The ascent to the summit is possible thanks to a surprising line of meadows on the Van del Pez (a suspended basin marked by the surrounding walls and punctuated by red spruces, or 'pez' as they are called in Belluno), bordering the precipices of the Boral di Lagunaz.

This is a typical trail for chamois, which go there in number to graze, and so reveal the natural weaknesses of the mountain. The summit also offers an unparalleled view, in all its breadth and strength, of the northern front of the Agner. If you were to drop an object there, it would land directly in the woods at the bottom of the valley!

From the car park near the last houses of Col di Prà, follow the signposted path until Pont. The path is a shortcut to the much longer forest road to Gares. Turn right for Casera Malgonera up a steep dirt track through the woods. Leave the path when a sign points to the right for the Forcella di Gardes. Continue through a sloping forest, still on a clearly visible track, until you reach the meadows of the upper Gardes valley. After passing a spring, you will come to the

now abandoned Casera Gardes and then to the water intake of an aqueduct at 1,925 metres of altitude. Continue to follow the markers, which can be hidden in summer by the tall grass of the flowering meadows, and climb to the Forcella di Gardes (1,998 metres). From the pass, between the Pale di San Lucano and the Cima Pape, turn south. At the beginning, no paths or cairns are visible, as the abundant vegetation covers everything, but near the first rocky strips, a discreet track quickly leads to the only place where it is possible to climb the upper slopes of the mountain. After crossing a short, rocky step with the help of good support points, you will arrive at the slopes that descend from the top of the Cime del Van del Pez. Although not very visible, you can see a crossroads with a small stone cairn: on the right, you can reach the summit directly by following the cairns. It is better to continue toward Monte San Lucano, gradually ascending on a faint track until you reach a spectacular depression in the ridge where the Torre and the Spiz di Lagunaz appear. The Boral di Lagunaz can be seen right in front of you. Leave the track, which soon leads to the Arco del Bersanel, and climb freely up the grassy ridge on the right that overlooks the impressive Boral chasm and the Agner walls that rise up in front. Continue to the first rocks that make up the Cime del Van del Pez and follow them on the eastern side along an impressive semicircle, making the most of the faint chamois tracks. This section is a must; there is no other way than to cross the entire Van del Pez amphitheatre and then climb the only grassy slope that leads up. When you reach the mugo pines that cover the summit cap and look like a spot in the landscape, you will find a providential track that cuts through the branches and leads, without any possibility of error, to the triangulation station on the summit (2,266 metres, 4 hours from Col di Prà). It is also possible to push on to the very top of the ridge, above the houses of Col di Prà, paying careful attention to the precipice on the right.

The Miola via ferrata, an enigmatic ghost trail

Until the end of the 1980s, it was possible to cross from Forcella di Gardes to Forcella Besausega by means of a via ferrata that climbed the walls of Monte San Lucano from the Arco del Bersanel. The route was dedicated to the shepherd Gianni Miola, who tragically fell into the precipice near the Forcella di Gardes while trying to pick edelweiss. Unfortunately, the via ferrata denatured places that were wild, opening the way to tourism that featured artificial routes, including on the Pale di San Lucano. It is said that all the metal equipment disappeared overnight and that no one has come up with a new initiative since. It seems that, for once, and contrary to the trend of the time, the desire to preserve the legendary natural environment of this unique atoll-like platform prevailed.

THE SAN LUCANO CAVE

In the sacred and mysterious cave of Agordino

Starting point: *Col di Prà (843 metres), in the San Lucano valley, accessible from Taibon Agordino via the asphalt road. Park near the last houses in the village*
GPS: *46.296679 11.926785*
Time: *5 hours*
Difficulty: *This hike is for experts*
Elevation gain: *900 metres*
Trail markers: *Good until Casera della Stua, sporadic after, but the path to follow remains obvious*
Cartography: *Tabacco 1:25.000, sheet 022*

The cave of San Lucano opens onto a rock face of the Pale dei Balconi and dominates the entire San Lucano valley. This is the cave where Lucano, the bishop of Chiusa in Isarco, fled to after being exiled from the Adige valley. It is said he spent the last years of his life in solitary meditation, assisted by Vazza, a local woman who was later beatified.

The hike to this sacred and mysterious place is an excellent opportunity to reach a perfect viewpoint over the entire spectacular valley, which was shaped like a horseshoe by the ancient glaciers.

The calm and austere magic of the cave and its great natural beauty,

along with the strength of the north face of the Agner, will surely invite you to a meditative walk.

The route is not difficult, but requires a certain amount of motivation and commitment, like all pilgrimages.

From the last houses of Col di Prà, follow the path and then the forest road to Gares as indicated, until the picturesque village of Pont, with its many small waterfalls. Continue in the direction of Forcella Cesurette until you reach Pont della Pita, at a higher altitude. Shortly before reaching it, turn left onto a small road leading directly to the Casera della Stua. Follow this road for a few metres until you see a rock on the left which indicates the direction to the cave. Turn left and go up a small path that runs along the entire wooded ridge overlooking the Colle di San Lucano (1,744 metres). The flattened ground is home to a small clearing. A signpost invites you to continue to the left on the steep slope of the Cime dei Balconi, where you'll notice a small path cutting through the wooded hillside. After a few exposed stretches, emerge from the woods to a superb view of the Agner. The cave is a little further on (1,764 metres), with a final steep passage facilitated by a short metal cable (3.5 hours from Col di Prà).

The waterfall from hell

The impressive Cascata dell'Inferno waterfall is the largest waterfall fed by the enormous impluvium of the San Lucano valley. At 38 metres high and enclosed in a sort of rocky apse, it projects a powerful jet onto the stony bottom of the Bordina stream, which is particularly powerful in the thaw period.

The bottom of the valley, hidden by dense beech forests, collects the waters of the grandiose volcanic valleys of the Cima Pape and the north-eastern foothills of the Pale di San Martino high plateau, exposing a sandstone base characterised by thin, multicoloured layers. From the car park where the hike to the cave begins, continue on the direct road to Pont, but leave it at the first bend to the left. Near a rock you will see the signs for the waterfall, which indicate the right-hand side of the Bordina torrent. The walk to the waterfall is pleasant, although some sections can be difficult if the ground is wet. There is also a short, rocky staircase with a metal rope.

The Agner and the San Lucano valley, as seen from the cave

THE COLLE CANALI

An easily accessible and amazing viewpoint between the Pale di San Martino

Starting point: *From Fiera di Primiero, drive toward Passo Cereda. After the ruins of Castelpietra, turn left on the road to Val Canali, until the Cant del Gal hotel. Turn right and park on the car park near Malga Canali (1,300 metres)*
GPS: *46.223875 11.891000*
Time: *7 hours*
Difficulty: *This is an easy hike, but it is long, with significant elevation*
Elevation gain: *1,250 metres*
Trail markers: *Excellent until Passo Canali, but absent after*
Cartography: *Tabacco 1:25.000, sheet 022*

Although the Colle Canali are more discreet than the imposing proportions of the surrounding mountains, they are a dream location in the heart of the southern Pale di San Martino. You can admire some of the lesser-known areas of the vast plain, such as the Angheraz valley, the Cime del Marmor, the Croda Granda and the gigantic, but forgotten, satellite mountains of the Agner (the Lastei, the Sass delle Caure and delle Snare and the Cima della Beta).

To the south, Val Canali, surrounded by countless ridges, stands out,

with the Feltre Dolomites, the Sass d'Ortiga and the Cima dei Lastei in the background.

This is an authentic viewpoint, which many hikers on their way to Passo Canali tend to ignore, leaving it blessed with peace, silence and exquisite views of the Dolomites.

From the car park, follow the signs for Rifugio Trevise, which can be reached in an hour by following the wide and busy CAI 707 trail. Continue following the same signpost toward the Canali pass, which is clearly visible at the head of the grandiose depression, one of the most spectacular in the Pale di San Martino. The ascent to the pass, with its varied and sublime landscapes over imposing mountains, is long and requires good training. It is also quite busy, as it is part of the group crossing and Alta Via delle Dolomiti no 2. At the pass (2,469 metres, 2.5 hours from the refuge), ignore all the markers that converge on this point and enter the wild mountain: move freely east, climbing over some rocky outcrops in view of the slender, isolated dome of Colle Canali (2,522 metres). The large stone cairns will make it easier to find your way around the summit rocks and will invite you to take a few pleasant detours to discover the surprising panoramas and chasms that open up toward the Val d'Angheraz (30 minutes from the pass to the summit).

BIVACCO MENEGAZZI

On the most picturesque meadows of the Pale di San Martino

Starting point: *On the national road between Agordo and Passo Cereda, take the road in the village of Sarasin that leads to the Domadori car park (1,339 metres)*
GPS: *46.217711 11.929231*
Time: *3.5 hours*
Difficulty: *Easy, for all hikers*
Elevation gain: *400 metres*
Trail markers: *Good*
Cartography: *Tabacco 1:25.000, sheet 022*

The Menegazzi bivouac is at 1,737 metres in the Pianlonch. Otherwise punctuated by massive rocks and surrounded by the towers and rock faces of the Pala della Madonna, the Sass d'Ortiga and the Croda Granda, the green and flat Pianloch is considered the most picturesque meadow of the Pale di San Martino. The bivouac is a small building leaning against a gigantic, erratic rock dedicated to the military hero Giovanni Menegazzi, who died in Russia after the old Casera Pianlonch was restored by the Associazione Nazionale Alpini of Gosaldo in 1980. The bivouac is located not far from Casera Cavallera, which welcomes shepherds throughout the summer and has recently started offering an agritourism service.

The great beauty of the alpine pastures and mountains, the tranquillity – even in summer – and the easy access make this an ideal place for a walk everyone can enjoy, whatever the time of year, even in the snow!

From the beautiful hill covered with meadows, continue uphill on the pastoral road that leads to the Casera Cavallera. Once you reach a flat area, you can either continue along the longer but no less interesting road or follow the signs to the CAI 720 trail on the left, which is more direct and quicker. In this case, you will quickly gain altitude before emerging from the woods directly onto the vast pasture of Casera Cavallera. Immediately after the casera, start climbing again until you reach the Pianlonch, where you will see the Bivacco Menegazzi, which you will quickly reach. To make a loop and return along a different route, it is advisable to descend into the valley along the pastoral road.

The Bivacco Menegazzi on the Pianlonch ▶

The Bivacco Menegazzi on the Pianlonch

BIVACCO REALI

A red eagle's nest and a high plateau petrified between grandiose peaks

Starting point: *On the national road between Agordo and Passo Cereda, take the road in the village of Sarasin that leads to the Domadori car park (1,339 metres)*
GPS: *46.217711 11.929231*
Time: *8 hours. It is possible to spend the night in the bivouac*
Difficulty: *This hike is for experts; it is long and strenuous and includes a grade 1+ section*
Elevation gain: *1,300 metres*
Trail markers: *Good*
Cartography: *Tabacco 1:25.000, sheet 022*

The small Bivacco Reali is a high mountain shelter with a classic metal half-barrel structure that stands on the high plateau of the Foch della Croda Granda, which forms a roof over the slopes of the Croda Granda and the Cime del Marmor, in the southern sector of the Pale di San Martino.

The easiest and most convenient way to reach it is undoubtedly the old southern path leading to the Menegazzi bivouac through the legendary amphitheatres of the Vani Alti, once known only to chamois hunters.

These large, hanging valleys hidden among the mountain peaks are the prelude to a magical area of the Pale di San Martino: a petrified setting out of this world, isolated and far from the valley floor. The more adventurous hikers can spend a night in this excellent bivouac to witness a unique sunset and dawn at high altitude.

Just as on the hike to Bivacco Menegazzi, climb to the Pianlonch meadows and continue toward the Forcella delle Mughe and the Rifugio Treviso until you reach a large rock in the centre of the depression. Leave the direction of the refuge and continue up the valley between the Sass d'Ortiga and the Torre di Sant'Anna, heading in long diagonals toward the head of the impluvium. The path passes under the Forcella Sant'Anna and the Forcella Vani Alti and then passes a short, vertical rocky strip with some easy climbing sections. This historic passage, known as La Scaletta ('The Ladder'), is equipped with excellent holds and should therefore not be a source of concern, even on the descent. Beyond this rocky jump is the Vani Alti, which extends immediately after and must be tackled in its entirety through the rocky debris, using the various notches on the side if necessary. Once on the flat area between the Sass da Camp and the Cima dei Vani Alti, the track crosses the slopes of these mountains, facing the mighty mass of the Croda Granda, until it reaches the bivouac (2,595 metres, 4 hours from Domadori). To climb the Croda Granda (2,849 metres), descend the scree toward the lower Forcella Sprit, carefully following the cairns and faded markings. Before reaching it, climb up to the right along the obvious track in long diagonals over the scree until you reach the Forcella delle Miniere, between the Cima Nord and the Croda Granda. Climb immediately to the left, leaving the track that descends into the scree valley between the peaks, and climb the ridge along some easy grade I sections, up to the small Madonna on the summit (1 hour from the bivouac). The view is particularly beautiful and panoramic: it embraces all the Dolomites and extends as far as the shores of the Adriatic Sea.

The Bivacco Reali on the high plateau of the Foch della Croda Granda, with the Cime del Marmor. In the background, the Cimon della Pala and the Vezzana, the highest peak of the Pale di San Martino

SENTIERO DEGLI SPIRITI DELL'ARIA

Tibetan meditation in the Dolomites

Starting point: *Forcella Aurine (1,297 metres), between Frassenè Agordino and Gosaldo*
GPS: *46.236745 11.973857*
Time: *4.5 hours*
Difficulty: *This is an easy hike which only requires a bit of extra attention when the ridge starts to become steeper*
Elevation gain: *650 metres*
Trail markers: *Good*
Cartography: *Tabacco 1:25.000, sheet 022*

This hike is never mentioned on topographical maps, and it is absent from almost all guidebooks. The Sentiero degli Spiriti dell'Aria ('Path of the Spirits of the Air') runs along the grassy ridge of the Coston di Luna, on the slopes of the Croda Granda, one of the most important peaks in the southern area of the Pale di San Martino.

Ideally elevated, the Coston and its velvety alpine meadows are a perfect viewpoint to admire the Agordino mountains, the wild Monti del Sole and the Feltre Dolomites.

The path is well marked and passes two domes with a small altar, bells and Nepalese votive flags, where you can rest and meditate, generally in absolute solitude, in a grandiose landscape which exudes strength and beauty.

From Forcella Aurine, follow the path up through the dense forest, passing the Col Fres and opening up onto the meadows close to the summit of the Col di Luna. You will quickly reach the top of this hill, where there is a cemetery in memory of Cesare Battisti and a large metal cross. Notice the Croda Granda and the Agner in the background. From the top, you quickly lose altitude and reach the Passo del Col di Luna, where there are CAI signs and purple and yellow markers for the Sentiero degli Spiriti dell'Aria. Leave the path that connects the Rifugio Scarpa to the Casera de Camp and go straight to the Coston di Luna, between meadows and small rocks, where the clearly visible track winds along safely and peacefully. As you gain altitude, the views open up and you will reach the first rocky dome, perched on a tower and marked by coloured flags (2.5 hours). It is possible to continue up, climbing to just below the first rocky jumps of the Croda Granda. There, you'll find a small altar, also decorated with flags (3 hours from the start). This can be the final destination of the hike because, higher up, the Coston di Luna rises vertically and connects directly to the wall of the Croda Granda.

The Casera de Camp: a delightful walk

The Casera de Camp is at 1,750 metres, on a ridge of meadows dotted with rocks at the foot of the Coston di Luna and the Croda Granda. Shepherds still climb there during the summer season. It can be reached after a beautiful walk from the Passo del Col di Luna, crossing its slopes in about half an hour. From there, it is possible to return to Forcella Aurine along the forest road that leads to the Val dei Molini and then along part of the asphalt road that leads to Villa Sant'Andrea.

The dome with the Nepalese flags on the path

PALA D'OLTRO

An orientation test in the largely unknown parts of the Pale di San Martino

Starting point: *From Fiera di Primiero, drive to Passo Cereda. After the ruins of Castelpietra, turn left on the road to Val Canali and continue until the Cant del Gal hotel. Turn right and park on the car park near Malga Canali (1,300 metres)*
GPS: *46.223875 11.891000*
Time: *5.5 hours*
Difficulty: *This hike is for experts. The terrain is a steep slope with a few short grade I and II climbing sections*
Elevation gain: *1,000 metres*
Trail markers: *Minimal, with good visibility required because directions are not obvious*
Cartography: *Tabacco 1:25.000, sheet 022*

The Pala d'Oltro is the highest point of a small castle made of peaks and towers in an almost unknown corner of the Pale di San Martino, between the Pala della Madonna and the Cima d'Oltro. One of the characteristics of this area is the sheer number of strange pinnacles, and the most imposing peaks of the group, which include Sass Maor and Cima Canali, in the background.

To reach the short final climb, you'll need to take the trail that leads to the enchanting amphitheatre of Caldrolon, which is a magnificent, rocky beach between vertical walls, still unknown to most tourists and as unspoilt as when the first pioneers discovered it. In fact, it wasn't until 1900 that local guides Michele Bettega and Bortolo Zagonel made their first ascent of the Pelabut and discovered an easy trail with a rather adventurous finale punctuated by climbing sections requiring sure-footedness and no vertigo. Even just approaching the Forcella del Caldrolon, which is extraordinarily photogenic due to the imposing tower facing it, is a small

adventure. This route is definitely not suitable for everyone. Rather, it is reserved for those who want to experience the mountain in the old-fashioned way, untainted by signs, comfortable paths or frequent markers.

From the car park, continue for a few minutes on the road to the Rifugio Treviso before taking the dirt road to the right that descends rapidly toward the Canali torrent. Pass the riverbank and continue uphill on the left-hand side of the Canali valley until you reach a signposted crossroad. From there, turn right onto the Troi dei Todesch, following the excellent signs that lead up a winding climb to the top of the forest, below the Torre Dresda, and then to the Campigol d'Oltro clearing. Take the CAI 718 trail of the Alta Via no. 2 from the Rifugio Treviso and follow it toward the Forcella d'Oltro. Beyond Val Canali are the mighty Sass Maor and Cima Canali, which look like they are being set ablaze by the early-morning sun. Ignore the diversions for the Sentiero del Passo Regale to the right and continue to climb a little further toward the Forcella d'Oltro. There, you should pay close attention to the cairns and signs on the left that indicate the start of the faint track for the Forcella del Caldrolon. As you follow them, you will enter the woods, going up and across the western slopes of the Pala d'Oltro, and gain altitude on a track that is easily recognisable but poorly marked, as the faded red markers are far apart. As soon as the forest clears and the mugo pines start to dominate the landscape, you will come across a rock face that slopes to the right then climbs steeply up the grassy sill below the Caldrolon basin. Once you have passed this very steep section, you will find yourself on the rocky debris of a valley dominated by superb walls, in particular the very slender Torre Dresda. Head toward the Forcella del Caldrolon, which is clearly visible on the right (2.5 hours). The solitary pass, certainly one of the most intimate and scenic in the Pale, can be the final destination of this hike, but those who feel confident with the climb can continue to the summit. The ridge, with the twisted shapes of its split boulders, bends to the left and skirts a large tower on the right. Further on, climb a grade II- rocky notch (it can also be bypassed more easily from the right, but the passage is exposed) to reach a grassy slope. Climb the slope along a track to the left until you reach a flat area. After going around a few obstacles, descend over the rocks into a grassy basin filled with boulders, then take an exposed ledge below the walls which climbs up to a stone pulpit facing the Torre del Caldrolon. All that remains is to tackle the summit tower with about 10 metres of grade I+ climbing. At that stage, you'll finally see the well-deserved peak of the Pala d'Oltro (2,288 metres, about 1 hour from the fork).

Flowers on the Caldrolon, with the fork of the same name at the top right ▶

THE ROCCHETTE DI GOSALDO ⑬

Discover a fantastic world in the Pale di San Martino

Starting point: *Passo Cereda (1,361 metres), on the road to the pass between Agordo and Fiera di Primiero*
GPS: *46.193096 11.905485*
Time: *5.5 hours*
Difficulty: *This is an easy hike for everyone, but it is tiring*
Elevation gain: *900 metres*
Trail markers: *Excellent*
Cartography: *Tabacco 1:25.000, sheet 022*

The name 'Rocchette di Gosaldo' refers to the Cima d'Oltro's proliferation of pinnacles, bell towers and rocky forks in the southern part of the Pale di San Martino. As their name suggests, they surround the villages and hamlets around Gosaldo Agordino much like the battlements (called 'rocca' in Italian) of a medieval fortress.

While it is usually the powerful, compact walls of the Agner and the Croda Granda that attract attention in this area of the Pale, the Rocchette display a particular charm even from a distance, as soon as you enter the unique fairy-tale setting of this mountain.

As you walk along the path that crosses the Rochette, you'll have the impression of being in a fantastic world, similar to the Stallo dei Camosci in Latemar or the slopes of the Cimon di Cajada on the Schiara. You'll discover enchanting landscapes that nature created in the most secluded and quiet places, mostly hidden from view and from the classic hiking routes.

From Passo Cereda, follow the forest road CAI 718 of the Alta Via no. 2 and, just before the Maso Brunet (1,434 metres) turn left into the forest (sign). Go up a wooded hill on a winding path to reach the steep meadows of Regade, with its typical chalet overlooked by impressive rock towers. You'll notice the scenery changes completely: the trees gradually give way to the rocky pinnacles that populate the slopes of the Cima delle Regade and, as you pass between them, you'll discover a bewitching and amusing path (we won't say more, for fear of spoiling the surprise). After the long climb, you will reach a crossroads at 2,138 metres above sea level, a little below the Passo delle Regade (2,192 metres). There are two possibilities: the first is the path to the left. It is the fastest and most panoramic route. It leads to the Regade pass and the summit of the same name (2,245 metres), which is a magnificent viewpoint over the long chain from Sass Maor to Sass d'Ortiga, Val Canali, the Dolomites of Feltre and Monte del Sol. In this case, you can reach the summit and its cross in about 2.5 hours along an easy path that follows the short ridge of the pass. The other option is to turn right, toward the Forcella d'Oltro, which offers a spectacular crossing of positive and negative gradients under Monte Feltraio, the Rocchette and the Cima d'Oltro with its rocky foothills. You can end the hike at the crossroads for the Forcella d'Oltro, but you can also push on to the Forcella d'Oltro, if you have the time and energy (3.5 hours from the Regade pass). From there, the views on the opposite slope are spectacular, in particular the view of the Sass Maor, with its slender silhouette rising from the bottom of the Pradidali valley.

◀ Monoliths in the Rocchette

Among the Rocchette

CIMA DEL LAGO

*An unknown mountain with one of the most
beautiful panoramic views of the Sass Maor*

Starting point: *From Fiera di Primiero, drive toward Passo Cereda. After the
ruins of Castelpietra, turn left on the road to Val Canali and drive until you
reach the Cant del Gal hotel. Turn right and park on the car park near Malga
Canali (1,300 metres)*
GPS: *46.223875 11.891000*
Time: *8 hours; we recommend spending the night at the Bivacco Minazio*
Difficulty: *This is an easy hike for everyone, but it is very long and there is a
significant difference in altitude*
Elevation gain: *1,500 metres*
Trail markers: *Excellent until Passo delle Lede, but absent after*
Cartography: *Tabacco 1:25.000, sheet 022*

Surrounded by the most grandiose mountains of the Pale di San Martino, which inevitably attract the attention of hikers, the Cima del Lago summit tends to go completely unnoticed. Yet this high point, which is even overlooked on topographical maps, offers one of the most beautiful and original views, thanks to its excellent position facing the Fradusta, the Cima Canali, the Pala di San Martino, the Altipiano and, above all, the Sass Maor, which stands perfectly opposite it like a gigantic obelisk overlooking the Pradidali valley.

This mountain takes its name from Lake Pradidali (*lago* means 'lake' in Italian), which lies peacefully at its base and closes the splendid Lede valley on the eastern slope. It is a true natural monument of mountains, walls and towers. It is in this unspoilt environment that the comfortable and well-equipped Bivacco Minazio is located.

Unlike the classic half-barrel bivouacs, this is a small house with plenty of space for eating and a dormitory with 12 beds, perfect to spend the night in the midst of these magnificent surroundings or to rest on your long climb to the summit.

From the car park, go to Rifugio Treviso along a small road. At a signposted crossroads, turn left onto the CAI 711 trail for the Bivacco Minazio, which initially climbs up a fairly strenuous path through the woods and then among the mugo pines to the Lede valley. Higher up, the path leaves the vegetation and leads toward the Pala dei Colombi and the Cima dei Lasti, climbing steeply in a beautiful landscape. After passing through some particularly rugged sections on rocky bands, you will reach the vertical section of the Fradusta and the plateau where the bivouac is located (2,250 metres, 3 hours). From there, continue on rocky slabs under the southern wall of the Fradusta, climbing the petrified cirque formed by the Cima delle Lede, the Cima Canali and the Cima Wilma, which is one of the most beautiful rocky places in the Dolomites. After a final steeper section on a detritus corridor, you will reach the narrow Passo delle Lede (2,695 metres, sign). Ignore the sign for the Passo della Fradusta and head south toward the Cima del Lago, passing some easy rocky reliefs on the sloping reverse side of the mountain. As you walk along an incredible path that offers so many wonders to see, you'll eventually reach the summit at 2,770 metres, which will leave you in awe of the emptiness above the Pradidali valley and its magnificent, mountainous landscape (1.5 hours from the bivouac).

◄ The Bivacco Minazio with the Sass d'Ortiga in the background

The Sass Maor, as seen from the Cima del Lago

THE DINO BUZZATI EQUIPPED PATH

Amazing views of the Sass Maor

Starting point: From Fiera di Primiero, drive toward Passo Cereda. After the ruins of Castelpietra, turn left on the road to Val Canali. Turn left at the junction near the Pizmador bridge and drive up to Chalet Piereni and then Prati Fosne (1,326 metres), where you can park
GPS: 46.206917 11.854221
Time: 8 hours. We recommend spending the night at Rifugio del Velo, if only to enjoy the exceptional sunset on the Sass Maor and the Cima della Madonna mountains. This option also enables you to hike down to Malga Zivertaghe and return to the starting point stress-free
Difficulty: This is a long and tiring hike along a moderately difficult via ferrata which requires appropriate kit. Good weather is essential as you make your way along the long sections on rocky ridges
Elevation gain: 1,350 metres, with frequent positive and negative elevation
Trail markers: Excellent
Cartography: Tabacco 1:25.000, sheet 022

The Sentiero Attrezzato ('equipped path') in memory of Dino Buzzati, one of the great Italian writers of the 20th century, was created in 1977 in one of the most remote, solitary and spectacular corners of the Pale di San Martino.

Although it leads to some striking scenery, this is the least known and travelled via ferrata of the mountain range. The views of the monolith mountain of Sass Maor are almost surreal and very impressive. The views alone are worth the hike. Dino Buzzati, born in Belluno in 1906, at the foot of the Dolomites, always combined his artistic commitment with his unconditional love for these mountains, a love that led him to climb and examine them all his life.

Buzzati was a skilled climber, often accompanied by famous alpine guides, such as Gabriele Franceschini, the inventor of the equipped trail that bears his name. He had a special affection for the Schiara, his home mountain, the Croda da Lago and the Pale di San Martino, which he dreamed of often when in Milan for work. In his 1940 masterpiece, *The Tartar Steppe*, as well as in many other writings, he seems to have been inspired by the petrified and eternal landscape of the Pale, probably the most grandiose vertical rock mass of the Dolomites.

The Cima della Madonna, the Sass Maor and the Pradidali valley, as seen from the Cimerlo ▶

From the Prati Fosne, follow the signs for the Sentiero Buzzati and climb up next to a bucolic clearing before tackling a very steep slope that first passes through the woods and then between the mugo pines. The path zigzags toward the rock faces and enters a maze of pinnacles that lead to a narrow, gravelly fork, where the metal equipment that secures the route in the most difficult places begins. After putting on your via ferrata kit, start climbing on an exposed sloping wall using a rope and some metal handles to move forward. At the end of the first section, the most difficult one, you will reach a meadow where the track climbs to a panoramic point overlooking the opposite Cima Canali. We recommend reaching a small, rocky peak nearby with its plunging view of the abyss above the Pradidali valley, and directly opposite the Cima Canali and Sass Maor. Once you have climbed up the entire meadow, you will reach the Cimerlo, from where you can admire the Cima della Stanga, the Sass Maor and the Cima della Madonna. Descend into a deep cleft between the rocks, with the help of the excellent equipment available. As you descend, the Lagorai range, mostly made of porphyry rocks, will appear to the west and you

will reach the grassy ridge between the Cimerlo and the Cima della Stanga. Follow the ridge almost on the edge, ignoring the Sentiero del Cacciatore (very strenuous) which descends into Val Canali, and continue on to the steep, grassy slopes dotted with rock fragments until you reach the Cima della Stanga (2,550 metres), the highest and most spectacular part of the hike. From the summit, descend on the opposite side, which is full of rocks, to the already visible Rifugio Velo della Madonna (2,358 metres), one of the most important places in international mountaineering (4.5 hours). From the refuge, under the immense walls of the Cima della Madonna, descend into the valley along the CAI 713 trail, first on easy detritus terrain and then on a steep slab secured by metal ropes. Once you have reached the Cadin de Sora Ronz, you will find yourself on the forest road a little above the Malga Zivertaghe. Go south, following the CAI 731 trail which stretches for a long time through the woods, until you reach the Forcella Col dei Cistri and the Malga Rodena. From this bucolic spot at the base of the Cimerlo, descend the slope to the Prati Fosne (about 4 hours from the Rifugio Velo della Madonna).

The Rifugio del Velo facing the Lagorai chain

THE PALE ALTE DEL PALUGHET ⑯

A spectacular view of the Feltre Dolomites amid monumental larches

Starting point: *Passo Cereda (1,361 metres); you can drive up the long and very steep road to Malga Fossetta (1,556 metres)*
GPS: *46.193096 11.905485*
Time: *3 hours*
Difficulty: *Easy, for all hikers*
Elevation gain: *400 metres*
Trail markers: *Good*
Cartography: *Tabacco 1:25.000, sheet 023*

The Pale Alte del Palughet are the northernmost peaks of the Feltre Dolomites. They face the Malga Fossetta mountain pasture, the western walls of the Piz de Sagron and the Sass de Mura. Despite their modest altitude, they offer one of the most complete and fascinating panoramic views of these two marvellous mountains which, at sunset, light up with the colours of the alpenglow. Their gentle slopes conceal a short circular path which is surprisingly unknown and deserted despite being close to the busy Malga Fossetta. The ancient and gigantic twisted larches that stand on the ridge are of incomparable beauty and compete with the rocky battlements of the surrounding mountains. Their branches tell of the ravages left by the wind, snow and years, like silent witnesses of the passing seasons and symbols of a superb but delicate, fragile nature.

The signs for the Passo del Palughet are visible just before descending to the meadows of the Malga Fossetta. Turn left and follow the path that enters the forest and stretches for a long time on the eastern slopes of the Pale Alte. The path goes up slightly until a corridor of large rocks that continues uphill for a short distance. Shortly after, follow the markers on the left to leave the corridor. You will arrive again on meadows with sparse trees between the Pale del Garofolo and the Pale del Palughet. Once you reach a clearing where the water tends to stagnate (hence the name Palughet, or 'palude', meaning 'swamp' in Italian), a sign indicates the crossing under the Pale Alte ridge to the west. The path, which is very well marked, winds between meadows and tightly packed mugo pines, with clear views of the walls of the Piz di Sagron and the Sass de Mura. Admire the large, monumental larches all around you. As you reach the crossroads, ignore the track that descends to the left toward the Giasinozza valley and, a little further on, follow a sign for the Malga Fossetta to the right. Cross the ridge and descend steeply through the woods toward the large meadow, where you'll notice the Malga in the distance.

Sunset on the Piz di Sagron and on the Sass de Mura from the Pale Alte

THE SOUTH-WEST SIDE OF SASS DE MURA ⑰

On the iconic ledge that surrounds the dolomite castle of Sass de Mura

Starting point: *Rifugio Fonteghi in Val Noana, accessible along the asphalt road from Imer, a little bit south of Fiera di Primiero. Continue by car until the car park of El Belo (1,157 metres)*
GPS: *46.078103 11.894089*
Time: *8 hours*
Difficulty: *This hike for experts is long and strenuous. A short grade II climbing section may require the use of a 30-metre rope*
Elevation gain: *1,250 metres*
Trail markers: *Good until Pass de Mura. Beyond that, the trail markers are sparse, and you will only find stone cairns*
Cartography: *Tabacco 1:25.000, sheet 023*

The Sass de Mura is the highest peak of the Feltre Dolomites and the second highest in the Belluno Dolomites National Park. This gigantic tower is made up of imposing rock walls on each side. Located a few kilometres from the town of Feltre, its dome can even be seen from the Adriatic coast and the Venetian plain.

It is one of the few mountains in the Dolomites that has a circular corniche around its summit, which marks a break halfway up in the regularity of its walls. The entire route of the banca ('corniche' in the local dialect) is very difficult, long, exposed, and neither marked nor equipped. It is therefore only suitable for the most expert hikers. The highest point of the corniche, commonly called Spalla Sud-Ovest, is easier to reach and a very satisfying destination for its wild, grandiose setting.

The landscape to the south is unrestricted: if visibility is good, the views are endless and include the profiles of the Vette Feltrine and the Prealps blending into the blue reflections of the Adriatic Sea.

From the car park, follow the signs for the Rifugio Boz, which lead to the left side of the valley dug by the Rio Neva (do not take the forest road on the right bank, which is longer and less scenic). The initial path will later merge with a forest road. As the forest road comes to an end, continue along a new path in an increasingly open and interesting setting, dominated by the imposing mass of the Sass de Mura. After reaching the upper part of the valley, continue alongside the stream, passing through the Due Nevette mountain pasture and reaching the meadows of the former Malga Neva, above which the refuge stands. Climb through the meadows following the CAI 801 signpost of the Alta Via no. 2 to the Pass de Mura where, on the opposite slope, the wild peaks of the Pizzocco group and the vast, majestic southern wall of the Sass de Mura can be seen. Higher up, you can clearly see the Finestra, a hole framed by a rock portal on the southern ridge, and the Birillo, a monolith standing on this portal. Leave the Alta Via no. 2 but remain on the slope of Val di Neva and continue on the CAI 748

trail, which crosses under the threshold of Cadin di Neva, until you reach a crossroads without signs. If you pay attention, you will see a path that stretches across the meadows toward the Cadin and leads (without signs but still clearly visible) to the Forcella Neva. The ascent to the pass is steep but very pleasant because of the rare beauty of its setting, which makes it one of the most interesting places in the Feltre Dolomites. The Forcella Neva is a pass that cannot be climbed on its northern side. Continue beyond it, on the ridge toward the walls of the Sass de Mura, until you reach a break in the large, rocky bumps on which the trail runs. Descend a rocky jump of about 10 metres, if necessary using a rope on a rock (leave it there for the ascent on the way back). This rocky jump leads to a narrow fork that follows the ascent of a fairly steep staircase on the opposite slope, and leads directly to the Banca Ovest, under the protruding walls. The corniche runs uphill on loose, wide, easy ground. At its highest point, you will reach the Spalla (2,403 metres, 4 hours).

THE CIMONEGA

In the stone heart of the Feltre Dolomites

Starting point: From Feltre, drive toward Cesiomaggiore, passing by Soranzen, where you should join the road from Val Canzoi. After crossing the valley, park near the Albergo Alpino Boz hotel (660 metres), a little before the dam on Lago della Stua
GPS: 46.128420 11.944647
Time: 8 hours
Difficulty: This long hike with a steep incline is for trained hikers
Elevation gain: 1,300 metres
Trail markers: Excellent
Cartography: Tabacco 1:25.000, sheet 023
Accommodation: Bivacco Feltre

You'll encounter the eastern wall of the mighty Sass de Mura, adorned with the Finestra, a rock portal, and the small monolith called the Birillo, which sits above it.

The site's charm is all the more unique because of how secluded it is. Its distance from the valley floor is such that you'll find the two stopping points particularly useful. They are: the ancient Casera Cimonega on the meadows below the Parete Piatta of the Sass de Mura and the Bivacco Feltre on the Pian della Regina, 300 metres higher. The access path to the ancient pastures, and the wild, unaltered setting during the ascent and the contrasting natural scenery from the starting point at an almost pre-Alpine altitude, make reaching the stopping points particularly satisfying.

At the instigation of the best climbers in the Feltre area, the casera was built as the first stopping point for the great mountaineering companies of the mid-20th century. It is in good condition and offers a rather spartan shelter with four beds on boards.

The Bivacco Feltre, on the other hand, is an excellent shelter, consisting of two sheet metal buildings. The large one is equipped with a living room and small, comfortable rooms. It is a welcome stopover along the demanding stretch of the Alta Via 2 between Passo Cereda and Feltre.

From the Albergo Alpino Boz hotel, climb to the dam and follow a small road on the right bank until the end of the artificial reservoir. Cross the small bridge over the Caorame mountain stream and follow the forest road, ignoring the road to the Pian Eterni a little further on. Cross the stream again and continue along the CAI 806 trail, which climbs for a long time on the wooded slopes. This will take you up the whole Val Caorame, with

its small waterfalls and ravines, until the Alpe Pendane clearing dominated by rocky walls. Turn left and cross the whole sloping meadow until you reach the bottom of an impressive fissure carved by the waters of the stream. After this amazing spot, climb again, over an area exposed to rock falls from the Col dei Bechi (some sections of the path have been damaged and are exposed) to reach a pleasant passage above the Caorame stream. Climb again, on an excellent path with a clear view of the surrounding peaks, before crossing in the direction of Casera Cimonega, which you can already

see at this stage (1,637 metres). Leave the track that climbs directly up to the Piani Eterni and descend again to the bottom of the valley, reaching this characteristic little shelter in the middle of the meadows (3 hours). Now cross the whole beautiful pasture until you reach the rock face that seems to block the road. The trail winds safely through a wonderful landscape of emerald pools and waterfalls. After passing a final notch in the rock and an easy ledge (equipped with a safety wire rope), you will reach the dome and the Bivacco Feltre's two shelters (1,930 metres, 1 hour from the casera).

MALGA ALVIS

The sun is back but time is forever fleeting!

Starting point: From Feltre, drive toward Cesiomaggiore, passing by Soranzen, where you should join the road from Val Canzoi. After crossing the valley, park near the Albergo Alpino Boz hotel (660 metres), a little before the dam on Lago della Stua
GPS: 46.128420 11.944647
Time: 5 hours
Difficulty: Easy, for all hikers
Elevation gain: 900 metres
Trail markers: Good
Cartography: Tabacco 1:25.000, sheet 023

Malga Alvis is at the foot of Col del Demonio and Monte Colsent, on one of the oldest pastures in Val Canzoi, the main valley of the Feltre Dolomites. The historic buildings of the alpine pasture have recently been restored by the Belluno Dolomites National Park. On the main building hangs a magnificent sundial reminding us of the relentless passing of time: 'El sol magna le ore' ('The sun swallows the hours') is the warning inscribed between the numbered notches. While the shadow inexorably moves around the sundial, the southern wall of the Sass de Mura looks on, motionless, a symbol of the greatness of nature in contrast with the brevity of human life. It is precisely the Sass de Mura with its ledges, the Finestra and the Birillo, clearly visible from the Malga, that

give the impression of a typically dolomitic landscape, despite being so close to the town of Feltre. Beyond the Val Canzoi, the enigmatic profiles of the Pizzocco del Tre Pietre stand out. These least-known dolomitic groups are still the exclusive kingdom of chamois and silence.

The alpine pasture is easily accessible from Lago della Stua in Val Canzoi via a pleasant hike, which gradually reveals beautiful, unusual features and many signs of the age-old presence of humankind. It is also possible to extend the walk to the Alvis pass and the Boz refuge on the Trentino side, in what was once an important high mountain pasture.

From the Albergo Alpino Boz hotel, go up to the Lago della Stua dam, where the CAI 811 forest road immediately turns left and leads to the alpine pasture. After the Casera il Pra di Faibon, continue to the left on a mule track that climbs the hillside along a rockfall. After the many steep hairpin bends and their charming views of the surrounding mountains and lake, the mule track continues to the right and crosses a small bridge over a rocky gorge, to the mountain pasture (1,573 metres, 2.5 hours). To climb to the Alvis pass, continue on the well-trodden mule track on the slopes of Monte Alvis and Monte Colsent. Cross the clear terrain with views overlooking the Piani Eterni, and the Pizzocco in particular, to reach the Passo Alvis (1,880 metres), just opposite the Sass de Mura. In addition to the pass, it is also possible to make a detour to the Rifugio Boz, visible in the distance (1,718 metres, 1 hour from the mountain pasture).

The Demonio pass: an old military mule track that is still clearly visible

The Demonio pass (1,722 metres) is a rocky outcrop covered with mugo pines and sparse forest that overlooks Val Canzoi and the Malga Alvis as far as the Valbelluna. This is why a military mule track was laid out there and a strategic artillery point was installed before the First World War.

In front of the alpine pasture is a track that leads south. Using red markings, it starts off flat then climbs on a moderate slope up the entire northern side of the pass. This old military mule track is still clearly visible but is only rarely used. After passing a cave carved into the rock, you will quickly reach the vast summit (30 minutes from the mountain pasture).

THE PIANI ETERNI

Karst labyrinths, meadows and underground chasms in the Belluno Dolomites National Park

Starting point: *From Feltre, drive toward Cesiomaggiore, passing Soranzen, where you should join the road from Val Canzoi. After crossing the valley, park near the Albergo Alpino Boz hotel (660 metres), a little before the dam on Lago della Stua*
GPS: *46.128420 11.944647*
Time: *6 hours*
Difficulty: *Long hike without difficulties*
Elevation gain: *1,100 metres*
Trail markers: *Excellent*
Cartography: *Tabacco 1:25.000, sheet 023*

The Piani Eterni plateau stands out in the multifaceted natural scenery of the Belluno Dolomites National Park because of the extraordinary originality of its landscape. In fact, it has two obvious features: the alpine meadows of Erera, Brandol, Campotorondo and Agnelezze, and the Piani Eterni themselves, a vast karst with crevasses, sinkholes and furrows on which a dense and intertwined vegetation made up of mugo pines, rhododendrons and larches grows.

Outside the few marked paths, it is almost impossible to find your way and advance safely. There are two sides to the Piani Eterni: beyond the visible side is a mysterious, worrying underground world full of cavities, caves and tunnels that stretch for kilometres and reach depths of more than 1,000 metres. The water that flows there feeds the numerous karstic springs of Val Canzoi and Val del Mis.

Set at the base of Monte Brandol, the ancient alpine pastures of the Piani Eterni were a major source of income for the local population, as evidenced by the harmonious buildings that blend into the landscape, such as the Pendana di Brendol, an imposing stone structure with 25 semicircular arches used to shelter livestock. Thanks to the park's restoration and improvement work, the *casere* of Brendol, Erera and Campotorondo are now very welcoming and can easily be used as emergency bivouacs. Erera even offers an agritourism service during the summer season. To fully appreciate the area, we recommend two hikes: one to the alpine pastures and the second to the Passo di Cimia pass, described on the next page.

From the Albergo Alpino Boz hotel, go up to the lake and follow a small road on the left bank to the end of the dam. Cross the Caorame stream and, shortly after, take the forest road CAI 802 on the right, with signs for the Erera and Brendol malghe. The climb will take you through a wonderful forest, on a wide military road (there are some rather steep shortcuts). At an altitude of about 1,400 metres, leave the road and enter a small valley

◄ Malga Erera and Malga Brendol from the Passo Cimia

among fir trees, which are present in this area due to the thermal inversion that keeps temperatures low, then climb up to the Sella del Porzil. The Piani Eterni appear with the two refuges (Erera and Brendol, at 1,700 metres) on the vast meadow at the foot of Monte Brandol and Monte Mondo. Descend toward this plain, pass the Malga Brendol to reach the Malga Erera (2.5 hours). Continue along the wide mule track that rises gradually and crosses the arid scree of the southern Pale Rosse and Monte Mondo mountains, where the chamois come to lick the salt contained in the rocks. At the large Forcella Pelse (1,847 metres), where you can admire the Pale di San Martino, you can descend without difficulty to the Busa del Toro and the Casera di Campotorondo (1,763 metres, 1 hour from Erera). Back at Malga Erera, we recommend descending into the valley on the forest service road of the refuges, which makes a wide loop along the Piani Eterni then joins the ascent route at 1,400 metres.

The Brandol lakes

The Brandol lakes are on a grassy saddle between Monte Brandol and the Demonio pass. From the time of the spring thaw until mid-summer, this is where a pool of water and a surrounding peat bog form. Many herds of chamois and mouflons graze and drink there, while the surrounding area offers vast panoramic views: to the south, the Piani Eterni and the Pizzocco, to the west, the peaks of the Cimonega and, to the north, the Dolomites. It is easy to reach, in about 45 minutes, along the CAI 851 trail which starts at the Malga Erera and leads to the Forcella dell'Omo and the Casera Cimonega. More adventurous hikers can push on to the summit of Monte Brandol (2,160 metres), the highest peak of the Piani Eterni.

GUSELA DELLA VAL DEL BURT

Gothic lines and dolomite cathedrals

Starting point: *From Feltre, drive toward Cesiomaggiore, passing Soranzen, where you should join the road from Val Canzoi. After crossing the valley, park near the Albergo Alpino Boz hotel (660 metres), a little before the dam on Lago della Stua*
GPS: *46.128420 11.944647*
Time: *8 hours*
Difficulty: *This is a long and strenuous hike, but it does not present any difficulties. Excellent visibility is essential as the Gusela can only be admired from afar*
Elevation gain: *1,450 metres*
Trail markers: *Good*
Cartography: *Tabacco 1:25.000, sheet 023*

The Gusela della Val del Burt (*gusela* means 'needle' in the local dialect) is a magnificent obelisk rising among the Cime di Picola, a minor, wild and little-known relief of the Feltre Dolomites, which extends toward Lago del Mis. Standing at an altitude of around 1,700 metres, the Gusela is 40 metres tall and was first climbed in 1954 by two young men from Feltre. They left a small bell on its summit, after dedicating it to Alberto Marini, a friend who died on the mountain. Although the valley where it is located has rather negative connotations (Val de Burt comes from *brutto*, meaning 'ugly' and 'bad' in Italian) for its rugged, harsh and hard-to-reach landscape, the writer and mountaineer Severino Casara described it as 'a stalagmite chiselled into the vault of heaven' because of the singular beauty of its forms.

The surrounding areas are only accessible to those who are used to them, and there are no marked trails leading to the base of the Gusela. It is precisely because it is inaccessible, not to mention the many hours of walking needed to admire it from a distance, that the Gusela has become a mythical point in the landscape.

In addition to there being only a few privileged viewpoints that reveal its slender silhouette, the clouds that tend to surround these medium-altitude mountains, including the peaks near Passo di Cimia on the Piani Eterni, often hide the enigmatic Gusela.

To get there, cross the summits from one side to the other along a journey that will allow you to appreciate their intertwining and wild character. Just a few kilometres from the town of Feltre, and overlooking the Dolomites and the mighty eastern wall of the Pizzocco nearby, is a pass that offers an unexpected panoramic point. At 800 metres high, like the Marmolada, the eastern wall of the Pizzocco has been the scene of legendary mountaineering exploits rarely repeated due to the difficulty and isolation of the place.

As in the previous hike, climb to the Malga Erera (2.5 hours). Head south along the CAI 851 trail for the Passo Forca, which leads to the magical and intricate Piani Eterni amid larches, mugo pines, sinkholes and karstic chasms, on a moderate climb. At the slopes of Monte Colsent – the only rise in relief amid the uniform expanse – leave the path that leads to the Passo Forca, which will now be visible in the distance. You'll notice a shortcut to the left, still on the slopes of the Colsent, that rises between alpine meadows and limestone plateaus until it joins the CAI 851 trail, again a little below the Passo di Cimia (2,080 metres). After a few bends, it climbs to the pass and then to the summit that borders it to the north until the end of the climb. You can admire the distant Gusela della Val del Burt (which you have to look for among the wooded peaks above the Piani di Cimia), the Lago del Mis and the grandiose Pizzocco (1.5 hours from the Malghe Erera and Brendol).

Grotta Isabella, the deepest abyss in the Dolomites

The karst phenomena of the Piani Eterni also occur at great depth, with a network of caves, galleries, and underground rivers. More than 400 caves and chasms have been explored and documented in the area. The main abyss is the Piani Eterni-Grotta Isabella complex, which is currently the deepest and most extensive abyss discovered in the Veneto Dolomites.

In January 2014, a record depth of 1,052 metres was reached, along a development of over 35 km. The entrance to the cave is approximately on the walls below the Gusela della Val del Burt at 1,640 metres, but the difficulties encountered in reaching it make it almost inaccessible to regular hikers. It was discovered in the 1970s during a hunting expedition and is named after the mother of the lucky man who found the entrance by chance, hidden in a fold in the mountain.

◄ The Gusela della Val del Burt, as seen from the Cimia Pass

The Pizzocco, Lake Mis and the lights of Valbelluna, as seen from the Cimia Pass

BUSA DI PIETENA

22

Among the most interesting places in the Feltre Dolomites, steeped in mystery and history

Starting point: *From Feltre, drive to Vignui then up Val di San Martino on a dirt track until you reach a small car park with signs*
GPS: *46.078103 11.894089*
Time: *8 hours*
Difficulty: *This is a long and strenuous hike along a very steep slope, but it does not present any difficulties*
Elevation gain: *1,550 metres*
Trail markers: *Excellent*
Cartography: *Tabacco 1:25.000, sheet 023*

Steeped in mystery and historical events, Busa di Pietena is one of the most interesting places in the Feltre Dolomites. It is also one of the first integral nature reserves (Reserve Integrali) of the Dolomites. It is located on the slopes of the Cima del Diavolo and the Pietena, an enormous basin lined with walls and shaped by glaciers that once stood there.

On each slope, steep rock faces run down to the valley below, guaranteeing the place is completely isolated and the continuity of a particularly rare endemic flora. On the endless meadows, you can still make out unique geological forms, mainly of stratified and jagged blocks, which have always inspired legends and popular beliefs.

As you admire its peculiar landscape, you will understand the power that the Busa exudes and why it was once said to be the meeting place of goblins, gnomes and witches and, as suggested by the name given to the chaotic expanse of scattered rocks known as Piazza del Diavolo ('Devil's Square'), the home of the devil. An enormous cross was even erected to protect the souls of the inhabitants in the valley. It was these same inhabitants who, after the armistice of 1943, became resistance fighters and organised their forces against the German invasion by exploiting the inaccessibility of the Pietena to escape the enemy. The Brigata Partigiana Gramsci ('Gramsci's Partisan Brigade') consisted of about 600 men supported by a handful of Englishmen under the leadership of Major Bill Tilman, a famous explorer, climber and writer, who set up camp at the Malghe Pietena and Pietenetta. These resistance fighters created serious problems for Hitler's troops, who were unable to move quickly over such difficult terrain. Tilman's account (in his book *When Men & Mountains Meet*) provides a vivid account of those days on the peaks that were tragically interrupted by a raid. After fierce resistance, and just before being captured, the inhabitants of Feltre managed to escape thanks to their perfect knowledge of the terrain, while the English soldiers hid on the impassable northern slope, taking advantage of the major's mountaineering skills. Unfortunately, these events led to the looting and burning of the magnificent chalets built on an idyllic alpine pasture that has now become a popular destination for one of the most fascinating hikes in the Belluno Dolomites National Park, full of significant places and points of interest.

◄ Ruins of the Malga Pietena

From the car park, continue along the road that crosses the river Stien to reach the village of Sass Sbregà, beyond which you will come across a calchera (a building formerly used for lime production) and then a crossroads at about 700 metres. Turn left to reach the Pian dei Violini at 900 metres, where there is another crossroads. This time turn right onto the mule track CAI 816 through a thick spruce wood until you reach the rocks where vegetation is scarce. After climbing all the way up the large, rocky valley called Scalon di Pietena, you will reach the edge of the Busa di Pietena and, immediately after, the Malga Pietenetta (1,856 metres), where the terrain finally levels out (about 3.5 hours). It is easier and less strenuous to continue around a hill to reach the Malga Pietena, in an extraordinarily beautiful alpine pasture. We recommend continuing the climb to the panoramic view of Passo Pietena, which is practically on the crest of the Vette Feltrine (30 minutes from Pietenetta). From this pass, continue on the Alta Via delle Dolomiti no. 2 toward the Rifugio Boz, cutting horizontally just below the ridge until you reach the depression beyond which the famous natural monument of Piazza del Diavolo can be reached after a slight climb.

Bill Tilman: 'Travelling in the wrong direction is probably better than walking in the footsteps of others!'

Born in 1898, Bill Tilman is best known for having made the first ascent of Nanda Devi, in 1936, and three expeditions to Everest, Kilimanjaro and Ruwenzori. His climbing activity took him to all the continents and every environment, making him one of the greatest mountaineers and explorers of the 20th century. His epic journey ended in 1977 at the age of 80, when he disappeared in the Atlantic Ocean on yet another adventure. He was one of the forerunners of light and self-sufficient mountaineering. He fought in the First and Second World Wars as an officer in the British Army and chose to fight in Italy so he could see the Dolomites for himself. His favourite motto was: 'Travelling in the wrong direction is probably better than walking in the footsteps of others!'

The Busa di Pietena, as seen from the ruins of the Malga Pietena

EREMO DI SAN MAURO IN VALSCURA

23

Between the Dolomites of Pizzocco and the lovely province of Belluno

Starting point: *From Busche, drive up to Cesiomaggiore, then to the villages of Cergnai and Campel. Park near the little church. It is also possible to drive to the last houses of Campel Alto, but parking options there are limited*
GPS: *46.105762, 12.007492*
Time: *3 hours*
Difficulty: *Easy, for all hikers*
Elevation gain: *550 metres*
Trail markers: *Sufficient*
Cartography: *Tabacco 1:25.000, sheet 023*

Recorded for the first time in 1530, on the slopes of Monte Tre Pietre in the Feltre Dolomites, the Eremo (hermitage) of San Mauro rises into the sky, high above the precipices of the imposing Valscura. Legend has it that the inhabitants of Cergnai and Campel decided to build their little church at the same height as San Felice, just opposite, but one night all the birds came out of the woods and carried the building materials to an even higher, steeper and more dangerous hill. This event was interpreted as a clear desire on the part of the Saint to watch over the villages and their inhabitants from much higher up! The backdrop to the magnificent building is twofold: to the south, at the base of the mountains, the province of Belluno extends with its gentle slopes down to the Prealps, while to the north, the western walls of the Pizzocco and the Cima di Valscura, the first real dolomite rampart to the south, stand out.

The value of this easy hike to this holy place is also twofold: to discover ancient places that bear witness to the vibrant life of the mountain people (mule tracks, lime factories, typical chalets, cable cars), and to enjoy the exceptional view of the Valscura and surrounding peaks. We recommend you do this walk at the end of autumn to enjoy the fresh air and the woods that are beginning to thin out and change colour. In the afternoons, the alpenglow magically illuminates the rock faces in the same way as it lights up the more famous dolomite mountains of the north.

From the small church of Campel, continue on foot along the steep asphalt road that leads to Campel Alto, which is dominated by the beautiful walls of Pizzocco and Cima di Valscura. After a sharp right-hand bend, pass the last house in the village, beyond which the asphalt road disappears to make way for a little forest. Continue for a long time on a gentler, uphill stretch until you reach the ruins of a typical calchera: a kiln used to produce quicklime, an artefact often found in the forests of the Belluno area. A little further, you will notice the departure point of a cable car that goes to the small church and a crossroads. Ignore the track toward the Casera Noia and turn left. Climb through a coppice forest, with good views of the valley below, and pass a crossing path protected by a solid wooden fence. After a few hairpin bends, a final climb leads to a clearing where the small church stands (1,175 metres). Right next to it is a room that serves as an emergency shelter and is also used by locals for parties and gatherings. For a better view of the surrounding peaks and the valley, it is better to continue climbing on the surrounding meadows and enjoy the clearings in the middle of the woods (1.5 hours).

EXCURSIONS

Excursions	Difficulty	Duration	Ascent	Shelter	Rating	Page
ANTELAO, MARMAROLE, SORAPISS						
Aieron Ridge	EE	6:00	1200	R	●●●	170
Chapel of San Dionisio	E	4:00	450	R	●●●	190
Croda Mandrin	EE	6:00	900	R	●●●	186
Monte Chiastelin	EE	5:00	750	R	●●●	174
Pian dello Scotter	E	8:00	1200	B	●●●	166
Pupo di Lozzo	T	4:00	200	R	●●●	178
Upper glacier of Antelao	EE	8:00	1550		●●●	182
CERNERA, CRODA DA LAGO, FORMIN						
Alpine Pastures of Possoliva	E	4:00	550		●●●	118
Journey across the Mesolithic	E	7:30	1000	B	●●●	132
Pennes di Formin and the lakes of Ciou de Ra Maza	E	6:00	650		●●●	128
Rocchetta di Prendera	E	6:30	800	R	●●●	122
CRESTE DI CONFINE, LONGERIN, RINALDO						
Geological path of the Quaternà Pass	E	4:30	650		●●●	194
Malga Dignas	T	3:00	350	A	●●●	202
Passo del Mulo	E	6:00	900		●●●	204
Path of the Waterfalls in Sappada	E	1:30	100		●●●	212
Sappada Vecchia	T	5:00	450	A	●●●	208
Val Vissada	E	3:00	450		●●●	196
CRISTALLO, DOLOMITES OF SESTO, AURONZO AND COMELICO						
Cresta Bianca	EE	7:00	1400		●●●	138
Fonda Valley	EE	8:00	1350		●●●	140
Guglia De Amicis	E	4:30	600		●●●	144
Lago Aiarnola	T	3:00	350		●●●	160
Lastron dei Scarperi	EE	7:00	1500		●●●	154
Mont Campoduro	EEA	7:00	1050	R	●●●	158
Monte Cengia	EE	8:30	1450	B	●●●	162
Trenches of the Alpe Mattina Pass	T	5:00	200	R	●●●	148
CRODA ROSSA D'AMPEZZO, SETTSASS, TOFANE, LAGAZUOI, CONTURINES						
Alpe di Fosses	E	7:00	900	R	●●●	74
Bivacco della Pace	E	8:00	1100	B	●●●	106
Cadin di Lagazuoi	EE	6:00	1100		●●●	114
Castello di Bancdalse	EE	8:00	1200	R	●●●	86
Cirques of Col Bechei	EE	7:00	1500		●●●	80
Collapse of the Piccola Croda Rossa	E	7:00	800	R	●●●	94
Forcella del Pin	EE	7:00	1000	A	●●●	90
Gran Piramide	E	8:00	1200	R	●●●	98
Piccolo Settsass	E	5:00	700		●●●	102
Ros di Tofana	EEA	3:00	150	R	●●●	110
FELTRE DOLOMITES						
Busa di Pietena	E	8:00	1550		●●●	478
Cimonega	E	8:00	1300	B	●●●	462
Eremo di San Mauro in Valscura	E	3:00	550	B	●●●	484
Gusela della Val del Burt	E	8:00	1450	B	●●●	472
Malga Alvis	E	5:00	900	B	●●●	466
Pale Alte del Palughet	E	3:00	400	A	●●●	454
Piani Eterni	E	6:00	1100	B	●●●	468
South-West side of Sass de Mura	EE	8:00	1250	R	●●●	458

EXCURSIONS

Excursions	Difficulty	Duration	Ascent	Shelter	Rating	Page
PELMO, CIVETTA, MOIAZZA, BOSCONERO						
Cantoni di Pelsa	EE	8:00	1200	R	●●●	248
Col Negro di Coldai	E	5:00	600	R	○○○	246
Labyrinth of Moiazza	EE	5:00	600	B	○○○	256
Lach di Pelmo	T	3:30	550		●●●	260
Monte Alto di Pelsa	E	7:30	1400	R	●○○	252
Sasso di Bosconero	EE	7:30	1650	R	●●●	274
Sassolungo di Cibiana	EE	6:00	1000		●●●	266
Sfornioi del Bosconero	EE	5:00	900		●●●	270
Spiz de Zuel	T	3:30	400	A	○○○	258
Val Tovanella	E	6:00	1150	B	○○○	280
Villages of Zoldo Alto	T	4:00	100		○○○	264
SCHIARA, SPIZ DI MEZZODÌ, PRAMPER, TAMER						
Bus del Buson	E	2:00	150		○○○	314
Cajada Forest	T	4:00	300		○○○	318
Canyon of Val di Piero	T	1:00	50		○○○	302
Casera di Col Marsang	T	3:00	500	B	○○○	288
Castello di Moschesin	EE	7:00	1000		○●●	296
Cima de Zità	E	8:00	1800	R	●●●	308
Cimon di Cajada	EE	4:30	700		●●●	326
Colcerver and its lake	T	3:30	350	A	○○○	294
Menadar Pass	E	2:30	250	A	○○○	300
Pala Alta	EE	5:30	1050		○○○	306
Pescors	E	4:30	600		○●●	322
Rifugio Angelini	E	3:30	400	R	○●●	282
SIERA, CLAP, TERZE, BRENTONI						
Casera Doana	T	3:00	250	A	○○○	240
Forcella della Terza Piccola	E	4:00	1000		○●●	224
Forcella Valgrande	E	5:00	400		○●●	234
Monte Brentoni	EEA	5:00	800		●●●	228
Passo dell'Arco	E	5:00	700		○○●	216
San Giacomo	T	4:00	300	A	○○○	236
Via Ferrata Simone and via Ferrata dei 50	EEA	8:00	1400	B	●●●	218

T = Tourist   R = Refuge   ○○● = Nice
E = Hiker   B = Bivouac   ○●● = Beautiful
EE = Expert Hiker   A = Agritourism/Alpine Pasture   ●●● = Spectacular
EEA = Expert Hiker with Equipment

ALPHABETICAL INDEX

Thomas Jonglez

It was September 1995 and Thomas Jonglez was in Peshawar, the northern Pakistani city 20 kilometres from the tribal zone he was to visit a few days later. It occurred to him that he should record the hidden aspects of his native city, Paris, which he knew so well. During his seven-month trip back home from Beijing, the countries he crossed took in Tibet (entering clandestinely, hidden under blankets in an overnight bus), Iran and Kurdistan. He never took a plane but travelled by boat, train or bus, hitchhiking, cycling, on horseback or on foot, reaching Paris just in time to celebrate Christmas with the family.

On his return, he spent two fantastic years wandering the streets of the capital to gather material for his first 'secret guide', written with a friend. For the next seven years he worked in the steel industry until the passion for discovery overtook him. He launched Jonglez Publishing in 2003 and moved to Venice three years later.

In 2013, in search of new adventures, the family left Venice and spent six months travelling to Brazil, via North Korea, Micronesia, the Solomon Islands, Easter Island, Peru and Bolivia.

After seven years in Rio de Janeiro, he now lives in Berlin with his wife and three children.

Jonglez Publishing produces a range of titles in nine languages, released in 40 countries.

Follow us on Facebook, Instagram and Twitter

Cartographie: Cyrille Suss – **Layout:** Emmanuelle Willard Toulemonde – **Translation:** Olivia Fuller – **Correction:** Lee Dickinson – **Proofreading:** Kimberly Bess – **Editing:** Clémence Mathé

© JONGLEZ 2023
Registration of copyright: April 2023 – Edition: 01
ISBN: 978-2-36195-624-0
Printed in Bulgaria by Dedrax